T0329948

Disequilibrium Sports Economics

NEW HORIZONS IN THE ECONOMICS OF SPORT

Series Editors: Wladimir Andreff, *Department of Economics, University of Paris 1 Panthéon Sorbonne, France* and Marc Lavoie, *Department of Economics, University of Ottawa, Canada*

For decades, the economics of sport was regarded as a hobby for a handful of professional economists who were primarily involved in other areas of research. In recent years, however, the significance of the sports economy as a percentage of GDP has expanded dramatically. This has coincided with an equivalent rise in the volume of economic literature devoted to the study of sport.

This series provides a vehicle for deeper analyses of the demand for sport, cost–benefit analysis of sport, sporting governance, the economics of professional sports and leagues, individual sports, trade in the sporting goods industry, media coverage, sponsoring and numerous related issues. It contributes to the further development of sports economics by welcoming new approaches and highlighting original research in both established and newly emerging sporting activities. The series publishes the best theoretical and empirical work from well-established researchers and academics, as well as from talented newcomers in the field.

Titles in the series include:

Economics, Uncertainty and European Football
Trends in Competitive Balance
Loek Groot

The Political Economy of Professional Sport
Jean-François Bourg and Jean-Jacques Gouguet

Contemporary Issues in Sports Economics
Participation and Professional Team Sports
Edited by Wladimir Andreff

The Economics of Sport, Health and Happiness
The Promotion of Well-being through Sporting Activities
Edited by Plácido Rodríguez, Stefan Késenne and Brad R. Humphreys

The Econometrics of Sport
Edited by Plácido Rodríguez, Stefan Késenne and Jaume García

Public Policy and Professional Sports
International and Australian Experiences
John K. Wilson and Richard Pomfret

The Economics of Competitive Sports
Edited by Plácido Rodríguez, Stefan Késenne and Ruud Koning

Disequilibrium Sports Economics
Competitive Imbalance and Budget Constraints
Edited by Wladimir Andreff

Disequilibrium Sports Economics

Competitive Imbalance and Budget Constraints

Edited by

Wladimir Andreff

Professor Emeritus, Department of Economics, University of Paris 1 Panthéon Sorbonne, France

NEW HORIZONS IN THE ECONOMICS OF SPORT

Edward Elgar
PUBLISHING

Cheltenham, UK • Northampton, MA, USA

Published by
Edward Elgar Publishing Limited
The Lypiatts
15 Lansdown Road
Cheltenham
Glos GL50 2JA
UK

Edward Elgar Publishing, Inc.
William Pratt House
9 Dewey Court
Northampton
Massachusetts 01060
USA

A catalogue record for this book
is available from the British Library

Library of Congress Control Number: 2015940694

This book is available electronically in the **Elgar**online
Economics subject collection
DOI 10.4337/9781783479368

ISBN 978 1 78347 935 1 (cased)
ISBN 978 1 78347 936 8 (eBook)

Typeset by Servis Filmsetting Ltd, Stockport, Cheshire

Printed and bound in Great Britain by
TJ International Ltd, Padstow, Cornwall

Contents

Contributors

Wladimir Andreff, Professor Emeritus in Economics, University Paris 1 Panthéon Sorbonne, France, Honorary President of the International Association of Sports Economists and of the European Sports Economics Association, Honorary Member of the European Association for Comparative Economic Studies, former President of the French Economics Association.

Egon Franck, Professor at the University of Zurich, Switzerland, former Vice-President of the University of Zurich, Member of the Union of European Football Associations' (UEFA) Club Financial Control Panel, then of the UEFA Club Financial Control Body, President of the Academic Sports Association Zurich.

Jean-Pascal Gayant, Professor in Economics, Groupe de Recherche sur les Itinéraires et Niveaux Salariaux (GAINS), University of Le Mans, France.

Nicolas Le Pape, Professor in Economics, Centre of Research in Economics and Management (CREM), University of Caen, France.

Robert D. Macdonald, Senior Fellow, Sports Law Program, Law School, University of Melbourne, Australia. He has consulted to the Australian Football League and published several articles and book chapters on labour market regulation and competitive balance in sporting leagues.

Klaus Nielsen, Professor of Institutional Economics, Birkbeck Sport Business Centre, Department of Management, Birkbeck University of London, UK.

Rasmus K. Storm, Head of Research at the Danish Institute for Sports Studies (Idan), PhD from the University of Southern Denmark and MSc in Public Administration from Roskilde University, Denmark.

Geoffrey N. Tuck, Senior Resource Modeller at the Commonwealth Scientific and Industrial Research Organisation (CSIRO) Oceans and Atmosphere and CSIRO Digital Productivity Flagships, Hobart, Tasmania, Australia.

Daam Van Reeth, Katholieke Universiteit Leuven, Campus Brussels, Belgium, Program Director of the Business Administration program and member of the Center for Research on Economic Markets and their Environments (CREME).

Athol R. Whitten, Senior Scientist and Director at Mezo Research, Melbourne, Australia. Honorary Fellow, School of Biosciences, Faculty of Science, University of Melbourne. Secretary of the ADMB Foundation, dedicated to improving data analysis and non-linear statistical modelling. Member of the Editorial Board for the Natural Resource Modeling Journal.

1. A new research area: disequilibrium sports economics

Wladimir Andreff*

Ever since Rottenberg's (1956) pioneering article, sports economics has been set within the framework of equilibrium economics, in particular when modelling team sport leagues. Four pillars of this mainstream approach are crystal-clear in the economics of team sport leagues. The first one of course is the concept of economic equilibrium assumed to be reached by a league for its product market and labour market for talent – its major input. Economic equilibrium is obtained through the usual marginal calculation achieved by all economic agents operating in a league's market, namely, the calculation of team owners driven by a profit maximization objective, both in the original model (El Hodiri and Quirk, 1971) and later in the standard model of a closed North American team sport league (Fort and Quirk, 1995). Therefore, the assumption of profit maximization is a second pillar. The equilibrium solutions in the labour market for talent (the marginal productivity of labour = the wage rate) and in the market for output (fan attendance equalizes marginal revenues with marginal costs) are supposed to prevail.

The league's labour market equilibrium in the standard model does not produce a perfect competitive balance where all teams would have an equal probability to win the championship and a 50–50 chance of winning any game. This first-best competitive balance is out of reach along with the league's economic equilibrium unless the market size of each team is absolutely identical (no big-market teams, no small-market teams). Therein lies all the debates about how much regulation (revenue redistribution between teams, a rookie draft, a salary cap and a luxury tax) is needed or not to make the league's economic equilibrium coincide with the best feasible competitive balance. Competitive balance is the third pillar of the standard model.

However, when it comes to open European team sport leagues with a promotion-relegation system, profit maximization is no longer considered as being relevant and has to be substituted by the assumption of team owners attempting to maximize some utility function (Sloane, 1971), which eventually boils down to a team's objective of win-maximization (Késenne, 1996). Késenne's model became standard for open leagues where an economic equilibrium is guaranteed if win-maximizing clubs stick strictly to their budget constraint or, in managerial terms, if clubs always attempt to break even. Thus, with a hard budget constraint or a break-even accounting rule, the team budget is always balanced, so that overall costs are neither higher nor lower than overall revenues. This is the fourth pillar of the equilibrium approach to team sport leagues.

A first motivation for launching a book dealing with disequilibrium sports economics is that such a thing just does not exist in the literature so far. All the authors in this volume have once embarked on research pathways that drove them away, to some extent, from the highway of mainstream equilibrium sports economics.

A second motivation is that a few recent papers have moved in the direction of something that looks like disequilibrium economics: this has happened when a few authors have examined some non-equilibrium solutions in actual labour markets for talent such as journeymen player unemployment, superstar excess wages and tanking. In particular, the *International Journal of Sport Finance* has played a crucial role as a springboard to this new disequilibrium approach to sports economics. This has been done when the journal published in the same year a rather theoretical article about the building blocks of a disequilibrium model of team sport leagues (Andreff, 2014) as well as a practical assessment of the Union of European Football Associations' (UEFA) Financial Fair Play facing the fact that many European football clubs actually do not break even because they face a soft – instead of hard – budget constraint (Franck, 2014). In the market for fan attendance, ticket touting expresses a local excess demand for a local sport show, whereas skyrocketing superstar wages express an excess demand for their talent. With regard to a club's soft budget constraint, the two aforementioned articles explicitly refer to a typical disequilibrium economist, Janos Kornaï – from Kornaï (1980) to Kornaï et al. (2003) – who emphasized soft budget constraints. This notion was first applied by Andreff (2007) when assessing the deficits and rising debts of football clubs through the lenses of a club's weak governance fuelled by a softening of its budget constraint. Not surprisingly, one more recently published paper has been entirely devoted to soft budget constraints in European professional football (Storm and Nielsen, 2012).

Alongside this new strain of sports economics literature about disequilibrium economics and soft budget constraints, the number of articles that call the notion of a league competitive balance into question is flourishing. Is a balanced league a precondition for its economic attractiveness in terms of attendance and gate receipts, and in terms of TV audience and TV rights revenues? The initial standard literature about the assumed strong relationship between sport outcome uncertainty and a fan's willingness to pay is no longer the unique train of thought in this research area. Among the renewed approaches, a simulation model has been used to explore complex stochastic dynamic systems such as sports leagues, where managers face difficult decisions regarding the structure of their league and the desire to maintain competitive balance (Tuck and Whitten, 2013). It has been found that reverse-order drafts can lead to some teams cycling between success and failure and to other teams being stuck in mid-rank positions for extended periods of time. Reverse-order drafts can also create incentives for teams to deliberately under-perform, or tank, due to the perceived gain from obtaining quality players at higher draft picks. With tanking, both a league's economic equilibrium and competitive balance may be in jeopardy. Another standpoint has been taken to push forward the concept of competitive imbalance (Gayant and Le Pape, 2012, 2015), thus going beyond the standard notion of competitive balance, an optimum that is never reached in reality. Revenue disparities between teams most often jeopardize competitive balance on the pitch.

All the above means, on the one hand, that a wide avenue for further research is opened up by applying concepts drawn from disequilibrium economics and Kornaï's analyses to the economics of team sport leagues and, on the other hand, that a small group of sports economists is already involved in this new research area. They are namely those who have contributed to the present volume.

A third motivation for this book is the conviction that in real life, more often than not, the situation of a team sport league does not coincide with general equilibrium solutions: everyone can witness disparities in sporting strengths, that is, in recruitment capacities, price rigidity or stickiness, excess demand or supply, revenue hyper-concentration, heavily imbalanced contests, superstar wages de-linked from their marginal productivity and more clubs in the red than in the black. One chapter in this volume, for the first time, offers some evidence that economic disequilibrium is not confined to sports leagues: it may affect the structure of supply in the market for televised sports as compared to the structure of demand.

The volume is divided into two parts. Part I focuses on economic disequilibrium in sports markets and competitive imbalance in sporting contests (four chapters). Part II concentrates on soft budget constraints and their consequences for club governance and management (three chapters).

Opening Part I, Chapter 2 by Wladimir Andreff starts by relaxing some unrealistic assumptions embedded in the equilibrium model of a team sport league, in particular with regard to open leagues. A next stage on the path to an alternative disequilibrium model is to realistically confront some hypotheses of the equilibrium model that do not fit empirical evidence gathered so far about the different markets of team sport leagues. The last stage is to introduce Kornaï's concept of a soft budget constraint and adjust it to the case of not-for-profit professional sports teams. Then, step by step, a simple disequilibrium model of an open team sport league is elaborated upon. It encompasses one labour market for heterogeneous talent with an excess demand for superstar players, and two markets for the league's final products: one is a market for live games with fans' excess demand, another is a market for televised games supplied by free-to-air TV channels with viewers' excess demand, and then the market is supplied by pay-per-view TV channels. However, this first attempt at disequilibrium modelling neglects some interactions and spillovers between markets that are observed in real European football leagues. This delineates avenues for further research.

An alternative approach to optimization modelling – which looks at how a team sport league reaches its first-best economic equilibrium – consists in resorting to a simulation model. Non-equilibrium simulation methods fit better with highly variable or unpredictable outcomes and complicated systemic feedback mechanisms often witnessed in a league. Geoff Tuck, Robert Macdonald and Athol Whitten (Chapter 3) stress that the role of simulation would be extremely useful for league managers in designing labour market regulations. Target reference points are derived from a team sport league's objectives (competitive balance, financial viability, integrity and quality of the sporting contest, public support and economic benefit of expansion clubs) and each target reference point is defined as a value of the indicator representing a desirable state of the system while a limit reference point is defined as an unacceptable system state. These reference points are linked to performance indicators in order to obtain performance measures of league management that may guide decision-making – namely, when negotiating collective bargaining agreements with the players' union – in a Monte Carlo simulation framework coined Management Strategy Evaluation.

After comparing the Australian Football League (AFL) to other closed leagues concerning player drafts, league expansion over time, sporting performances of expansion clubs and the design of detailed labour market regulation, Geoff Tuck, Robert Macdonald and Athol Whitten apply their Sports Synthesis simulation framework (initially used in marine resource modelling) and the reference point methodology to the competitive balance implications and other performance measures of various allocations of player draft selections to two expansion clubs recently admitted into the AFL. Running a number of simulations enables the calculation of performance statistics related to management objectives and reference points when a new team has benefited from player draft selections granted to expansion clubs joining a closed league.

At odds with an optimization model, many alternative allocations of draft selections to the expansion club, and not a single one, may satisfy the objectives of the league manager. With regard to the last two AFL expansion clubs, only three out of six simulation scenarios exhibit a high probability of success within ten years of their establishment. Expansion clubs are relatively weak in the years that follow establishment due to a preponderance of young players. This initial poor performance secures them high draft picks so that the clubs rapidly grow in team productivity, as the high draft picks mature as quality players, and move upwards to the top eight ranks in the league within five years.

Jean-Pascal Gayant and Nicolas Le Pape start a new train of analysis with a metrics of competitive imbalance (Chapter 4). If one is concerned about the effective level of competitive imbalance in a league, or if one seeks to define a socially desirable level of imbalance, then a suitable metric is needed. The first requirement is an index calculated through an appropriate point system, such that the index has its maximum value for the distribution that is most imbalanced, and its minimum value for the distribution that is most balanced. The second requirement is that the index must be robust with respect to any change in the size of the league. Finally, employing an analogy between measuring imbalance in a league and measuring inequality in a community, it seems worthwhile to construct an index that satisfies good properties and importantly, the so-called principle of transfers. This underlines that some of these good properties should be (a) specific to imbalance measurement and (b) separate for closed leagues and for open leagues (with promotion and relegation).

In Chapter 5, Daam Van Reeth studies TV broadcasts of Olympic events. With the addition of women's boxing, the 2012 Olympics in London became the first Games in which women competed in every sport on the Olympic programme. The presence of parallel competitions for men and women is one of the appealing features of the Games. Many studies have therefore used the Olympic Games for analysing gender balance in media coverage of sport. Most of these studies focus exclusively on the supply side of the media market by measuring how much time/space TV channels or newspapers dedicate to the coverage of both genders. Daam Van Reeth's study is different and original in its approach because it uses data on TV audiences, the demand side of the market. This creates an opportunity to check for evidence of a disequilibrium situation between, on the one hand, the supply of Olympic TV broadcasts and, on the other hand, the TV demand revealed by sports consumers. The analysis is based on a dataset of almost 1000 sport-specific Olympic TV broadcasts on

Dutch national television, totalling about 144 hours of television. The results show a disequilibrium situation on the Dutch TV market for Olympic sports broadcasts: while broadcasters provide significantly more coverage of male events, Dutch TV viewers slightly prefer broadcasts of women competitions over broadcasts of men competitions.

Part II of the volume begins with Rasmus Storm and Klaus Nielsen's (Chapter 6) presentation of soft and hard budget constraints as theoretical concepts according to Janos Kornaï that perfectly fit with the disequilibrium model dealt with in Chapter 1. The focus is on the soft budget constraint syndrome that had developed in former socialist economies but also in certain environmental conditions in capitalist market economies. That soft budget constraints prevail in European football is evidenced once again with a high survival rate of clubs despite continuous financial problems, namely, in the Big Five first-tier leagues. Storm and Nielsen extend the soft budget constraint approach to North American team sport leagues – a highly original extension. The argument runs from major league franchises enjoying a guaranteed survival because of their legally guaranteed, unregulated monopoly position to this position enabling them, as price-makers, to subtract profits that would not be possible to obtain if they were facing harder environmental conditions – a sort of inverse budget constraint softness. Empirical evidence is provided as regards soft pricing, soft taxation, soft subsidies and soft investment financing, soft credit and soft accounting in the National Football League (NFL), as the authors note that financial support is delivered to burdened teams *ex ante* in North American leagues while it is done *ex post* in European leagues. The analysis ends with a matrix outlining various ideal types of professional team sport clubs and leagues on both sides of the Atlantic.

In Chapter 7, Wladimir Andreff examines how to assess the quality and efficiency of governance in clubs that operate in a team sport league. Two theoretical standpoints can be adopted: the principal-agent model that is supposed to fit with profit-maximizing teams and economic equilibrium, and Kornaï's soft budget constraint that seems more suitable for win-maximizing clubs in disequilibrium leagues. With the principal-agent model a good corporate governance structure is such that profit is maximized under the control of either a single capital owner or core stockholders who stand last in line for the distribution of profits or losses. Thus, they have the appropriate incentives to make accurate profit-maximizing decisions and control free-riding managers through contractual, takeover and bankruptcy disciplines. The chapter assesses whether North American sport teams behave accordingly and are consequently profitable and whether they resort to asset sales in view of disciplining managers. This is definitely the case in the NFL, less so in Major League Baseball (MLB) and the National Basketball Association (NBA) and definitely not the case in the National Hockey League (NHL). Further challenging evidence is that most European football win-maximizing clubs that float their shares on the stock market are not profitable either and do not improve their governance.

Good governance in not-for-profit organizations boils down to breaking even and balancing the budget. Bad governance is associated with recurrent soft budget constraints. European football exhibits more clubs in the red than in the black. French football is used as an example with a detailed study of the clubs' deficits and the structure of their debts, confirming that a lasting soft budget constraint prevails. Recommendations are derived in favour of hardening the budget constraints of football clubs; the French football auditing system and UEFA Financial Fair Play are briefly assessed through the lens of the soft budget constraint approach.

The final chapter by Egon Franck (Chapter 8) tackles the issue of regulation in leagues where clubs turn out to have soft budget constraints and its impact on managerial incentives and the league outcome uncertainty. The author first reminds us of the detrimental managerial incentives that result from a soft budget constraint, as it triggers a runaway demand for talent and the emergence of a salary bubble. Managerial moral hazard and rent-seeking crowd out incentives for good management and fuel a kind of financial doping of football clubs. New UEFA Club Licensing and Financial Fair Play Regulations create harder budget constraints for football club managers and introduce a cap on payroll injections for football club benefactors. The chapter analyses how hardened budget constraints would presumably affect managerial incentives and decision-making in football clubs and how the cap on payroll injections would affect suspense and outcome uncertainty in European football competitions.

NOTE

*   I would like to thank Marc Lavoie for his final review of this chapter.

REFERENCES

Andreff, W. (2007), 'French football: a financial crisis rooted in weak governance', *Journal of Sports Economics*, **8**(6), 652–61.
Andreff, W. (2014), 'Building blocks for a disequilibrium model of a European team sports league', *International Journal of Sport Finance*, **9**(1), 20–38.

El Hodiri, M. and J. Quirk. (1971), 'An economic model of a professional sports league', *Journal of Political Economy*, **79**(6), 1302–19.

Fort, R. and J. Quirk (1995), 'Cross-subsidization, incentives, and outcomes in professional team leagues', *Journal of Economic Literature*, **XXXIII**, 1265–99.

Franck, E. (2014), 'Financial Fair Play in European club football – what is it all about?', *International Journal of Sport Finance*, **9**(1), 193–217.

Gayant, J.P. and N. Le Pape (2012), 'How to account for changes in the size of sports leagues: the iso competitive balance curves', *Economics Bulletin*, **32**, 1715–23.

Gayant, J.P. and N. Le Pape (2015), 'Mesure de la *competitive balance* dans les ligues de sports professionnels: faut-il distinguer les ligues fermées des ligues avec promotion et relégation?', *Revue Economique*, **66**, 427–48.

Késenne, S. (1996), 'League management in professional team sports with win maximizing clubs', *European Journal of Sport Management*, **2**(2), 14–22.

Kornaï, J. (1980), *Economics of Shortage*, Amsterdam: North Holland.

Kornaï, J., E. Maskin and G. Roland (2003), 'Understanding the soft budget constraint', *Journal of Economic Literature*, **LXI**, 1095–136.

Rottenberg, S. (1956), 'The baseball players' labor market', *Journal of Political Economy*, **54**(3), 242–58.

Sloane, P.J. (1971), 'The economics of professional football: the football club as a utility maximiser', *Scottish Journal of Political Economy*, **18**(2), 121–46.

Storm, R.K. and K. Nielsen (2012), 'Soft budget constraints in professional football', *European Sport Management Quarterly*, **12**(2), 183–201.

Tuck, G.N. and A.R. Whitten (2013), 'Lead us not into tanktation: a simulation modeling approach to gain insights into incentives for sporting teams to tank', *PLoS ONE*, **8**(11), 1–8.

PART I

Economic disequilibrium and competitive imbalance

2. An attempt at disequilibrium modelling a team sports league

Wladimir Andreff

INTRODUCTION

This chapter attempts to show how beneficial it would be to drop some simplifying and unrealistic assumptions that underlie the standard equilibrium model of a team sports league that have prevailed in the sports economics literature so far. Its aim is not only to discuss how to better adjust economic modelling to empirical evidence, in particular in the case of open leagues, but also to pave the way for an alternative disequilibrium model of – and approach to – team sports leagues. The next section briefly describes the core relationships that are found in the standard model of a North American closed league with profit-maximizing teams and a European open league with win-maximizing teams. It discusses why some of the most crucial assumptions underlying this model are extremely restrictive from the viewpoint of both general theoretical modelling and fitness to empirical evidence of open team sports leagues. The following section elaborates, step by step, on a new, though simple, disequilibrium model of an open team sports (football) league with two markets – one for talent and one for the league's final product – that does not rely on the restrictive assumptions of the standard equilibrium model. The final section assesses how much this first attempt at modelling is far from a comprehensive disequilibrium model of a team sports league given all the different interacting markets that are found in the real economic life of European football leagues. It delineates an entire programme for further research that would be needed to close the gap between the present attempt and a genuine general disequilibrium model.

ASSUMPTIONS UNDERLYING EQUILIBRIUM MODELS OF A TEAM SPORTS LEAGUE

An equilibrium model of a North American closed team sports league emerged in the sports economics literature in the early 1970s. Since then it became standard among sports economists and was adapted to European open leagues. Some of its underlying assumptions were called into question by some of the model's promoters themselves, in particular regarding the assumed fixed supply on the market for player talent. More unheeded or less discussed assumptions are moved to the forefront here since they call for a switch from an equilibrium to a disequilibrium approach of an open team sports league. The most crucial of these assumptions is about teams' budget constraints.

The Standard Equilibrium of a Closed Team Sports League

Since El Hodiri and Quirk (1971) a Walrasian equilibrium model has been used to represent a two-team closed league with profit-maximizing and wage-taker teams in the labour market for talent. Each team i maximizes its profit through unlimited marginal variations of its quantity of talent t_i:

$$Max\,\pi_i = Max\,(R_i - C_i) \tag{2.1}$$

$$R_i = R_i(m_i, t_i) \tag{2.2}$$

$$\text{with } \frac{\partial R_i}{\partial m_i} > 0,\, \frac{\partial R_i}{\partial t_i} > 0 \text{ or } \frac{\partial R_i}{\partial t_i} < 0,\, \frac{\partial^2 R_i}{\partial t_i^2} < 0,\, \frac{\partial^2 R_i}{\partial t_i \partial m_i} > 0$$

$$C_i = s.t_i + c_i^0 \tag{2.3}$$

It is assumed that a number of homogeneous talent units are embodied in each player. Fort and Quirk (1995, p. 1271) 'assume that talent is measured in units such that an additional unit of talent increases win per cent by one unit. Under this convention:

$$\frac{\partial w_i}{\partial t_i} = 1\text{'} \tag{2.4}$$

The aforementioned assumption allows the substitution of the win per cent w_i of team i by the quantity of recruited talent t_i in its revenue function R_i. The supply of talent is assumed to be fixed ($\sum_i t_i = 1$) since the labour market is closed by league regulation (rookie draft, salary cap). With a fixed supply of talent, team owners internalize the following externality: recruiting an additional unit of talent will deprive the other team from this unit, which will deteriorate league competitive balance. Team revenue R_i is a function of local market size m_i, ticket price[1] and the number of wins – or win per cent w_i (therefore t_i). The revenue function is concave in win per cent and thus wins have a decreasing marginal effect on revenues. The marginal revenue of a win is:

$$a_i - b_i \cdot w_i \tag{2.5}$$

with $b_i > 0$ and $\sum_i t_i = 1$, if the revenue function is assumed to be quadratic:

$$\left[a_i - \left(\frac{b_i}{2} \right) w_i \right] w_i + k_i \tag{2.6}$$

Team revenue is increasing together with wins until a maximum, then it decreases when the team is prevailing over the championship. Thus, talent has an increasing and then a decreasing return. In the team cost function, s is the salary per unit of talent and c_i^0 represents a fixed cost (stadium, management). Equilibrium wage is provided by either a Smithian invisible hand or a Walrasian central auctioneer. Team i augments its talent recruitment until marginal revenue of talent is equal to its marginal cost and to exogenous equilibrium unit wage:

$$MR_i = \frac{\partial R_i(m_i, t_i)}{\partial t_i} = s \text{ for } \forall i \tag{2.7}$$

Figure 2.1 shows a big market team 1 (big team) and a small market team 2 (small team) with $m_1 > m_2$. Since market 1 is bigger than market 2, this creates a revenue disparity between the two teams. For any given wage, team 1 demand for talent is bigger than team 2 demand. In equilibrium (E*), the two teams' demand for talent is equal to the supply of talent, at the unit equilibrium wage s^*. Then the big team recruits more talent units than the small team: $t_1 > t_2$, and the league does not reach the best level

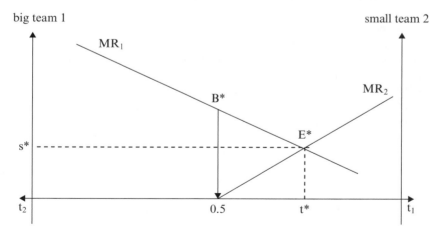

Figure 2.1   Competitive balance with profit maximization

of competitive balance ($t^* \neq 0.5$), the one that occurs when the two teams have an equal probability to win. League economic equilibrium is associated with disparities in team payrolls. Win per cents are uneven, $w_1 > w_2$, and the league is imbalanced. Economic equilibrium definitely generates competitive imbalance in a closed league, on the one hand. On the other hand, the best level of competitive balance does not coincide with economic equilibrium since in B* the marginal revenue of talent is neither equal among teams nor equal to equilibrium wage.

Thus, the core standard equilibrium model of a team sports league itself pushes forward the logical conclusion that there is either disequilibrium between marginal revenues of talent and market wage if the sport contest is to be balanced or the league endeavours a competitive imbalance when economic equilibrium is to be reached. There followed long-lasting debates that had lavishly nurtured the literature about closed league regulation: a reserve clause hindering perfect talent mobility is not an obstacle to economic equilibrium in the talent market if the invariance principle holds (Rottenberg, 1956). The standard model does not support two existing regulations since revenue sharing does not improve competitive balance in the league except under very precise conditions of revenue redistribution (Késenne, 2000a), and since a salary cap lowers overall league revenues (Késenne, 2000b). It is not easy to fill the gap between economic equilibrium E* of a closed league and its best suitable competitive balance B* (supposed to attract the highest attendance) without putting a regulator's hands in.

The Standard Equilibrium of an Open Team Sports League

The standard equilibrium model has been adapted to open leagues by Késenne (1996) by altering three assumptions: (a) now teams are win-maximizers; (b) therefore they recruit as much talent as possible within their budget constraint; (c) in a now globalized labour market triggered by Bosman jurisprudence ruling open leagues, free entry of players makes irrelevant the assumption of a fixed supply of talent. Teams are still wage-takers in this market so that:

$$Max \ t_i \tag{2.8}$$

$$R_i\,(m_i, t_i) - s.\,t_i - c_i^0 = 0 \tag{2.9}$$

Using the Lagrangian, first order conditions are:

$$1 + \lambda_i\!\left(\frac{\partial R_i}{\partial t_i} - s\right) = 0 \tag{2.10}$$

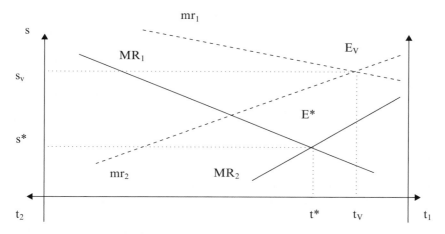

Figure 2.2   Competitive balance with win maximization (compared to profit maximization)

$$\text{hence } RM_i = s - 1 / \lambda_i < s \qquad (2.11)$$
$$R_i - s. \, t_i = 0 \qquad (2.12)$$

From (2.11), marginal revenue of talent is seen to be lower than its marginal cost. For a given talent unit cost, the team demand for talent that maximizes its wins is bigger than if the team were profit-maximizing; thus the team spends more to recruit more talent than in a closed league with profit-maximizing teams (Figure 2.2). The consequence is an arms race between teams in the league. Equation (2.12) shows that a team demand for talent is no longer given by its marginal revenue curve but by its average revenue curve: $\overline{R} = R_i / t_i = s$. Equilibrium is no longer located in E^* but instead in E_v. Again economic equilibrium does not coincide with the best competitive balance ($t_v \neq 0.5$). Equilibrium wage is higher with win-maximizing teams ($s_v > s^*$) and talent distribution is more uneven, that is, an open league with win-maximizing teams is more imbalanced than a closed league with profit-maximizing teams. Overall league revenue is lower than in the latter since all talents comprised between t^* and t_v play in the big team where their marginal revenue is lower than it would have been in the small team.

In an open league, revenue sharing improves competitive balance (Késenne, 2000a). The invariance principle does not hold. Revenue sharing enhances equilibrium wage compared with a no revenue sharing situation: players benefit from it.

Relaxing the Assumption of a Fixed Supply of Talent in Open Leagues

The Walrasian model successfully passed econometric testing of its assumptions with regard to closed leagues though its fitness with the reality is somewhat blurred. For instance, some econometric studies of the National Football League (NFL) had shown a weak profit incentive to win (Zimbalist, 2002) calling the profit-maximizing hypothesis into question. Lavoie (2005) stressed repeated financial deficits and team bankruptcies in North American leagues, a series of facts remote from the theoretical economic equilibrium of a closed league. Downward and Dawson (2000) consider that the standard model has paid too much attention to competitive balance. In this respect, the most striking empirical observation was a long-lasting worse competitive balance in closed than open leagues (Buzzachi et al., 2003; Andreff, 2011) at odds with model expectations. Empirical testing of the standard model for open leagues demonstrated that revenue concentration on a few big teams deteriorates neither league competitive balance nor game attendance (Szymanski, 2001) while other studies showed that post-Bosman deregulated open leagues are imbalanced since revenue disparities across teams impact team standings, competitive balance and attendance (Hall et al., 2002; Gerrard, 2006).

The standard model of team sports leagues has been reassessed within the past decade. The assumption of a fixed supply of talent does not hold any longer with globalization of the labour market for talent after the Bosman case in open leagues, but it is also doubtful in closed leagues (Osborne, 2006). Assuming that an increase of one talent unit augmenting win per cent by one unit (relation 2.4 above), for any win per cent, is not neutral (Szymanski, 2003). That marginal revenue of a win being equal for all teams is conditional on such an assumption. When in reality teams of nearly all national leagues recruit in a global market, an additional talent hired by one team is no longer lost by another team in the same league, namely, if the player is transferred from a foreign or lower league. Fixed supply of talent is no longer internalized by teams in their strategies. The Walrasian model must be substituted by a Nash conjecture in a two-team non-cooperative game when a team determines its quantity of talent without knowing the effect of the recruitment choice made by its opponent team (Szymanski, 2004a).

A number of results have been derived from this Nash equilibrium model that jeopardize the convincing power of the standard model. The invariance principle is not valid in a Nash conjecture and gate revenue sharing deteriorates competitive balance with profit-maximizing teams (Szymanski and Késenne, 2004) but if teams are win-maximizing, revenue sharing still improves competitive balance (Késenne, 2005). With win-maximizing teams, talent distribution is the same in Nash conjecture and Walrasian equilibrium (Késenne, 2007). A team that intends to win as many games as possible within its budget constraint will spend all its revenues on talent recruitment without considering other teams' recruitment strategies.

A controversial debate followed the emergence of the Nash model of team sports leagues. Some economists contended that the Walrasian model consequently is outdated and can no longer coexist with the Nash conjecture since only one single general theory of professional sports leagues can prevail (Szymanski, 2004b; Késenne, 2006). Some advocated that the assumption of a fixed talent supply and the Walrasian model are still valid (Eckard, 2006). Some put forward that the Walrasian model remains relevant for closed leagues with profit maximization while a Nash conjecture applies to open leagues where team owners have non-cooperative strategies (Fort, 2006). Beyond such outcome uncertainty about what the theoretical standard model of a team sports league is relevant for, it appears that some of its other underlying assumptions do not perform successfully in the face of real open leagues – like, for instance, European football leagues.

Equilibrium Model Assumptions versus Open Leagues' Empirical Evidence

Attention must be drawn to some assumptions that are crucial for the standard model of a team sports league to reach economic equilibrium; namely, those hypotheses that are required to write a balanced team's budget constraint such as (2.9) above. First, an infinite flexibility must be assumed in the variations of either quantity of talent t_i or market wage s or both in the market for team i's input. The same assumption would pertain to team i's product market for it to reach equilibrium had such a market been considered in the standard model. The problem is that, regards the team sports league's product market, such an assumption is at odds with a demand for games inelastic to price or given the fact that teams fix their price in the inelastic portion of their demand curve, as various studies have empirically tested. References are many in the sports economics literature – Noll (1974), Fort and Quirk (1995), Coates and Harrison (2005), Coates and Humphreys (2007) and for European football leagues (Andreff, 1981; Bird, 1982; Dobson and Goddard, 1995; Falter and Pérignon, 2000). In the European context, the league monopsony in the labour market, on the one hand, and player unionization and collective bargaining, on the other hand, though much less widespread than in North American leagues, fuel stickiness in wage determination. A fixed or even a sticky price immediately generates market disequilibrium (Benassy, 1982). With a fixed or sticky price, market adjustment will operate in quantity, defined as market rationing; whatever their demand, fans will have to adjust to the supply of games at a fix price $\bar{p}$.

Another required assumption in the standard model is that all talent units are identical and can always be marginally added or substituted for by a team, which assumes an infinitely divisible and homogeneous unit of talent. No differentiation between any two talent units or two genuine live players is taken into account even though, in the real world, journeymen players are not as talented as superstars. Assuming a homogeneous talent unit is a rather abstract concept. How many homogeneous talent units are embedded in Lionel Messi compared, for instance, with Jean-Marc Bosman? The metrics to check this are missing. The managers of a real team actually do not know what a talent unit is; they can only assess how much talented one player is – as a bundle of several heterogeneous talents. Thus, a team maximizes the number of heterogeneously talented units enshrined in live and entire players it recruits. In an open league, a team also maximizes its win percentage in order to be promoted in the upper league or avoid being relegated in the lower league whatever its quantity of talents and given its roster of live and entire players. Consequently, it must be considered that a team maximizes both its win percentage and quantity of talented players but the two variables cannot be substituted for each other as with the unrealistic assumption $\frac{\partial w_i}{\partial t_i} = 1$ adopted in the standard equilibrium model. Maximizing a quantity of live talented players and not simply a quantity of homogeneous talent leads to less convenient and less stylish modelling, the price to pay for avoiding the previous unrealistic assumption.

Moreover, the terms of trade and wage determination are dramatically different for players that face a high demand for their talents – superstars – than those for journeymen players. A superstar effect in wage determination has been clearly exhibited, namely, in Italian football (Lucifora and Simmons, 2003) and for European migrant footballers with a superstar status (Bryson et al., 2014). The arms race observed in European football targets superstars in excess demand, not journeymen players. Each superstar holds an exclusive specificity embedded in his or her talents and a monopoly position on the supply side of the labour market, and thus benefits from a rent included in his or her wage (Borghans and Groot, 1998) and transfer fee, a quite different market situation from excess supply of sometimes unemployed journeymen players. Segmentation of the football labour market has been confirmed by several studies since Bourg (1983). That a qualitative differentiation between player talents triggers labour market segmentation though in American baseball was also referred to in Hill and Spellman (1983) and Vrooman (1996) since there are two different wage rates for differently talented players in their models.

Another assumption is questioned by some of the standard model builders themselves who do not consider acceptable that, in a competition among the few teams of a league, teams are to be considered as wage-takers. For instance, Szymanski (2004a) stresses that in a 20 teams league, it is not sensible to assume that teams are wage-takers since some teams (for example, Manchester United, Chelsea, Manchester City in the English Premier League – EPL) are more influential in the market for talent: a pure competition model is not relevant. Big football teams definitely influence wage determination – they are wage-makers – and, though less so, a league and its teams are price-makers on their product market in particular when the league is pooling TV rights for sale (Andreff and Bourg, 2006).

In the standard model, a team i sticks to its budget constraint in augmenting its revenues R_i by increasing its market size m_i; in practice this means attracting more gate receipts and/or TV rights revenues in its output market. This may happen through either a flexible ticket price or TV subscription fee, on the one hand, or an unrestricted variation in the number of ticket holders and pay-per-view TV viewers, on the other hand. Analysing a team's trade-off between output price and quantity flexible variations implies integrating the detailed functioning of a second (product) market in the model, which is rare in the theoretical literature about team sports leagues. A major exception is found in Késenne (2007) who demonstrates that equilibrium ticket price with price assumed to be infinitely flexible is higher in a league with win-maximizing teams than in a league with profit-maximizing teams. However, in this model, neither stadium attendance and gate receipts nor TV rights revenues depend on any consumer demand function that would differentiate fans, season ticket holders, occasional spectators, TV viewers and couch potatoes who may have different behaviours in the face of a league supply of sport fixtures, and its price. A more recent and realistic hypothesis is that fans and TV viewers do not have the same consumer demand function. This means that a sport show is a differentiated (and not homogeneous) product. Consequently, the product market of a team sports league is segmented according to different varieties of a sport show consumed either in attending a stadium or switching on a TV set, laptop or cell phone.

An increasing trend in the empirical literature has exhibited and tested a distinction between two varieties of sport show consumers, with fans and season ticket holders, on the one hand, and TV viewers, casual spectators and couch potatoes, on the other hand (Simmons, 1996). There is a fans demand for attending games in stadia that is distinguished from a demand for televised games (Buraimo, 2008). Thus, there are two products, that is, two sport shows derived from the same game. The demand for seating close to the pitch is registered at stadium gates while the demand for televised games is registered through audience records on public and free-to-air TV channels and the number of subscribers to pay-per-view and commercial TV companies. Fans demand a maximum number of their favourite team games with an individual utility growing with as many attended games as possible, and with a wishful expectation of home team wins;[2] fans often turn away from a losing favourite team. TV viewers and couch potatoes rather demand uncertain and high quality games; thus, they are attracted to more balanced games, that is, showing a sufficiently high uncertainty of outcome (Forrest et al., 2005), and switch off when the game is boring.

At first glance it is not obvious that equilibrium prevails in both fan and TV viewer markets. The first one is very often witnessed to be either in excess demand – when fans are queuing at the gate and then touting – or excess supply when a game is played in a nearly empty stadium. Both happen in European football, for example. It is more difficult to assess which equilibrium or disequilibrium affects the TV viewer market. A preliminary quantitative signal leans towards the reality of an excess supply of non-free televised sport overall though it is not an academic proof: in the French market in 2010, 98,000 hours of sport were televised by pay-per-view and commercial TV companies against 2,000 hours by public and free-to-air channels (CSA, 2011). A TV viewer willing to subscribe to all the supply of sports broadcasts would have been asked to pay over €2,000 per year. If addicted TV viewers can envisage spending such an amount to watch sports all day and all year long, nobody can spend more than 24 hours (98,000/365 = 268 hours) per day watching his or her TV screen. None of the aforementioned hypotheses is required for a disequilibrium model of a team sports league; they are dropped in the model elaborated below.

Teams' Soft Budget Constraint

The most crucial assumption in the standard equilibrium model of a league with win-maximizing teams is that teams are run in such a way as to exactly break even in accounting terms, that is, they are supposed to strictly stick to their budget constraint having simultaneously a zero profit and a zero deficit. However, a strictly balanced budget constraint introduces a strongly restrictive assumption in the model; relax this assumption and the equilibrium solution can no longer be taken for granted because teams' expenditures in excess of teams' revenues would translate into an excess demand for talent. With a deregulated labour market, win-maximizing teams overbid and overspend for talents, run deficits season after season and sink into debt. Lasting deficit and debt without going bankrupt suggest that teams enjoy a soft budget constraint in their maximizing calculation, which points to disequilibrium models in which teams can either endeavour a hard (> 0) or enjoy a soft (< 0) budget constraint, and not only a balanced budget ($= 0$).

First, the assumption of a hard budget constraint – never a team deficit – is not that realistic compared with current weak governance and bad financial performance of many European football teams and leagues (Andreff, 2007). According to the Union of European Football Associations (UEFA, 2014), 51 per cent of all European top division football clubs were making losses in 2007, 54 per cent in 2008, 61 per cent in 2009 and 2010, 63 per cent in 2011 and 48 per cent in 2012.[3] Repeatedly being in the red – revealing a soft budget constraint – is more the rule than exception, which translates into leagues operating off their economic equilibrium. Recurrent teams' financial deficits and debts in European football drew sports economists' attention already one decade ago as to what was then coined a financial crisis[4] – rather improperly since deficits and debts seem to be chronic and structural in open leagues.

Storm and Nielsen (2012) underlined that a number of European professional football teams chronically operate on the brink of insolvency for over a decade or so, without going out of business. They correctly conclude that European professional football clubs have many characteristics in common with enterprises in former communist economies. A state-owned enterprise would never disappear in centrally planned economies. It is nearly the same in professional football leagues: clubs are promoted or relegated according to their sporting outcomes, but they almost never disappear from the football business due to financial issues. Kornaï (1980) demonstrated that firms which enjoy a soft budget constraint take stock of it to form an excess demand for inputs.[5] When all or most firms (teams) are run with a soft budget constraint, the whole economy (league) is all the time in a typical disequilibrium of a shortage economy. It never returns to equilibrium: there are always a number of teams in the red. Following Kornaï, there are five circumstances that *ex ante* ensure a firm (a team) enjoys a soft budget constraint:

a. The team is price-maker on its input and/or output markets. If a team is wage-taker as in the standard equilibrium model, then its budget constraint is hard or balanced (never a deficit).
b. The team can influence taxation rules, avoid or postpone tax payment (tax arrears are tolerated by tax authorities). If the team cannot, then its budget constraint is hard.
c. The team can receive state or municipality grants or subsidies to cover current expenses or finance investment. If not, the team's budget constraint is hard.

   d. The team can be granted credit by banks whatever its deficit, debt and insolvency. If it does not find any credit due to its deficit, debt or insolvency, its budget constraint is hard.

   e. The team's investment is not dependent on retained profits because it can find external finance for investing or overinvesting, including from fans or sugar daddies. When investment is strictly constrained by the amount of profits, a team's budget constraint is hard.

Therefore, when its budget constraint is soft, spending more than its revenues is not a matter of life and death for a firm (team), as Kornaï states, which will permanently survive its deficit.[6] A high survival rate of teams in a league, even when they are in the red, would confirm that it is so. For instance, teams' survival rate is very high[7] despite football business generating losses. Spanish football teams are used to spending larger amounts on player wages and transfers than their revenues, and exhibit a rising indebtedness – 89 per cent of clubs were operating losses in 2008 (Barajas and Rodriguez, 2010) without bankruptcies. The French football league experimented quite a few more years in the red than in the black over more than a decade (Aglietta et al., 2008; Andreff, 2015a) though deficits and debts were smaller than in English, Italian and Spanish leagues. Even in the German league, professional football teams are not run as if they were compelled to break even since they are non-profit associations (*Vereins*) committed to win as many games as possible for the fans, not to make profit.

Moreover, with regard to Kornaï's five preconditions for a budget constraint to be soft, empirical evidence in European football open leagues is there. Big teams are wage-makers. Many teams fail to pay taxes without being liquidated, and when they enter administration the reconstructed tax arrears are almost always among the debt obligations that are not being met (Storm and Nielsen, 2012). A number of football teams rent sports facilities to a municipality at a subsidized rate. The enforcement of European Union competition policy has restricted the possibility of direct municipal subsidies to professional football teams but subsidization still occasionally happens, like in the Italian *calcio*, with the government having stepped in with league financing (the *salve calcio* state plan in 2002, see Baroncelli and Lago, 2006). Catalan banks grant credits to FC Barcelona and Castillan banks to Real Madrid whatever their balance sheets (Ascari and Gagnepain, 2007). Teams often succeed in renegotiating and rescheduling repayments to the banks.

Many European football teams are seen as too big to fail by their stakeholders, and they always find some institution (bank, TV company and so on) to bail them out or grant them a loan even though irrecoverable;

soft subsidies are provided by sugar daddies (Abramovich, Glaser, sheik Mansur, the Qatari sovereign fund and others) or sponsors in the form of additional cash and capital in cases of looming insolvency (Storm and Nielsen, 2012). This is widespread enough to be under the scrutiny of the UEFA Financial Fair Play initiative (Franck, 2014). TV companies either take over some teams or finance a league (including its deficit) again and again through inflating TV rights from one broadcasting contract to the other (Andreff, 2011). Such money inflows redistributed across the league allow overinvestment in talent at team level. German teams are used to gambling on success from which ensues a constant overinvestment in talents and players (Dietl and Frank, 2007), a characteristic behaviour of organizations with a soft budget constraint. Whatever the case, those teams in the red were not liquidated even after heavy payment arrears, social contribution and tax arrears in all European football leagues. Many European football teams purchase more inputs than they can afford with their revenues; they attempt to endlessly recruit more expensive players and the richest clubs overbid each other to attract the best superstars.

A SIMPLE DISEQUILIBRIUM MODEL OF AN OPEN TEAM SPORTS LEAGUE

Given the above-underlined empirical evidence about European football open leagues, it is worth exploring the potential offered by disequilibrium economics to move forward on the path towards a more adapted, realistic and comprehensive model than the standard equilibrium of a team sports league.

Disequilibrium Economics: A Brief Reminder

A non-Walrasian economics approach had been initiated by Clower (1967) and Leijonhuvfud (1968) starting from the evidence that a Walrasian central auctioneer required for a market to converge towards equilibrium is usually absent in market economies so that decentralized economic agents are not likely to be price-takers – of prices sent by the central auctioneer. Therefore, convergence towards equilibrium may take a long time or may not show up at all, and eventually in the short term a number of adjustments will proceed through quantity variations, and not only through marginal price adjustments as in the Walrasian model. Such was the inception to disequilibrium economics that led to a general disequilibrium model of repressed inflation (Barro and Grossman, 1971, 1974) with mixed market adjustments both in price and quantity.

Then a major hindrance against the general equilibrium model emerged from within the mainstream equilibrium theory itself. In a Walrasian trial-and-error process, the equilibrium solution is reached if and only if for any good and all goods, at any time, the Arrow-Debreu net demand (demand minus supply) has an appropriate shape guaranteeing that if net demand is positive the price of this good increases, and if net demand is negative the price decreases – that is, the gross substitutability property is satisfied. Otherwise the Walrasian interdependent system of equations and prices do not converge towards equilibrium. A theorem simultaneously and independently demonstrated by Sonnenschein (1973), Debreu (1974) and Mantel (1974) establishes that Arrow-Debreu net demands may have any sort of shape and there is no logical or theoretical reason why they will necessarily comply with the gross substitutability property. Thus, a positive net demand does not necessarily trigger a price increase while a negative net demand does not necessarily lead to a price decrease. That the whole system of equations and prices will unavoidably converge to equilibrium can no longer be taken for granted whatever the shape of net demand. Therefore, lasting excess demand and excess supply rather than equilibrium are likely to result from the Walrasian trial-and-error process.

It is in the wake of the first attempt by Barro-Grossman and the so-called Sonnenschein-Debreu-Mantel theorem that disequilibrium modelling sprang up: Younes (1975), Weitzman (1977), Muellbauer and Portes (1978), Drazen (1980) and others elaborated on different fixed or sticky price rationing models, that is, disequilibria regimes reacting to quantity signals rather – or more swiftly – than to price signals (Varian, 1975). In particular, Malinvaud (1977) and Benassy (1975, 1982, 1983) developed a disequilibrium model combining either open or repressed inflation with either employment or unemployment in three different economic regimes. A disequilibrium regime may turn out to be a repressed inflation regime, a classical unemployment regime or a Keynesian unemployment regime, considering the different arrangements of excess demand and excess supply exhibited in Table 2.1. When an economy exhibits a double excess demand in both labour and product markets, it is known to reproduce a repressed inflation regime. In the variety of disequilibrium models à la Malinvaud-Benassy the focus is on price rigidity or inelasticity.

Since repressed inflation, rationing and quantitative adjustments were usually associated with communist economies, Manove (1973), Howard (1976), Portes and Winter (1977, 1980) and Charemza and Quandt (1982) applied disequilibrium models to former centrally planned economies. The latter were the context in which Kornaï (1980) stressed the role of enterprises' budget constraints in generating excess demand in some markets and excess supply in other markets. When the budget constraint is soft,

Table 2.1   Economic disequilibrium regimes

	Repressed inflation	Classical unemployment	Keynesian unemployment	Fourth regime[a]
Product market	excess demand	excess demand	excess supply	excess supply
Labour market	excess demand	excess supply	excess supply	excess demand

Note: a. This regime is mathematically unstable and eventually degenerates into a repressed inflation regime.

Source: Andreff (2014b).

one is referred back to the above-described situation (preconditions a, b, c, d, e) as a shortage economy and, according to Kornaï, the demand for some inputs may be infinite if enterprise budget constraint is definitely soft. If soft budget constraint pertains to all or most firms the whole economy or industry (or league)[8] will lastingly function off equilibrium. The resulting shortage economy characterized former centrally planned economies, but it can also emerge in a number of sectors, industries and activities in market economies as soon as their organizations (firms, teams, clubs) do not maximize profit and are run under a soft budget constraint. Kornaï et al. (2003) provided a model generalization to all the situations where a soft budget constraint is a self-reproducing and self-sustaining phenomenon, in particular in those industries encompassing non-profit organizations. An open team sports league with win-maximizing teams is one case in point. In this variety of disequilibrium models the focus is no longer on price rigidity but on imbalanced budget constraint.

Moreover, a disequilibrium model is more general than an equilibrium model, which is the solution reached when the budget constraint exactly equals zero (Equation 2.9). In all the many (infinite number of) events[9] when the budget constraint is either > 0 or < 0, disequilibrium self-sustains and lasts. A unique solution ($= 0$) is not crucially looked for in disequilibrium modelling where supply–demand equilibrium is considered as pure hazard or strictly theoretical. Kornaï (1980) compares Walras economic equilibrium with the point of absolute congealing in physics. Both have no empirical existence while being at the roots of theoretical reasoning and practical metrics. Equilibrium belongs to the realm of theoretical pure and utopian economics whereas disequilibrium is the harsh reality of everyday economic life and actual markets.

None of the famous disequilibrium economists like Barro,[10] Grossman, Kornaï, Malinvaud and others was appealed to sports economics in the making so that there is no application of disequilibrium economics to sports so far. Searching the sports economics literature shows no analytical article devoted to a disequilibrium team sports league model. Some sports markets in disequilibrium were empirically surveyed (Andreff, 2012) such as an excess demand for some sports events, possible excess demand or excess supply in the different markets for sporting goods, and an excess supply of some sport arenas and televised sports. Regards team sports leagues, the only departure from a standard equilibrium model is due to Tuck and Whitten (2013). Their dynamic simulation model of a win-maximizing sports league allows for non-equilibrium solutions when the complex stochastic dynamic characteristics of a league provide teams with incentives to under-perform and tank. However, this mathematical model is not a direct application of disequilibrium economics strictly speaking.

Now that most clubs in European football leagues actually face a soft budget constraint, one interpretation of such a situation is in terms of club and league weak governance (Andreff, 2007; Chapter 7, this volume). Another implication is that a more realistic model of an open team sports league should be a disequilibrium model and no longer the Walrasian equilibrium model. A disequilibrium model of a team sports league should encompass at least two markets that may be both in excess demand or both in excess supply, or one each, and where teams do not break even because of a soft budget constraint.

A Labour Market in Excess Demand

The simplest disequilibrium model of a European team sports league comprising win-maximizing teams that operate in a labour market with wage rigidity would be:[11]

$$Max \; t_i \qquad\qquad (2.13')$$

$$R_i\,(m_i, t_i) - s.\, t_i - c_i^0 \le or \ge 0 \qquad\qquad (2.14')$$

Assuming that the stadium and club management are not significant inputs of a team's revenue function, the fixed cost can be left out and then it follows:

$$R_i\,(m_i, t_i) \le or \ge s.\, t_i \qquad\qquad (2.15')$$

If wage is not assumed to be infinitely flexible, talent mobility across the teams is limited enough to hinder equality occurring between marginal cost and average talent revenue as in Equation (2.7) – while market wage will not adjust to its equilibrium level. Thus, compared to equilibrium, team i will form either excess demand for talents when the budget constraint (2.14') is < 0 or a too short demand when it is > 0. In the first event, team i spends more on acquiring talents than it makes in revenues, which fits with the above-mentioned football leagues' empirical evidence. In the second case, team i does not spend all its revenues on talent purchase; it is left with surplus (above normal) profit, and demands a shorter quantity of inputs than in equilibrium, which is not very realistic with win-maximizing teams in a system of promotion and relegation.

Now assume that team i meets a soft budget constraint, (2.13') to (2.15') transform into:

$$Max \ t_i \tag{2.13}$$

$$R_i(m_i, t_i) - s. \ t_i - c_i^0 \leq 0 \tag{2.14}$$

and without fixed cost:

$$R_i(m_i, t_i) \leq s. \ t_i \tag{2.15}$$

If most teams behave this way, two logical consequences are:

a. the league itself repeatedly is in the red when aggregating the net financial results of all its teams as soon as the profits of some teams are more than compensated by losses of most teams, and
b. there is necessarily a permanent excess demand on the labour market for talents, triggering an endless arms race. Without a hard or balanced budget constraint, there is no brake on an ever growing demand for talent while the number of players talented enough to play in professional football leagues is limited, say to T_0. The labour market for talents is in disequilibrium due to a team's aggregated excess demand in the face of a limited supply of player talents to the league T_0:

$$\sum_{i=1}^{n} t_i = T; T \geq T_0 \tag{2.16}$$

where the number of teams in the league is $n(i = 1, \ldots, n)$.

With an excess demand for talents, marginal revenue productivity of labour $RM_i = \frac{\partial R_i(m_i, t_i)}{\partial t_i}$ cannot equalize marginal unit cost of labour when the last unit of the T_0 talents is recruited and the disequilibrium in the labour market for talents implies:

$$RM_i = \frac{\partial R_i(m_i, t_i)}{\partial t_i} \leq s \tag{2.17}$$

All the labour units, up to the last one recruited, are overpaid when excess demand prevails in the labour market. Due to their aggregate overall excess demand, teams are rationed by a short supply of talents and are eager to pay a salary much higher than marginal labour productivity of talent, that is, to overpay players in order to attract them in a context of relative player shortage and harsh competition across the teams on the demand side of the labour market.[12] Then, recruited players provide a lower labour productivity than the salary they are paid, which sounds like the exact opposite of Scully's sense of player exploitation (Scully, 1974). In European leagues with win-maximizing teams operating under a soft budget constraint, players are paid more than they would have been at equilibrium wage. Since all wage-maker teams are embarked on an arms race to recruit players, namely, the few available superstars, they accept paying a wage quite higher than marginal revenue productivity of labour in order to outbid competing teams – evidenced in all European leagues after the Bosman case; at the end of the day, teams are cursed in paying too much wages for the marginal labour productivity they obtain from players (Andreff, 2014b). Paying more than the equilibrium wage and recruiting less than the quantity of talents they demand, rationed teams are involved in an endless skyrocketing race of payroll increases, which is observed in European football as regards superstars.

Another implication of excess demand in the labour market for player talents is that football teams with soft budget constraints attempt to recruit too many players, although they cannot afford as many as they would have wished due to the short supply of superstars. Teams spend their money without counting losses – and sometimes they cook the books to hide this reality – due to soft budget constraints. Moreover, operating on the demand side of an excess demand input market teams are always scared of being short of inputs without being able to find one more superstars in the market – due to inequality (2.16). In such an event, like enterprises in former centrally planned economies, teams hoard labour (talents) as a reaction to circumvent the consequences of operating on a short supply input market. In European football, the very existence of a reservation and transfer system until the Bosman ruling in 1995 enabled teams to keep their players. After the Bosman case, teams recruited on their rosters more players than they really needed.[13] Thus, there is some slack in each team; teams are overmanned – look at the rosters of various European football teams and the number of substitutes never used over a season. This slack is beneficial to players in terms of the relationship between wages and both working time (very few players play all the season games during 90 minutes) – that is, work intensity – and labour productivity.

Genuine Players: Beyond a Homogeneous Unit of Talent

Now let us give up the unrealistic and simplifying assumption of a homogeneous unit of talent, and introduce a qualitative differentiation between the most talented superstars and less talented journeymen players. It was assumed above that the supply of player talents is limited. Is it as likely to be true for journeymen players as for superstars? Obviously not since one can witness in all European top football leagues a number of journeymen players who are unemployed at the start of every season.[14] Unemployment is a crucial index of excess supply. Such an observation apparently contradicts inequality (2.16), which means excess demand on the labour market for player talents. Therefore, for a journeymen player segment of the labour market excess supply is to be modelled instead of excess demand on a superstar segment.

The next point to consider is whether a team's excess demand for superstars in one market segment is compensated by excess supply of journeymen players in the other market segment. It is assumed here that there is not full compensation: excess demand for superstars exceeds excess supply of journeymen players and the inequality (2.16) still remains relevant for the labour market overall.

Let T_s stand for the overall number of available superstars and T_a the overall number of available journeymen players. It follows that:

$$T_s + T_a = T_0 \qquad (2.18)$$

Now a team has to maximize an assortment of superstar and journeymen player talents in order to maximize its wins (2.19), and its soft budget constraint is to be rewritten in such a way as to take this assortment into account (2.20). Below t_{si} is defined as the demand for superstars by team i, t_{ai} the demand for journeymen players by team i, s_s the market wage for superstars and s_a the market wage for journeymen players. Thus, for team i:

$$Max\ (t_{si} + t_{ai}) \qquad (2.19)$$

Under a soft budget constraint:

$$R^i\ (m_i, t_{si} + t_{ai}) - s_s \cdot t_{si} - s_a \cdot t_{ai} \leq 0 \qquad (2.20)$$

and

$$\sum_{i=1}^{n} (t_{si} + t_{ai}) \geq T_0 \qquad (2.21)$$

If, as assumed, excess demand for superstars more than compensates excess supply for journeymen players, the labour market disequilibrium in the superstar segment becomes:

$$\sum_{i=1}^{n} t_{si} \geq T_s \tag{2.22}$$

In the superstar segment of the market, excess demand coincides with a wage higher than the marginal revenue productivity of labour:

$$RM_{si} = \frac{\partial R_i(m_i, t_{si})}{\partial t_i} \leq s_s \tag{2.23}$$

Superstars are not directly competing against each other, with every superstar being in a monopoly position over his or her practically non-substitutable specific talent. In the journeymen player segment of the market, excess supply of talents (2.24) drives market wage down lower than the marginal revenue productivity of labour (2.25) for these lower quality and more competing talents:

$$\sum_{i=1}^{n} t_{ai} \leq T_a \tag{2.24}$$

$$RM_{ai} = \frac{\partial R_i(m_i, t_{ai})}{\partial t_i} \geq s_a \tag{2.25}$$

Inequality (2.25) shows that journeymen players are subject to exploitation in Scully's sense; they are paid less than their marginal productivity. They suffer from being in excess supply as well as from the monopsonistic situation of the league encompassing coordinated wage-maker team owners in the labour market; thus journeymen players bear a rent levied by owners on their salaries. An opposite asymmetry prevails on the superstar segment where the league's monopsony is countervailed by a strong monopoly situation of each superstar due to the uniqueness of his or her talents, skills, reputation, performances, record of achievements and so on, and his or her absolute exclusivity over them. Thus wage-maker team owners have to overbid in terms of wage for recruiting Lionel Messi, Cristiano Ronaldo and other superstars.

A disequilibrium model of a league with win-maximizing teams operating under soft budget constraints in a segmented labour market describes an arms race for superstar talents fuelled by excess demand, superstars' skyrocketing wages that trigger teams' payroll overruns, the unemployment of journeymen players in excess supply used as a safety valve or an adjustment variable by team owners, and their lower wages paid at a rate below their marginal labour productivity.

A Fan's Excess Demand in the Market for Live Games

Turning now to the output market where a league and its clubs supply games, let us assume for a while that there is no difference between team fans attending a game at stadium and TV viewers. Thus, on the demand side are found only homogeneous fans who basically demand to attend as many games of their favourite team i as they can financially afford;[15] d_{hi} stands for a fan h demand of team i games. A fan's utility is assumed to increase in strict proportion to the number of games attended. Since a European top football league is a cartel of teams supplying professional football games in a country, it is in a monopoly position to fix its output supply, that is, the number of fixtures once given the number of teams in the league; n_i stands for all the team i games supplied by the league over a season This monopoly supply creates a game shortage on the supply side of the market for live football matches and enables teams to maintain a price high enough to make a profit that includes a monopoly rent.

Consider one fan h: as any consumer, her demand function of team i games depends on her initial money endowment m_{0h} (savings, assets), her income share available for paying tickets at the gate Inc_h,[16] and the fixed ticket price of a game $\bar{p}$[17]. First, imagine that there was just one fan per team i; her behaviour could be described as:

$$Max\ d_i \qquad (2.26)$$

$$d_i\,(m_0, Inc, \bar{p}) \geq n_i \qquad (2.27)$$

$$\bar{p} > 0 \qquad (2.28)$$

In European football, each team plays twice against all other teams, one home and one away game, so that the supply of team i games is $n_i = 2(n - 1)$ while the overall league supply of games over a season is $n(n - 1)$. This is the total supply of professional football games in a country since creating another top football league in the same country is prohibited by the international Fédération Internationale de Football Association (FIFA). Stadium capacity is assumed to be constant over a season and then the supply side overall is fixed by multiplying all stadiums' capacities by the overall number of games $n(n - 1)$.

Now assume that the overall number of a team sports league fans is $g(h = 1, \ldots, g)$ and the number of team i's fans is gi ($h_i = 1, \ldots, g_i$), with $g_i \leq g$. All team i's fans are subject to the same constraint, a shortage in the supply by the league of their favourite team games, of which the number is restricted to $n_i = 2(n - 1)$. Thus, for any team i's fan h, maximizing utility boils down to:

$$Max \; d_{hi} \tag{2.29}$$

$$d_{hi} \, (m_{0h}, Inc_h, \bar{p}) \geq 2(n - 1) \tag{2.30}$$

$$\bar{p} > 0 \tag{2.31}$$

Whatever fans' expenditures over a season, the number of games they actually attend cannot be bigger than the number of their favourite team i games supplied by the league: $2(n - 1)$. They are rationed by the league to this maximum number of team i's games over the whole season.[18] Inequality (2.30) expresses the potential excess of a fan's demand facing the league's short supply of her favourite team games. With a fixed price the market will adjust in quantity, through market rationing; fans will have to adjust to the available supply of games at a given price $\bar{p}$. The short side of the market, that is, the league's supply of games, rations the longer side, that is, fans' demand. Moreover, since fans' demand is trivially inelastic to a game at fixed price, the price variable can be dropped, as in most disequilibrium models with price rigidity. Then the constraint (2.30) simplifies to:

$$d_{hi} \, (m_{0h}, Inc_h) \geq 2(n - 1) \tag{2.32}$$

At the level of a whole league, that is, for all games and all fans, market disequilibrium clearly is in short supply of games compared to fans' demand; from the fans' standpoint, they are in excess demand written as:

$$\sum_{i=1}^{n} \sum_{h=1}^{g_i} d_{hi}(m_{0h}, Inc_h) \geq n(n - 1) \tag{2.33}$$

At first sight, it could be objected that fans' demand does not take into account some variable reflecting game quality. There are various candidates for a game quality variable such as the team i's standing in the championship (Andreff and Scelles, 2014), its win percentage, its quantity of talents t_i or bookmakers' odds. With regard to overall market disequilibrium (2.33), one could think of introducing some index of competitive balance on the left-hand side demand function d_{hi}. However, this variable is not considered here under the assumption that a genuine team i's fan is not attracted to the stadium by game quality, the opponent team quality or his or her favourite team quality. A typical fan attends simply because this is the emotional and usual fan behaviour whatever their favourite team standing, win percentage, competitive balance and so on. This assumption will specify fan behaviour when other game spectators, such as TV viewers or couch potatoes, are differentiated from fans below.

Finally, relations (2.13) to (2.33) describe two building blocks of a team sports league's economy that exhibit a double excess demand in labour and product markets, which is known to reproduce a repressed inflation regime (Benassy, 1983), also coined a shortage economy by Kornaï (1980), to which labour market segmentation has been added. As long as the budget constraint on football teams is soft – that is, the break-even point is not actually reached or enforced as a permanent governance rule – European football leagues will remain in such a regime. The arms race among the clubs to acquire the most talented players in the market will go on. Fans will go on being frustrated by waiting (queuing) for more games of their favourite team since their willingness to attend and pay is bigger than the number of their favourite team games fixed by the league.

A Market for Televised Games Supplied by Free-to-air TV Channels

Following the above-mentioned distinction between two sorts of sport attendance that emerged in the sports economics literature, it is assumed that fans and TV viewers do not behave the same way in the market for sports matches. The latter is to be split into two segments for two differentiated products. As regards fans' demand and the corresponding market for live sport shows nothing is changed compared to above inequalities (2.29) to (2.33). However, a second market for televised sport shows must be introduced into the model together with a consumer demand function for televised games by TV viewers.

Assuming that the TV viewers' audience is attracted by outcome uncertainty and not by a specific team i games, the variable of interest is no longer the number of their favourite team i's games attended. One variable that encapsulates a game uncertainty of outcome lies in respective win percentages of two opponent teams i and j, that is, w_i and w_j. Thus, TV viewers' utility is maximized when the outcome uncertainty of a televised game is the highest, that is, when win percentages of the two teams are the highest; their utility function is assumed to increase in win percentages. It is only beyond a given threshold of the couple $(\overline{w}_i, \overline{w}_j)$ that a game is considered attractive enough to represent a high quality product worth watching.[19] Beyond this threshold, that is, for $\overline{w} = \min(\overline{w}_i, \overline{w}_j)$, viewers switch on their TV, otherwise they do not. It follows that TV viewers' demand is high for high quality games while only a proportion of overall games supplied by the league (assumed all to be televised) over a season will pass the quality threshold and will be effectively viewed. Let d_{kij} stand for the number of high quality games between a team i and an opponent team j that a TV viewer $k(k = 1, \ldots, r)$ demands. A TV viewer utility is assumed to increase in strict proportion with the number of high quality games watched. Assume also that TV viewers of the k vintage only like watching televised games for free and address their demand exclusively to free-to-air TV channels. Since all the games televised by these channels are not high quality, that is, do not pass the $\overline{w}$ threshold, TV viewers k are rationed. If, say, only a proportion $\lambda(0 \leq \lambda \leq 1)$ of all televised games on free-to-air channels are high quality, then it follows for any TV viewer k:

$$Max \ d_{kij} \tag{2.34}$$

$$d_{kij} \ (m_{0k}, \ Inc_k, \ \overline{w}) \geq \lambda \ n(n - 1) \tag{2.35}$$

$$p = 0 \tag{2.36}$$

Overall market excess demand derives from aggregating all the individual TV viewers' demands:

$$\sum_{k=1}^{r} d_{kij} (m_{0k}, Inc_k, \overline{w}) \geq \lambda n(n - 1) \tag{2.37}$$

This was the observed real situation when there was just one public free-to-air monopoly TV channel in operation per country in Europe. It may still be so now, when there are a few coordinated or collusive oligopolistic public and private TV companies. In practice, this translates into high audience ratios (or high TV market shares) when the $\lambda \ n(n - 1)$ high quality games, with high outcome uncertainty, are broadcast on the one hand. On the other hand, only a low audience is reached for a number $n(1 - \lambda)$ of boring games without enough outcome uncertainty. Relation (2.37) paves the way for empirical studies about audiences of televised sport on free-to-air channels in order to check whether they are low or not and for which game quality.

A Market for Televised Games Supplied by Pay-per-view TV Channels

Now consider that televised games are no longer broadcast for free by public and free-to-air but by pay-per-view and commercial TV companies at a subscription fee p^*. The market situation (equilibrium or disequilibrium) will crucially depend on the level of the subscription fee fixed ahead over the season by TV companies in an oligopsony situation. Of course, TV viewers $v(v = 1, \ldots, z)$ – those willing to pay for televised sport – will take p^* into account in their demand function d_{vij} when maximizing their utility so that:

$$Max\ d_{vij} \tag{2.38}$$

$$d_{vij}\ (m_{0v}, Inc_v, \overline{w}, p^*) \geq \text{or} \leq \alpha\ n(n-1) \tag{2.39}$$

$$p^* > 0 \tag{2.40}$$

with α the proportion ($0 \leq \alpha \leq 1$) of all games televised on pay-per-view channels that are high quality and that TV viewers are willing to pay for.

If by chance a TV channel exactly fixed *ex ante* the single value of the subscription fee p^* that transforms inequality (2.39) into an equality, then this TV company would have found the price that TV viewers are exactly willing to pay for a proportion α of all the broadcast games without spending more than they can afford given their savings m_{0v} and incomes Inc_v. In such circumstances, p^* is the market equilibrium price. In the current functioning of TV channels that overbid to obtain the broadcasting rights of European major football leagues, a TV channel that besides must cover the cost of such rights can find the equilibrium subscription fee only by chance. If a TV channel *ex ante* fixes a subscription fee lower than p^*, inequality (2.39) will be $\geq$ and TV viewers will be rationed in high quality games but will pay a low subscription fee for this ration, lower than their willingness to pay. If, as more likely to happen with oligopsonistic commercial TV companies,[20] a TV channel *ex ante* fixes a subscription fee higher than p^*, a number of potential subscribers will not subscribe, inequality (2.39) will be $\leq$ and the sport (football) broadcast market will be in excess supply.

The above model (2.13) to (2.40) has some major implications that can be briefly sketched. As long as the budget constraint on football clubs is not hard – until sticking to the break-even point is not the rule – top European football leagues will remain in a repressed inflation regime. The arms race across the clubs to acquire the most talented players will go on. The fans will be frustrated at queuing to attend football matches since their willingness to pay for more games is higher than the league supply of their favourite team's games. UEFA Financial Fair Play rules would probably alleviate repressed inflation in somewhat hardening clubs' budget constraints, and this would slightly curb superstar wage inflation (superstar wages would come closer to, though remaining still higher than, labour productivity) and put a brake on the arms race for superstars. However, if one wants to definitely phase out the existing repressed inflation regime, measures are needed to get rid of excess demand in the labour market for talent, which means tightening the financial belt or strictly hardening the budget constraint of European football clubs and leagues. Though UEFA Financial Fair Play rules are going in the right direction in this respect,[21] the deadline is not fixed yet when all teams qualified on the pitch for UEFA competitions would only be admitted to participate under the precondition that their revenues exactly balance their expenditures (balanced budget constraint).

A following implication is that fans' excess demand of their favourite team games is hard to satisfy. One option is to increase the number of opponent teams in the league but such a solution is not too realistic beyond 20 teams because it would multiply the number of boring games without much reward to the winners in terms of prize or league standing. Another option is to augment the number of fixtures, for instance, playing two instead of one home and away games or adding a final play-off stage probably with the same effect of diluting the attractiveness of many games, namely, in the second half of the season. Creating a rival league is not an option in European open team sports leagues since it is not allowed by international sports federations. Attracting more TV viewers seems to be easier because it would consist in increasing the share a of high quality games. A number of tools – the championship format, revenue redistribution across teams, UEFA Financial Fair Play, a regulation of player recruitment (if not infringing the Bosman jurisprudence) – may improve competitive balance and the league standing effect, a question that goes beyond this first attempt at disequilibrium modelling of a team sports league. In order to compare with the classical sports economics approach, at least to some extent, competitive balance should be introduced in the model, not only as a threshold to be reached such as in (2.35), but also in the labour market block of the model. Then competitive balance will be one of the interactive variables between the labour and product markets to be examined. An interesting question will emerge: is a sport contest more – or less – balanced with a team sports league in economic equilibrium or disequilibrium?

A PROGRAMME FOR FURTHER RESEARCH: TOWARDS A COMPREHENSIVE DISEQUILIBRIUM MODEL OF AN OPEN TEAM SPORTS LEAGUE

A lot of work remains to be done in order to achieve a comprehensive disequilibrium model of an open team sports league. Once completed the disequilibrium model should be resolved, and its mathematical properties exhibited. Then, before data collection, some indices should be designed in order to assess the existence and handle metrics of excess demand (for example, outlying inflation for superstar wages, length of fans' waiting lists, touting) and excess supply (for example, journeymen player unemployment, rates of stadium utilization, TV audience ratios). A further step should be robust econometric testing after including appropriate disequilibrium indices.[22] However, the first step should be to complete as much as possible the disequilibrium model of a team sports league in two ways: first, the model must take on board a number of markets pertaining to a team sports league that are usually unheeded in equilibrium modelling of a league and, at best, encompass all of them. Second, since different spillover effects across markets usually appear in a disequilibrium model, it is absolutely crucial to model interactions between markets.

Missing Markets

A first missing market in the above-sketched disequilibrium model is the one for TV rights to be acquired for broadcasting team sports league games. Indeed, TV viewers are not supplied with televised sport games directly by the league but through an intermediary market for sport TV broadcasts on the supply side, which are either a monopolistic league that pools TV rights for sale or the different teams that negotiate with TV companies in their own right.[23] On the demand side, oligopsonistic competition[24] between TV companies does not usually translate into flexible prices (TV rights), all the more so when purchasing channels are facing a league monopoly with a rationing behaviour. Thus, this intermediary market is likely to operate off equilibrium and must be modelled accordingly.

Nowadays all football teams are used to signing contracts with sponsors. Teams are demanders for such contracts and associated finance offered in the market for football sponsorship. On the demand side, each football team negotiates its own sponsorship contracts – this business is not pooled at league level – in potential competition with all the teams of the league but also with teams from foreign football leagues in a globalized market for sport sponsorship. A team negotiates with companies located in different countries, not only companies from the league's domestic economy. On the supply side, any enterprise or organization willing to pay for having its brand exposed on T-shirts, football shoes, in stadia and on football TV broadcasts is a potential supplier in the market for sport sponsorship. The number of potential sponsors is big with sport (football) economic globalization (Andreff, 2012), so that the supply side is close to having the characteristics of a competitive market.[25] Moreover, each sponsorship contract is signed after a face-to-face secret negotiation between one competing team and one competing sponsor usually on the basis of a standardized contract form that is a rather homogeneous product. Thus, the market for sport sponsorship is likely to move close to equilibrium compared with other markets of a team sports league. Nevertheless, it should be integrated in disequilibrium modelling of an open league.

The market for sport (football) wagering and gambling is absolutely unheeded in equilibrium models of a team sports league. On the supply side, bookmakers, gambling companies and on-line betting operators compete in offering betting opportunities on the outcome of sports events, primarily football games, while the demand side is crowded with occasional betters, addicted and professional gamblers and even some gamblers connected to organized crime (Forrest et al., 2008). With the development of on-line sporting bets in the past decade this market has become both global and extremely close to a pure competitive market. Now it is not only possible to bet before but also during the course of a game, and at any second of the game; bets are not only about a game's outcome or scoring but also about specific in-match events (such as the probability of a corner, a penalty, a yellow card and so on, and the time of its occurrence); money can be placed in spread betting and betting exchanges; variations of traded quantities (of bets and their amounts) instantaneously adjust to changing odds (prices) without any demand inelasticity to price. With each bookmaker or on-line betting operator the odds are instantaneously evolving (adjusted) in reaction to variations of betting amounts; there is no price rigidity. Rather similarly to a stock exchange, on-line sport betting is the closest reality to a pure competitive market in the sports industry; its instant adjustments in quantities and prices should drive it to the Walrasian market equilibrium solution. However, this remains to be rigorously demonstrated before integrating the market for sport betting into the disequilibrium model of a team sports league since the context is changing: a concentration of the supply side[26] in the market for on-line sport betting is currently witnessed.

Team sports leagues as well as other sports are increasingly plagued with betting-related match fixing due to both intertwined market globalization and on-line betting. Athletes, football players, in particular journeymen players with lower salaries, and some greedy sport managers or coaches are sensitive to monetary incentives for throwing the outcome of a match (Andreff, 2015b); in a sense, they are potential suppliers of fixes, thus creating the supply side of a market, though underground, for match fixing. On the demand side, organized crime as well as corrupted and corrupting people involved in sports, on the one hand, and entire networks of small coordinated gamblers primarily located in Asia (Hill, 2010), on the other hand, demand fixed matches to bet on, primarily those of European major team sports leagues (Forrest, 2012). They do not contract with registered bookmakers and on-line betting operators in the regulated gambling business but instead place their bets in the streets with coordinating corrupted gamblers and unregistered ('illegal') on-line operators. Awareness surfaced in the sports economics literature in the past decade that an 'illegal' market for match fixing had emerged that might jeopardize the whole industry of professional sports leagues (Dietl and Weingärtner, 2012; Andreff, 2014c). Further studies are needed before including the market for match fixing in the above-sketched disequilibrium model of a team sports league but such an underground, illegal and rigged market would hardly deliver Walrasian equilibrium prices and quantities.

Interacting Markets though Spillovers

There are two sorts of interactions between disequilibrium markets. The first consists of spillover effects triggered by those economic agents who are rationed on the short side of a market and switch their unsatisfied demand or supply to another market. A rationed demander (supplier) is not queuing until new sellers (buyers) will appear in the market since it may take a long time due to market imperfections, frictions and so on, or may never happen; then he or she spills over his or her demand (supply) to the market of another more or less substitutable product. Thus, quantity constraints on one market influence effective demands and supplies on other markets. Spillover effects transmit initial disequilibrium from market to market. This is a major difference with an equilibrium model where all individual demands and supplies are assumed to instantaneously adjust or economic agents are assumed to wait until the Walrasian central auctioneer finds the system of equilibrium prices (as assumed until the Sonnenschein-Debreu-Mantel theorem). A second interaction is most typical in disequilibrium models when rationed economic agents in an upstream (input) market in disequilibrium spill over to a downstream (output) market or the other way round; being rationed on their downstream (upstream) market in disequilibrium, they react on their upstream (downstream) market.[27]

Spillover effects in a team sports league are to be identified before introducing them in disequilibrium modelling. A first example is when fans are queuing at the stadium gates or on a team's ticket reservation system while all tickets are already sold. They will not be happy or satisfied waiting until the next game played by their favourite team. Instead, a number of them will decide to watch on a TV screen the game for which they have missed a ticket. In so doing, they switch their excess demand from the market for live games to the market for televised games. Such switching has been coined a spillover effect (Benassy, 1982) or a forced substitution (Kornaï, 1980), here of a televised game to a – no longer available – live game.

Another spillover occurs because the global market segment for superstar players is often in excess demand in the face of sports leagues with win-maximizing teams. Those teams that have unsuccessfully queued for superstars will spill over their excess demand to the market segment of journeymen players, thus forced to substitute the recruitment of lower quality players to recruiting one superstar. Another case in point is the one of journeymen players in excess supply in the market of a given domestic team sports league. Those potentially unemployed football players queuing for recruitment often cannot avoid spilling over their supply of talent to another league abroad or to a lower football division in the same domestic league. In both events, rationed suppliers are forced to spill over to another market and re-contract on less desirable terms. Finally, in case of too short supply by a domestic league – say the French *Ligue* 1 – of football games that meet the above-defined quality threshold in the market for televised games, unsatisfied (rationed) fans will switch their demand to a foreign market for game broadcasts, for instance, those played in the English Premier League. This again is a spillover effect or a forced substitution reacting to excess demand.

Now, with regard to spillover between disequilibrium upstream and downstream markets in a team sports league, a first task is to check for, and analyse, plausible interactions between the labour and product markets, as suggested in note 14. Fans whose demand for their favourite team's wins on the downstream market for live games is frustrated (they are left with an excess demand for wins) may spill over – and often do so – their demand on to the team's upstream labour market in claiming and pressing for more investment in talents or a new coach. This interaction between the product and labour markets is not the only one. Another example is the virtuous or vicious circle (Andreff, 2011) between increases in revenues obtained by a football league on the downstream market for TV broadcasting rights and the related increase in teams' payrolls (thus, in the aggregated payroll at league level) due to their arms race in the upstream market for talent. Clubs' excess demand on the latter spills over through league centralization towards the market for league televised output and translates into inflation in TV broadcasting rights.

Késenne (2012) correctly states, though in the framework of a league equilibrium model, that two markets interplay in the relationship between sports and the media, the upstream market for TV broadcasting rights and the downstream market of televised sports, with the latter broadcasters on the supply side and TV viewers on the demand side. Since broadcasters are on one (demand) side of the upstream market and on the other (supply) side of the downstream market, there are obviously deep interactions between the two markets and a wide room for spillover both ways. Therefore, in a next step, once a market for sport TV broadcasting rights is added to the disequilibrium model its interactions with the downstream market modelled in (2.34) to (2.40) should be taken on board.

Moreover, Késenne (2012) sketches an interaction between the market of televised sport and the market of advertising that uses sport as a support for brand promotion, primarily sponsorship. Assuming that board and shirt advertisers are interested in TV exposure and spectators' aversion for TV advertising, Késenne's model shows that pay-TV is not always more profitable than free-TV for a profit-maximizing broadcaster due to a larger number of TV viewers attracted by free-TV than those willing to pay for sport broadcasts. Therefore, it is clear that the market for advertising and sport sponsorship is downstream in the sense that advertisers and sponsors use sport TV broadcasts as inputs that enable them to extend the size of their brand exposure to more people (viewers). The price that upstream sport organizers sell the broadcasting rights, beyond the quality and audience of supplied sport shows, is also influenced by its attractiveness to advertisers and sponsors. Such interactions between the market for sport sponsorship/advertising and the market of televised games are likely to generate spillover effects as well.

The market for live football matches is upstream to the market of football betting since the basic inputs of bets are outcomes, scores and in-match events of football games. Similarly, the market for fraudulent sport betting utilizes match fixes as its inputs. A model of bet-related match fixing has recently been elaborated with at its core such a relationship between an upstream market for fixes and a downstream market for rigged bets (Andreff, 2014c). A further interaction should be checked and analysed: are not the underpaid journeymen players, according to (2.25) above, the most targeted prey for match fixers? If it were so, this would suggest spillover behaviour of these players compensating on the downstream market of match fixing for their low salaries in the upstream market for labour talent, an assertion that requires further research.

A last avenue for further research would be in fragmenting each side of a market into sub-groups of teams with different budget constraints – hard (> 0), soft (< 0) and balanced ($= 0$) – and then comparing within a same model the effect of soft, hard and balanced budget constraints. It would be of particular interest to theoretically allow a deficit for a given sub-group of teams and fix the precondition of breaking even on other teams in the league, a differentiation that corresponds to reality in most European football leagues. Then the model resolution would exhibit how excess demand for superstars and competitive balance evolve under such an assumption. Disentangling the three theoretical situations fits with the real world of some teams in the black, some strictly sticking to their budget constraint while others are overinvesting in talent and in the red, a major concern for policy makers in charge of European football today.

CONCLUSION

After describing the major characteristics of the standard Walrasian model of a team sports league, this chapter has pointed out some of its restrictive assumptions that make it unfit for the economic reality of actual leagues, in particular, regarding football open leagues with win-maximizing teams. Through dropping the most unrealistic assumptions and stressing the soft budget constraints met by many European professional sport teams, disequilibrium economics has been introduced. A first simplified disequilibrium model has been sketched with two markets for talent and for live games and then extended to televised games and to market segmentation. On the path towards a more comprehensive disequilibrium model of a team sports league, some markets usually unheeded in equilibrium models are to be integrated as well as spillovers across markets due to excess demand or excess supply.

Once achieved, this more comprehensive disequilibrium model should be compared in depth with the standard equilibrium model of a team sports league, namely, with regard to mathematical properties, fitness to empirical evidence of European open leagues and policy recommendations. A preliminary intuition derived from this first attempt at disequilibrium modelling is that a salary cap would not moderate payroll growth as long as the labour market for superstars was in excess demand, that is, as long as teams' budget constraints were not hardened up to tolerate no financial deficit at all. From the disequilibrium model standpoint, assessing UEFA Financial Fair Play should be different from those criticisms often applied to it from a standard equilibrium model viewpoint. Financial Fair Play rules are likely to alleviate repressed inflation and somewhat curb superstar wage inflation in hardening teams' budget constraints, a topic covered in Chapter 8 in this volume.

NOTES

1. Ticket price is assumed to be formed in a perfect competitive market and is given as a parameter (or a price announced by a virtual central auctioneer) taken on board in teams' economic calculation – like in the standard Walrasian model; as a parameter, it does not show up as an active variable in the model.
2. Tested for National Basketball Association (NBA) basketball, fans wish that at least two-thirds of their favourite team wins (Rascher and Solmes, 2007). Buraimo and

Simmons (2008) found that fans at EPL games, who are predominantly supporting the home team, prefer to see their team play a much more inferior team (and beat that team) rather than attend a game that is predicted to be close in score. Essentially, home fans prefer to see their team win rather than watch a draw or see the home team defeated. Késenne (2015) demonstrates theoretically that the winning percentage of a large-market team should not be larger than $w_x = 0.67$ and eventually between 0.5 and 0.67.

3.   12 per cent of all clubs have spent more on wages than they have earned in total revenue in 2012.

4.   See the *Journal of Sports Economics*, **7** (1) 2006 special issue on the financial crisis of European football and a part of the *Journal of Sports Economics*, **8** (6) 2007 issue.

5.   Such a 'Kornaï effect' has been tested successfully by Goldfeld and Quandt (1988, 1993).

6.   When the budget constraint is hard, spending more than its revenues drives a firm into bankruptcy and liquidation.

7.   A high survival rate is clearly verified in English football by Kuper and Szymanski (2009).

8.   A dividing line between Kornaï's and Clower-Barro-Grossman's approaches to economic disequilibrium modelling is that Kornaï contests the relevance of the concept of an aggregated excess demand or excess supply. His point is that at any moment of time there may be (and indeed there are) coexisting economic agents in excess demand and in excess supply on a same market for a same product whose demand and supply do not match due to market imperfections, inflexibilities, frictions, adjustment time lags, geographical distances and institutional constraints on prices and/or quantities. The tentative model below sticks to this view since it pertains to the markets of just one industry (a team sports league).

9.   The solution of an equilibrium model is just one point on a graph whereas a disequilibrium model exhibits a wide (infinite) range of solutions that is either the whole part of the graph where demand exceeds supply (excess demand) or the whole part of the graph where supply exceeds demand (excess supply).

10.   With the anecdotal exception of Barro (2000).

11.   For equations and inequations from (2.13) to (2.40), the formal presentation is similar to the one adopted in Andreff (2014a).

12.   When a market is in disequilibrium, one side (for instance, supply) of the market is shorter than the other one (demand); therefore excess demand. In an excess supply situation, the demand side is shorter than the supply side. This means that, in an excess demand market, aggregating all the microeconomic demands (of all teams) results in a bigger quantity of talents than the aggregated quantity supplied by suppliers (all players). In excess supply, the aggregate quantity of supplied talents is bigger than the aggregated demand of all teams. Usually those economic agents on the shorter side of a market have a stronger bargaining power than those on the longer side; they successfully negotiate and bargain on their own terms – prices (thus they are price-makers) and transaction conditions –, and obtain a better payoff for what they deliver to the market. While those agents on the longer side of the market have to adjust, revise down their demand or supply, and accept forced substitutions.

13.   Since a soft budget constraint leads to labour hoarding within the enterprise (team) – thus hedging against future labour market shortage – all European football teams are eager to recruit as many players as possible, including disposing of a great number of potential substitutes to sit on the touch-bench.

14.   Some of them, often not accounted for as unemployed, simply revise downwards the terms of their supply of talent and spill over their labour supply to a lower division team or a weaker foreign league. Supply (and demand) revision by spilling over from one market to another are basic effects that result from rationing schemes and quantitative adjustment processes in disequilibrium models.

15.   In addition, they wish, expect or even bet on their favourite team winning as many games as possible (see note 2). However, they realistically cannot have a straightforward demand for home and away wins, due to outcome uncertainty. Their demand for wins is

indirect and often takes the form of their support (or request) to their team overinvesting in talents, which exactly fits with team behaviour as described in inequalities 2.13 to 2.15. This is a spillover-type interaction between product and labour markets.

16. Inc_h is the share of overall income that a fan h can afford to pay for game attendance.
17. This assumption materializes price rigidity in tune with the literature mentioned above.
18. Here it is assumed that a fan wants to attend all his or her favourite team's games, home and away, and that he or she can financially afford it. Of course, it could easily be assumed that he or she wants to attend only home games, then the supply he or she faces would simplify to $(n - 1)$ without any major change in the model.
19. Alavy et al. (2010) contend that 'people may be turned off by a boring 0-0 stalemate' (p. 80) and other 'boring characteristics such as non-attacking play, few goals, etc., which could reduce viewership'. In the same vein, see Andreff and Raballand (2011).
20. Usually oligopsonistic TV companies compete to broadcast the same sport event supplied by a single sport organization (league) – thus in a monopoly position. Since the monopolistic supplier allocates the event to the most optimistic overbidding broadcaster through an auction, the latter is cursed and bears an excessive cost (Andreff, 2014b). Such a cost on its input market is spilled over by the winning TV channel to its product market for televised sport through a high price (subscription fee).
21. From 2004/05 to 2013/14, 44 teams from 20 countries have missed out on UEFA Champions League/Europa League places due to poor financial management (not complying with the licensing and then financial fair play rules, FFP), in particular six teams in 2012/13 and seven teams in 2013/14; nine other teams (of which Paris Saint-Germain, Manchester City, Zenith Saint Petersburg and Galatasaray) have been financially sanctioned (fined) for non-compliance with FFP during this last year.
22. Just to give an example, derived from (2.24), $T_a - \sum_{i=1}^{n} t_{ai}$ is an unemployment index signalling an excess supply in the labour market for journeymen players.
23. Some insights are found in Andreff and Bourg (2006) while Késenne (2007, pp. 22–5) presents tentative modelling of this market in an equilibrium framework.
24. Empirical evidence of a league's monopoly pooling TV rights that faces oligopsonistic TV companies in European football (Cave and Crandall, 2001; Buraimo, 2006; Gratton and Solberg, 2007) suggests that prices are not often flexible.
25. An empirical measure that the sport sponsorship market is actually competitive lies in the mobility of sponsors across sports teams, which increased in the aftermath of the financial crisis when several traditional sponsors gave up sport sponsorship (Andreff, 2009) while newcomers stepped in.
26. Empirical evidence of such concentration can be found in Paul and Weinbach (2010) for the US market and Andreff (2012) for the French market, which has recently opened to foreign competition.
27. The following example is highlighted (Malinvaud, 1977; Benassy, 1982): an involuntarily unemployed worker will not maintain his or her Walrasian demand on the consumer goods market, nor will a firm that is experiencing sales difficulties of its output continue to employ the Walrasian profit-maximizing quantity of labour on its input market.

REFERENCES

Aglietta, M., W. Andreff and B. Drut (2008), 'Bourse et Football', *Revue d'Economie Politique*, **118**(2), 255–96.

Alavy, K., A. Gaskell, S. Leach and S. Szymanski (2010), 'On the edge of your seat: demand for football on television and the uncertainty of outcome hypothesis', *International Journal of Sport Finance*, **5**(2), 75–95.

Andreff, W. (1981), 'Prix du spectacle sportif et comportement du spectateur', in F. Alaphilippe and E. Bournazel (eds), *Le spectacle sportif*, Paris: Presses Universitaires de France, pp. 60–83.

Andreff, W. (2007), 'French football: a financial crisis rooted in weak governance', *Journal of Sports Economics*, **8**(6), 652–61.

Andreff, W. (2009), 'Public and private financing of sport in Europe: the impact of global crisis', Paper presented at the 84th Annual Conference of Western Economic Association International, Vancouver, 29 June–3 July.

Andreff, W. (2011), 'Some comparative economics of the organization of sports: competition and regulation in North American vs. European professional team sports leagues', *European Journal of Comparative Economics*, **8**(1), 3–27.

Andreff, W. (2012), *Mondialisation économique du sport. Manuel de référence en Economie du sport*, Bruxelles: De Boeck.

Andreff, W. (2014a), 'Building blocks for a disequilibrium model of a European team sports league', *International Journal of Sport Finance*, **9**(1), 20–38.

Andreff, W. (2014b), 'The winner's curse in sports economics', in O. Budzinski and A. Feddersen (eds), *Contemporary Research in Sports Economics – Proceedings of the 5th ESEA Conference*, Frankfurt a.M.: Peter Lang Academic Research, pp. 177–205.

Andreff, W. (2014c), 'A wrong future for sport? Corruption and betting-related match fixing', Paper presented at the XIVth IASE Conference, Fundaçao Getulio Vargas, Rio de Janeiro, 3–5 December.

Andreff, W. (2015a), 'French professional football: how much different?', in J. Goddard and P. Sloane (eds), *Handbook on the Economics of Football*, Cheltenham, UK and Northampton, MA, UK: Edward Elgar, pp. 298–321 (forthcoming).

Andreff, W. (2015b), 'Corruption', in T. Byers and S. Gorse (eds), *Contemporary Issues in Sport: An Introduction*, London: Sage (forthcoming).

Andreff, W. and J.-F. Bourg (2006), 'Broadcasting rights and competition in European football', in C. Jeanrenaud and S. Késenne (eds), *The Economics of Sport and the Media*, Cheltenham, UK and Northampton, MA, USA: Edward Elgar, pp. 37–70.

Andreff, W. and G. Raballand (2011), 'Is European football's future to become a boring game?', in W. Andreff (ed.), *Contemporary Issues in Sports Economics: Participation and Professional Team Sports*, Cheltenham, UK and Northampton, MA, USA: Edward Elgar, pp. 131–67.

Andreff, W. and N. Scelles (2014), 'Walter C. Neale fifty years after: beyond competitive balance, the league standing effect tested with French football data', *Journal of Sports Economics*, available at http://jse.sagepub.com/content/early/20 14/11/04/1527002514556621, 5 November.

Ascari, G. and P. Gagnepain (2007), 'Evaluating rent dissipation in the Spanish football industry', *Journal of Sports Economics*, **8**(5), 468–90.

Barajas, A. and P. Rodriguez (2010), 'Spanish football clubs' finances: crisis and player salaries', *International Journal of Sport Finance*, **5**(1), 52–66.

Baroncelli, A. and U. Lago (2006), 'Italian football', *Journal of Sports Economics*, **7**(1), 13–28.

Barro, R.J. (2000), 'Economics of golf balls', *Journal of Sports Economics*, **1**(1), 86–9.

Barro, R.J. and H.I. Grossman (1971), 'A general disequilibrium model of income and unemployment', *American Economic Review*, **61**(1), 82–93.

Barro, R.J. and H.I. Grossman (1974), 'Suppressed inflation and the supply multiplier', *Review of Economic Studies*, **41**(1), 87–104.

Benassy, J.-P. (1975), 'Neo-Keynesian disequilibrium theory in a monetary economy', *Review of Economic Studies*, **42**(4), 502–23.

Benassy, J.-P. (1982), *The Economics of Market Disequilibrium*, New York: Academic Press.

Benassy, J.-P. (1983), 'The three regimes of the IS-LM model: a non-Walrasian analysis', *European Economic Review*, **23**(1), 1–17.

Bird, P.J.W.N. (1982), 'The demand for league football', *Applied Economics*, **14**(6), 637–49.

Borghans, L. and L. Groot (1998), 'Superstardom and monopoly power: why media stars earn more than their contribution to welfare?', *Journal of Institutional and Theoretical Economics*, **154**(3), 546–71.

Bourg, J.-F. (1983), *Salaire, travail et emploi dans le football professionnel français*, Paris: FFF & LNF.

Bryson, A., G. Rossi and R. Simmons (2014), 'The migrant wage premium in professional football: a superstar effect?', *Kyklos*, **67**(1), 12–28.

Buraimo, B. (2006), 'The demand for sports broadcasting', in W. Andreff and S. Szymanski (eds), *Handbook on the Economics of Sport*, Cheltenham, UK and Northampton, MA, USA: Edward Elgar, pp. 100–111.

Buraimo, B. (2008), 'Stadium attendance and television audience demand in English league football', *Managerial and Decision Economics*, **29**(6), 513–23.

Buraimo, B. and R. Simmons (2008), 'Do sports fans really value uncertainty of outcome? Evidence from the English Premier League', *International Journal of Sport Finance*, **3**(3), 146–55.

Buzzachi, L., S. Szymanski and T. Valletti (2003), 'Equality of opportunity and equality of outcome: open leagues, closed leagues and competitive balance', *Journal of Industry, Competition and Trade*, **3**(3), 167–86.

Cave, M. and R.W. Crandall (2001), 'Sports rights and the broadcast industry', *Economic Journal*, **111**, F4–F26.

Charemza, W. and R.E. Quandt (1982), 'Models and estimation of disequilibrium for centrally planned economies', *Review of Economic Studies*, **49**(1), 109–16.

Clower, R.W. (1967), 'A reconsideration of the microfoundations of monetary theory', *Economic Inquiry*, **6**(1), 1–8.

Coates, D. and T. Harrison (2005), 'Baseball strikes and the demand for attendance', *Journal of Sports Economics*, **6**(3), 282–302.

Coates, D. and B.R. Humphreys (2007), 'Ticket prices, concessions and attendance at professional sporting events', *International Journal of Sport Finance*, **2**(3), 161–70.

CSA (2011), 'Sport et télévision. Quels défis pour le régulateur dans le nouvel équilibre gratuit-payant?', *Les Etudes du CSA*, Conseil Supérieur de l'Audiovisuel, June.

Debreu, G. (1974), 'Excess demand functions', *Journal of Mathematical Economics*, **1**(1), 15–21.

Dietl, H.M. and E. Franck (2007), 'Governance failure and financial crisis in German football', *Journal of Sports Economics*, **8**(6), 662–9.

Dietl, H.M. and C. Weingärtner (2012), 'Betting scandals and attenuated property rights – how betting related match fixing can be prevented in future', Working Paper No. 154, Institute for Strategy and Business Economics, University of Zurich.

Dobson, S.M. and J.A. Goddard (1995), 'The demand for professional league football in England and Wales, 1923–1992', *Journal of the Royal Statistical Society*, Series D, **44**(2), 259–77.

Downward, P. and A. Dawson (2000), *The Economics of Professional Team Sports*, London: Routledge.

Drazen, A. (1980), 'Recent development in macroeconomic disequilibrium theory', *Econometrica*, **48**(2), 283–306.

Eckard, W. (2006), 'Comment (on Stefan Szymanski, 2004b)', *Journal of Sports Economics*, **7**(2), 234–9.

El Hodiri, M. and J. Quirk (1971), 'An economic model of a professional sports league', *Journal of Political Economy*, **79**(6), 1302–19.

Falter, J.-M. and C. Pérignon (2000), 'Demand for football and intra-match winning probability: an essay on the glorious uncertainty of sports', *Applied Economics*, **32**(13), 1757–65.

Forrest, D. (2012), 'The threat to football from betting-related corruption', *International Journal of Sport Finance*, **7**(2), 99–116.

Forrest, D., R. Simmons and B. Buraimo (2005), 'Outcome uncertainty and the couch potato audience', *Scottish Journal of Political Economy*, **52**(4), 641–61.

Forrest, D., I. McHale and K. McAuley (2008), 'Say it ain't so: betting-related malpractice in sport', *International Journal of Sport Finance*, **3**(3), 156–66.

Fort, R. (2006), 'Talent market models in North American and world leagues', in P. Rodriguez, S. Késenne and J. Garcia (eds), *Sports Economics after Fifty Years: Essays in Honour of Simon Rottenberg*, Oviedo: Ediciones de la Universidad de Oviedo, pp. 83–106.

Fort, R. and J. Quirk (1995), 'Cross-subsidization, incentives, and outcomes in professional team leagues', *Journal of Economic Literature*, **XXXIII**, 1265–99.

Franck, E. (2014), 'Financial Fair Play in European club football – what is it all about?', *International Journal of Sport Finance*, **9**(1), 193–217.

Gerrard, B. (2006), 'Analysing the win-wage relationship in pro sports leagues: Evidence from the FA Premier League, 1997/98–2001/02, in P. Rodriguez, S. Késenne and J. Garcia (eds), *Sports Economics after Fifty Years: Essays in Honour of Simon Rottenberg*, Oviedo: Ediciones de la Universidad de Oviedo, pp. 169–90.

Goldfeld, S.M. and R.E. Quandt (1988), 'Budget constraints, bailouts and the firm under central planning', *Journal of Comparative Economics*, **12**(4), 502–20.

Goldfeld, S.M. and R.E. Quandt (1993), 'Uncertainty, bailouts and the Kornaï effect', *Economics Letters*, **41**(2), 113–19.

Gratton, C. and H.A. Solberg (2007), *The Economics of Sports Broadcasting*, London: Routledge.

Hall, S., S. Szymanski and A. Zimbalist (2002), 'Testing causality between team performance and payroll. The cases of Major League Baseball and English soccer', *Journal of Sports Economics*, **3**(2), 149–68.

Hill, D. (2010), 'A critical mass of corruption: why some football leagues have more match-fixing than others', *International Journal of Sports Marketing and Sponsorship*, **11**(3), 221–35.

Hill, J.R. and W. Spellman (1983), 'Professional baseball: the reserve clause and salary structure', *Industrial Relations*, **22**(1), 1–19.

Howard, D.H. (1976), 'The disequilibrium model in a controlled economy: an empirical test of the Barro-Grossman model', *American Economic Review*, **66**(1), 871–9.

Késenne, S. (1996), 'League management in professional team sports with win maximizing clubs', *European Journal of Sport Management*, **2**(2), 14–22.

Késenne, S. (2000a), 'Revenue sharing and competitive balance in professional team sports', *Journal of Sports Economics*, **1**(1), 56–65.

Késenne, S. (2000b), 'The impact of salary caps in professional team sports', *Scottish Journal of Political Economy*, **47**(4), 431–55.

Késenne, S. (2005), 'Revenue sharing and competitive balance. Does the invariance proposition hold?', *Journal of Sports Economics*, **6**(1), 98–106.

Késenne, S. (2006), 'The win maximisation model reconsidered. Flexible talent supply and efficiency wages', *Journal of Sports Economics*, **7**(4), 416–27.

Késenne, S. (2007), *The Economic Theory of Professional Team Sports: An Analytical Treatment*, Cheltenham, UK and Northampton, MA, USA: Edward Elgar.

Késenne, S. (2012), 'Can advertising make free-to-air broadcasting more profitable than pay-TV?', *International Journal of Sport Finance*, **7**(4), 358–64.

Késenne, S. (2015), 'The optimal competitive balance in a sports league?', in P. Rodriguez, S. Késenne and R. Koning (eds), *The Economics of Competitive Sport*, Cheltenham, UK and Northampton, MA, USA: Edward Elgar, pp. 85–92.

Kornaï, J. (1980), *Economics of Shortage*, Amsterdam: North Holland.

Kornaï, J., E. Maskin and G. Roland (2003), 'Understanding the soft budget constraint', *Journal of Economic Literature*, **LXI**, 1095–136.

Kuper, S. and S. Szymanski (2009), *Why England Lose & Other Curious Football Phenomena Explained*, London: Harper Collins.

Lavoie, M. (2005), 'Faut-il transposer à l'Europe les instruments de régulation du sport professionnel américain?', in J.-J. Gouguet (ed.), *Le sport professionnel après l'arrêt Bosman: Une analyse économique internationale*, Limoges: Pulim, pp. 61–84.

Leijonhuvfud, A. (1968), *On Keynesian Economics and the Economics of Keynes*, Oxford: Oxford University Press.

Lucifora, C. and R. Simmons (2003), 'Superstar effects in sport', *Journal of Sports Economics*, **4**(1), 35–55.

Malinvaud, E. (1977), *The Theory of Unemployment Reconsidered*, Oxford: Basil Blackwell.

Manove, M. (1973), 'Non-price rationing of intermediate goods in centrally planned economies', *Econometrica*, **41**(5), 829–52.

Mantel, R. (1974), 'On the characterization of aggregate excess demand', *Journal of Economic Theory*, **7**(3), 348–53.

Muellbauer, J. and R. Portes (1978), 'Macroeconomic models with quantity rationing', *Economic Journal*, **88**(352), 788–821.

Noll, R.G. (1974), 'Attendance and price setting', in R.G. Noll (ed.), *Government and the Sports Business*, Washington, DC: Brookings Institution, pp. 115–57.

Osborne, E. (2006), 'Baseball's international division of labor', *Journal of Sports Economics*, **7**(2), 150–67.

Paul, R.J. and A.P. Weinbach (2010), 'The determinants of betting volume for sports in North America: evidence of sports betting as consumption in the NBA and NHL', *International Journal of Sport Finance*, **5**(2), 128–40.

Portes, R. and D. Winter (1977), 'The demand for money and for consumption goods in centrally planned economies', *Review of Economics and Statistics*, **60**(1), 8–18.

Portes, R. and D. Winter (1980), 'Disequilibrium estimates for consumption goods markets in centrally planned markets', *Review of Economic Studies*, **47**(1), 137–59.

Rascher, D.A. and J.P.G. Solmes (2007), 'Do fans want close contests? A test of the uncertainty of outcome hypothesis in the National Basketball Association', *International Journal of Sport Finance*, **2**(3), 130–41.

Rottenberg, S. (1956), 'The baseball players' labor market', *Journal of Political Economy*, **54**(3), 242–58.

Scully, G. (1974), 'Pay and performance in Major League Baseball', *American Economic Review*, **64**(6), 915–30.

Simmons, R. (1996), 'The demand for English league football: a club-level analysis', *Applied Economics*, **28**(2), 139–55.

Sonnenschein, H. (1973), 'Do Walras identity and continuity characterize the class of excess demand functions?', *Journal of Economic Theory*, **6**(4), 345–54.

Storm, R.K. and K. Nielsen (2012), 'Soft budget constraints in professional football', *European Sport Management Quarterly*, **12**(2), 183–201.

Szymanski, S. (2001), 'Income inequality, competitive balance and the attractiveness of team sports: some evidence and a natural experiment from English soccer', *Economic Journal*, **111**(469), F69–F84.

Szymanski, S. (2003), 'The economic design of sporting contests', *Journal of Economic Literature*, **XLI**, 1137–87.

Szymanski, S. (2004a), 'Professional team sport are only a game: the Walrasian fixed-supply conjecture model, contest-Nash equilibrium, and the invariance principle', *Journal of Sports Economics*, **5**(2), 111–26.

Szymanski, S. (2004b), 'Is there a European model of sports?', in R. Fort and J. Fizel (eds), *International Sports Economic Comparison*, Westport, CT: Praeger, pp. 19–37.

Szymanski, S. and S. Késenne (2004), 'Competitive balance and gate revenue sharing in team sports', *Journal of Industrial Economics*, **51**(4), 513–25.

Tuck, G. N. and A.R. Whitten (2013), 'Lead us not into tanktation: a simulation modeling approach to gain insights into incentives for sporting teams to tank', *PLoS ONE*, **8**(11), 1–8.

UEFA (2014), *The European Club Footballing Landscape: The 6th UEFA Club Licensing Benchmarking Report*, Nyon (and previous years).

Varian, H.A. (1975), 'On persistent disequilibrium', *Journal of Economic Theory*, **10**(2), 218–27.

Vrooman, J. (1996), 'The baseball players' labor market reconsidered', *Southern Economic Journal*, **63**(2), 339–60.

Weitzman, M.L. (1977), 'Is the price system or rationing more effective in getting a commodity to those who need it the most?', *Bell Journal of Economics*, **8**(2), 517–24.

Younes, Y. (1975), 'On the role of money in the process of exchange and the existence of a non-Walrasian equilibrium', *Review of Economic Studies*, **42**(2), 489–501.

Zimbalist, A. (2002), 'Competitive balance in sport leagues: an introduction', *Journal of Sports Economics*, **3**(2), 111–21.

3. Management reference points for sporting leagues: simulating league expansion and the effect of alternative player drafting regulations

Geoffrey N. Tuck, Robert D. Macdonald and Athol R. Whitten

INTRODUCTION

Most research on the economic design of sporting leagues has assumed that league managers, who are often club owners, seek an optimal mix of regulatory settings in the labour market, the product market and in the sharing of revenue between the league clubs (and league manager). From a normative perspective, the optimal league model identifies the regulatory settings that maximize a variable such as the aggregate profits or revenue of league clubs, or the social welfare of club owners, players and fans. From a positive perspective, such league models, as originally formalized by El-Hodiri and Quirk (1971), are generally solved to identify the equilibrium level of competitive balance and player wages given actual regulatory settings; with the profit, revenue or social welfare outcomes compared to the ideal normative models (Szymanski, 2003; Késenne, 2014).

In contrast to this dominant Walrasian equilibrium approach, there are few disequilibrium or non-equilibrium models in the sports economics literature. Recent work by Andreff (2014, Chapter 2, this volume) offers first steps towards a robust disequilibrium model of the labour and product markets of a league. Other non-equilibrium approaches to league modelling have also developed, but have received little attention in the mainstream sports economics literature. In this chapter, we therefore build on the earlier modelling of labour markets and competitive balance by Tuck and Whitten (2012, 2013, 2014) to show how dynamic non-equilibrium simulation represents a viable tool to aid league managers in the design of labour market regulations. Specifically, we consider the expansion of a closed league, where a player draft is the primary player recruitment regulation. Using Tuck and Whitten's 'Sports Synthesis' simulation framework, we assess the competitive balance implications of various allocations of player draft selections to the expansion club. This research is motivated by the expansion of the Australian Football League (AFL) from 16 to 18 clubs, with the entry of the Gold Coast Suns and Greater Western Sydney Giants to the AFL competition in 2011 and 2012, respectively.

League managers must allocate draft selections to an expansion club in the first year (or early years) of the club's existence. This allocation of draft selections may be motivated by performance criteria set by league managers. For example, league managers may desire the expansion club to achieve a particular level of on-field performance within a defined time period, or for league-wide competitive balance to be maintained above a minimum level during the foundation years of an expansion club. Our approach formalizes the objectives of league managers in the league expansion scenario by establishing performance 'indicators' of the system state and 'reference points', which define the target and limit points for optimal and acceptable levels of club performance and league-wide competitive balance. Simulation allows league designers to assess the probability of such outcomes across various timeframes and under alternative regulatory scenarios.

SIMULATION

Simulation as a Management Tool

Simulation is a well-established feature of education and practice in many fields of commerce and not-for-profit activity. Applications are wide-ranging and include, inter alia, financial risk analysis and the analysis of business strategies, the design of supply chains and production workflows, and the management of natural resources such as fisheries, oilfields and forests (Sainsbury et al., 2000; Jahangirian et al., 2010; Mun, 2010; Bunnefeld et al., 2011; Punt et al., 2014). Small- and large-scale simulation models are also central to policy analysis in fields ranging from macroeconomics (Welfe, 2013) to climatology (Flato et al., 2013).

Non-equilibrium simulation methods can have advantages over equilibrium methods when the product(s) of interest (and the factors that influence their dynamics) are highly variable or unpredictable, and where the system and feedback mechanisms are complicated and therefore do not lend themselves to analytic solutions (Caddy, 1984). For natural resource management, these advantages include better estimation of resource status and a clearer description of how system uncertainty can impact management decisions (Hilborn and Walters, 1992; Punt et al., 2014). The analogies to natural resource management are clear, for league managers face similar problems due to the 'peculiar economics' of sport (Neale, 1964). Unpredictable sporting contests – due to complex team production functions and the creation of a joint product by separate producers (teams) – as well as great uncertainty about the strength of consumer preferences for winning teams or competitive balance create multiple challenges for league managers and league modellers. This chapter and book explore the utility of non-equilibrium approaches to these problems.

Simulation in Sports Research and Practice

Recent examples of how Monte Carlo simulation can be used in sports economics research are found in Lahvička (2013), Rockerbie (2014) and Owen and King (2015). These studies respectively assess the effect of ice hockey tournament formats, basketball scoring patterns, and league size and season length upon uncertainty of outcomes/competitive balance. Relative to the 'traditional' sports economics literature and journals, simulation-based approaches are arguably more common in the field of operations research, which has a long-established tradition of empirical research, dynamic programming and simulation modelling of sporting rules, league regulations and game strategies (Haigh, 2009; Wright, 2009, 2014; Coleman, 2012 offer literature surveys). Such operations research applications both predate and run in parallel with the contemporary sports analytics research. These trends are exemplified by the modern classic, *Moneyball* (Lewis, 2004), Alamar (2013) and new journals such as the *Journal of Quantitative Analysis in Sports*, which has published simulations of strategic decision-making by clubs in a player draft (Fry et al., 2007) as well as simulation-based studies of the consequences of league/conference realignments (Pettigrew, 2014) and league tournament formats (Puterman and Wang, 2011).

Simulations of vastly different kinds have also been adapted as teaching tools for sports business students (Einolf, 2005; Drayer and Rascher, 2010; Szymanski, 2010), while the 'game engine' of electronic sports games, such as the highly popular EA Sports *Madden NFL* and *FIFA* titles, rely upon simulation of both individual sporting contests and whole seasons. Electronic games may also have academic applications as the generator of simulation results (such as Adams, 2006). Simulation, often in conjunction with empirical sports analytics, has also aided decision-making in player recruitment, fantasy sports and sports betting (Sargent and Bedford, 2010; Silver, 2012).

Less well known is the role, extent and sophistication of simulation used by league managers in the economic design of labour market and product market regulations, which are commonly seen as the product of negotiations between league managers, clubs and player unions (Gahan and Macdonald, 2001). Leagues occasionally provide limited insight into the simulation and modelling of labour market regulation. For instance, AFL National Talent Manager Kevin Sheehan (2010) briefly summarizes the process – including modelling of alternative proposals – undertaken to devise the regulations governing initial player recruitment by 2011 expansion club, the Gold Coast Suns.

THE AUSTRALIAN FOOTBALL LEAGUE

Background

While the Sports Synthesis model has general application across leagues and sports, the AFL is the primary inspiration for our simulation application in this chapter. Founded in 1896 and commencing play in 1897 with eight clubs that broke away from the older Victorian Football Association, the AFL is one of the oldest continuously operating sporting leagues in global sport. Originally known as the Victorian Football League (VFL), the league had expanded to 12 clubs by 1925, after which no new clubs joined for another 62 years. Commencing in season 1987, the VFL expanded from 12 to 18 clubs in the next quarter-century, with the entry of the Brisbane Bears and the West Coast Eagles (1987), the Adelaide Crows (1991), the Fremantle Dockers (1995), Port Adelaide Power (1997), the formation of the Brisbane Lions via the merger of Fitzroy and Brisbane Bears (1997), Gold Coast Suns (2011) and Greater Western Sydney Giants (2012). The AFL is a closed league with no promotion or relegation of clubs to second-tier Australian football competitions at the state or territory level.

Australian football is a sport played between teams of 22 players, with 18 players on the playing field at any one time. Unlike other codes of football there are no specialist roles such as a goalkeeper or quarterback. All players are interchangeable in theory, though taller players are typically designated the key offensive and defensive roles and different skill sets are required for players in offensive, defensive and midfield roles on the playing field. All clubs play 22 matches in the AFL Premiership Season, with the top eight clubs contesting the AFL Finals Series, a nine-game tournament

Disequilibrium sports economics

with both single- and double-elimination elements, which culminates in the AFL Grand Final on the last Saturday in September or in early October.

AFL Labour Market Regulations

The *AFL Rules* and the collective bargaining agreement (CBA) between the AFL and the AFL Players' Association (AFLPA) define the key labour market regulations of interest here. These include the number of players employed by AFL clubs, the minimum salary of individual players, the minimum and maximum salary expenditure of AFL clubs, as well as player recruitment processes including three kinds of player drafts, player trading and player eligibility for free agency.[1]

In ordinary circumstances, the AFL clubs each employ a maximum of 47 players, including 38 to 40 Primary List players and six to nine Rookie List players. Of these, 40 players, including all Primary List players, are eligible for team selection each week. In 2015, the Total Player Payment Cap (TPPC) per club is AUD $10.07 million, with an 'Additional Services Agreements' (ASA) cap of AUD $992,000 per club for the employment of players for legitimate marketing purposes. Table 3.1 summarizes key labour market and financial details of the AFL for recent seasons.

The AFL conducts three player drafts each season. The National Draft (held in November) and the Pre-Season and Rookie Drafts (held on the same day in December) are the primary player recruitment mechanisms and all players enter the league via a draft.[2] For all three drafts, the basic premise

Table 3.1   Key AFL labour market and financial statistics, 2011–2015

Season	AFL clubs	Total AFL players	Primary List/ eligible AFL players	Average salary	TPPC per club	ASA cap per club	AFL revenue
2010	16	742	638	$226,165	$7.95 m	$0.555 m	$335.862 m
2011	17	796	684	$237,388	$8.21 m	$0.573 m	$343.017 m
2012	18	841	725	$251,559	$8.79 m	$0.613 m	$428.623 m
2013	18	817	729	$265,179	$9.14 m	$0.852 m	$446.505 m
2014	18	811	719	$283,029	$9.63 m	$0.963 m	$458.157 m
2015	18	818	n.a.	n.a.	$10.07 m	$0.992 m	n.a.

Notes: TPPC = Total Player Payments Cap, ASA cap = Additional Services Agreements cap. The AFL calculates the average salary on the basis of TPPC + ASA payments to Primary List players and those Rookie List players nominated pre-season to be eligible for team selection (column 5). AFL revenue excludes that revenue generated independently by the AFL clubs. Monetary values are in Australian dollars (AUD).

Sources: AFL (2012, 2013a, 2014b), Lovett (2010, 2011, 2012, 2013, 2014, 2015) and Ryan and Bowen (2015).

is that AFL clubs select players in reverse order to their final league ranking in the previous AFL season. Over the years, the AFL has implemented different regulations to modify this basic order of selection. 'Special assistance' is provided to expansion and/or poorly performed clubs via the granting of additional draft selections, while clubs are sanctioned for breaching the *AFL Rules* by the removal of draft selections as well as monetary fines.

The National Draft has become the primary player recruitment mechanism since it was first held after the 1986 season. Since the 1994 National Draft, clubs have been required (in ordinary circumstances) to exercise a minimum of three National Draft selections each year, creating a natural minimum level of annual player turnover. The trading of existing AFL players and National Draft selections was first introduced for the 1988 National Draft. Trading may only occur during the designated 'Exchange Period' ahead of the National Draft selection meeting each year. The Pre-Season Draft was introduced ahead of the 1989 season and was initially a mechanism allowing existing, but out-of-contract, Primary List AFL players to move between clubs. Over time the Pre-Season Draft has evolved to a point where all prospective players eligible for selection in the National Draft are also eligible for the Pre-Season Draft.[3] The Rookie Draft was introduced ahead of the 1997 season to provide a 'second chance' for prospective players to be drafted to the Rookie List of each club.[4] The most significant reform to this system of labour market regulation was the introduction of a system of limited free agency ahead of the 2013 AFL season.[5]

As outlined further below, Gold Coast (2011–14) and Greater Western Sydney (2012–18) were entitled to employ additional players, enjoyed a higher TPPC and were granted additional player draft selections and recruiting opportunities in order to build the playing lists of each club and field competitive teams. These draft selections (particularly the National Draft selections) form the basis of the simulations analyzed in this chapter.

League Objectives and Reference Points

Three general classes of league objectives are relevant to this study. Competitive balance is a common theme, but is a difficult policy objective to quantify.

First, there are the broad philosophical objectives of the league, as seen from the perspective of the league owners/members and founders. These are stated in the policy statements, constitutional objects of the legal entity or unincorporated association that governs the league, as well as in the regulations defining the economic structure of the league. The AFL Commission – the independent board of directors of the AFL – has previously stated its broad goal 'is to achieve competitiveness and evenness on the field and uncertainty of outcomes which in turn maximises public interest' (AFL Commission, 1999, p. 3) while readily acknowledging that 'deciding how much equalisation is enough is a judgement call and a rough one at that. We are not pursuing complete equality and would want to minimise the disincentives to clubs' (AFL Commission, 1999, p. 30). In explaining the most recent reforms to AFL competitive balance policy, AFL Commission Chairman Mike Fitzpatrick offered a more specific statement by noting '[t]he AFL competition has been built on the basic philosophy of ensuring supporters of every Club believe that their team has a chance to win in any game, regardless of the Club's financial strength' (Fitzpatrick 2014, cited in AFL, 2014c).

As with other leagues, AFL labour market regulation is heavily influenced by competition law, in particular the common law doctrine of restraint of trade (Macdonald, 2012). In a clear reflection of the language adopted by the High Court of Australia in *Buckley v Tutty* (1971),[6] the first stated object of the *AFL Rules* is:

'OBJECTIVES:
> (a)   The AFL and the Clubs wish to ensure that the teams fielded in the competitions conducted by the AFL are as strong and well matched as possible. The support of the public and the opportunity for Players to develop and employ their skills both depend upon the AFL continuing to conduct vigorous competitions between evenly matched and financially viable Clubs. . . .' (AFL, 2014a, p. 13)

Both practically and legally, these objectives may be difficult to quantify. In 1991, a single judge of the Federal Court of Australia concluded 'there is no objective test accepted by experts in the field and upon which I could rely to measure the competitiveness of playing talent of teams in a competition' (*Adamson v New South Wales Rugby League* (1991) 27 FCR 535, 562).[7] The literature on the measurement, causes and consequences of competitive balance is still described as being 'large and contentious' (Humphreys and Watanabe, 2012, p. 19).

Second, there are the specific operational objectives of the league manager, relating in particular to four attributes of the sporting contest: (1) the absolute quality of the athletic performance of individual players, teams and the sporting contest itself; (2) the competitive balance and uncertainty of outcome of the sporting contest; (3) the significance of the sporting contest to the participants and to the fans in the context of the league season and in the wider historical context; and (4) the integrity of the sporting contest (Macdonald and Smith, 2015). Examples highlight an emphasis upon alternative dimensions of club performance, *ex ante* uncertainty of outcomes and *ex post* competitive balance.

Over 20 years ago, the AFL specifically identified two performance criteria, 'a maximum differential between the top and bottom sides of ten wins . . . [and] . . . the bottom [ranked] team winning at least 25% of games per season' (AFL, 1993, p. 4). While this does not represent current policy, it is arguably the clearest specification of a quantifiable reference point in documents available from the AFL. Instead of the absolute measurement of *ex post* wins and losses, the Major League Baseball (MLB) Commissioner's Blue Ribbon Panel on Baseball Economics concentrated upon *ex ante* uncertainty of outcomes. Yet, in suggesting that '[p]roper competitive balance will not exist until every well-run [MLB] club has a *regularly recurring reasonable hope of reaching postseason play*' (Levin et al., 2000, p. 5, emphasis in original), the Blue Ribbon Panel highlights the same problem encountered by courts in Australia and other jurisdictions that rely upon 'reasonableness' or 'rule of reason' criteria in the assessment of the legality of labour market regulations (Davies, 2005; McKeown, 2011). A specific target or limit reference point can be difficult to specify (Berri et al., 2007).

Third, league managers may set objectives regarding the on- and off-field performance of (expansion) clubs during the initial foundation period for an expansion club. For example, Sheehan (2010, p. 367) notes the 'two primary considerations' when devising the labour market regulations governing the entry of the Gold Coast and Greater Western Sydney clubs were the assembly and development of competitive playing lists for the expansion clubs, while minimizing the negative impact upon the 16 existing AFL clubs.

It is clear that on balance, fans prefer winning teams and high-quality sporting contests, but the strength of consumer demand for competitive balance or uncertainty of outcomes is ambiguous. Reviews of the literature suggest the relationship is context specific and varies, inter alia, with the dimension of competitive balance or uncertainty of outcomes in question, with the type of sporting product consumed (for example, live match attendance or consumption of a sports broadcast), as well as the price of sports consumption (Borland and Macdonald, 2003; Szymanski, 2003; Garcia and Rodríguez, 2009). These empirical problems lead Budzinski and Pawlowski (2014) to the conclusion that the relevant considerations in consumer demand for sport are the minimum acceptable level of competitive imbalance or poor team performance, along with the perceived uncertainty of outcomes in 'sub-competitions' within the league season between different subsets of league clubs. The sub-competitions include the race for the premiership, or different groups of clubs vying for higher league ladder rankings, or the battle to avoid relegation in an open league. All such sub-competitions offer potential target or limit reference points for simulation.

Table 3.2   Performance criteria for granting of Gold Coast Suns AFL licence

Criteria	Headline objective
Revenue	The ability to generate sufficient revenue to compete in the AFL (individual club memberships, business support, long-term sponsorships)
Assets	The capacity to establish a positive net asset base
Facilities	The ability to deliver first-class training and administration facilities
Brand and identity	Development of a brand identity for the new club that reflects the Gold Coast community
Community	The ability to build community support (including social and community programmes) that engages the whole Gold Coast community
Game development	The capacity to build the football team in partnership with the state governing body, AFL Queensland
Corporate governance	The ability to build a strong organization based on appropriate governance and business principles
Business planning	Preparation of business plans for 2008–10 and 2011–15

Source: AFL (2008, p. 20).

Other League Reference Points

While our focus in this chapter is upon on-field club performance and league competitive balance, other reference points of interest to league managers will be necessarily related to the financial viability of an expansion club, the public support for such a club and the net economic and social benefit of an expansion club to the sport, the league and existing league clubs. The criteria set by the AFL Commission (Table 3.2) for the granting of an AFL competition licence to the Gold Coast Suns Football Club reflect such considerations.

LABOUR MARKET REGULATION, PLAYER DRAFTS AND LEAGUE EXPANSION: GLOBAL PERSPECTIVES

Player Drafts

Before explaining the central elements of the Sports Synthesis model, it is necessary to outline the central elements of the economic design of a player draft, which has been utilized by at least 12 closed leagues around the world. In addition to the five types of drafts of the VFL/AFL and the short-lived New South Wales Rugby League Internal Draft, the Australian National Water Polo League also briefly employed a draft to allocate playing talent to clubs in the early 2000s (Fairweather, 2010). In the United States, the National Football League (NFL) was the first league to adopt a player draft in 1936. Other North American leagues currently using player drafts of different kinds include MLB, the National Basketball Association (NBA), the NBA Development League (NBADL) and the Women's National Basketball Association (WNBA), the National Hockey League (NHL), Major League Lacrosse (MLL), Major League Soccer (MLS) and the National Women's Soccer League (NWSL), as has the Kontinental Hockey League (KHL) of Eastern Europe and Russia.

Conventional wisdom on the effect of player drafts in leagues of profit-maximizing clubs (Siegfried, 1995; Kahane, 2006; Quinn, 2008) is founded upon the Rottenberg invariance principle (Rottenberg, 1956, 2000) and the Coase theorem (Coase, 1960); the long-run allocation of playing talent (and thus competitive balance) is expected to be invariant to the initial allocation of playing talent. While elegant in its simplicity, the Rottenberg–Coase arguments have been empirically refuted (Grier and Tollison, 1994; Richardson, 2000) as well as supported (Fort and Quirk, 1995; Maxcy, 2012). Alternative assumptions also challenge the Rottenberg–Coase conclusions with Booth (2000) showing a player draft in conjunction with a salary cap can improve competitive balance in a closed league of two win-maximizing clubs. One common problem with the economic literature on player drafts has been the tendency to offer insufficient consideration of the specifics of the economic design of the player draft (Borland, 2006). More detailed analysis of player draft systems is found in support of the econo-metric (Taylor and Trogdon, 2002; Borland et al., 2009; Price et al., 2010) and simulation models (Tuck and Whitten, 2012, 2013) of the perverse incentive effect of a player draft (the incentive to 'tank' in matches to secure earlier draft selections), in proposals for modification of the 'basic' reverse order of selection in different circumstances (Bedford and Schembri, 2006; O'Shaughnessy, 2010; AFL, 2015), as well as in the legal commentary on labour market regulation (Dabscheck and Opie, 2003; Davies, 2006).

Several issues must be considered in the economic design of a player draft, starting with a clear understanding of the objects of the regulation. As noted above, clear specification of target and limit reference points can be challenging, but ought to include consideration of the strength of the (perverse) incentive effects of the regulations, as shaped by the prevailing understanding of player productivity and the relationship between individual and team performance for that sport. Important elements of the design of a player draft – including the interaction between the draft itself and other labour market regulations – include:

(a) the eligibility of an individual to be selected in the draft, including:
   (i)   voluntary or automatic registration/consent requirements
   (ii)   age, nationality, residency, playing experience, education, contract status, family history, other qualifying criteria
(b) the 'basic' order of club selection in the draft:
   (i)   the degree of inverse correlation between draft selections in season t and league rankings in season $t - 1$ (and/or earlier seasons)
   (ii)   the required minimum and/or maximum number of draft selections per club
(c) regulatory modification of the 'basic' order of club selection in the draft, via:
   (i)   the granting of additional draft selections in cases such as sustained poor club performance, league expansion or other special circumstances
   (ii)   the removal of draft selections as a penalty for the breach of league regulations or in other special circumstances
   (iii) the right of clubs to draft players characterized by various eligibility criteria
(d) voluntary modification of the order of selection via trades (transactions) between clubs, subject to the allowable:
   (i)   mediums of exchange – including current and/or future season draft selections, players, cash or salary cap credit
   (ii)   timeframe for trading – whether prior to, during or immediately after the player draft
   (iii) rights to re-trade draft selections or players previously acquired via trade
(e) the consequences of being drafted, including:
   (i)   required minimum and maximum terms and conditions of employment
   (ii)   the status of drafted players on the playing list/roster of a club
   (iii) the length of the period during which a club enjoys exclusive contract negotiation rights with a drafted player.

League Expansion and the Design of Labour Market Regulation

Table 3.3 identifies 49 expansion clubs across seven of the most prominent closed leagues to operate a player draft in the past 30 years, while Table 3.4 compares the first decade of on-field performance of the seven recent

Table 3.3   Expansion clubs, selected national leagues, 1985–2015

League	Season	Expansion clubs
Australian Football League (AFL)	1987	Brisbane Bears, West Coast Eagles
(18 clubs in 2015)	1991	Adelaide Crows
	1995	Fremantle Dockers
	1997	Port Adelaide
	2011	Gold Coast Suns
	2012	Greater Western Sydney Giants
Canadian Football League (CFL)	1993	Sacramento Gold Miners
(9 clubs in 2015)	1994	Baltimore Stallions, Las Vegas Posse, Shreveport Pirates
	1995	Birmingham Barracudas, Memphis Mad Dogs
	2002	Ottawa Renegades
	2014	Ottawa Redblacks
Major League Baseball (MLB)	1993	Colorado Rockies, Florida Marlins
(30 clubs in 2015)	1998	Arizona Diamondbacks, Tampa Bay Devil Rays
National Basketball Association	1988	Charlotte Hornets, Miami Heat
(NBA)	1989	Minnesota Timberwolves, Orlando Magic
(30 clubs in 2015)	1995	Vancouver Grizzlies, Toronto Raptors
	2004	Charlotte Bobcats
National Hockey League (NHL)	1991	San Jose Sharks
(30 clubs in 2015)	1992	Ottawa Senators, Tampa Bay Lightning
	1993	Mighty Ducks of Anaheim, Florida Panthers
	1998	Nashville Predators
	1999	Atlanta Thrashers
	2000	Columbus Blue Jackets, Minnesota Wild
National Football League (NFL)	1995	Carolina Panthers, Jacksonville Jaguars
(32 clubs in 2015)	1999	Cleveland Browns
	2002	Houston Texans
Women's National Basketball	1998	Detroit Shock, Washington Mystics
Association (WNBA)	1999	Orlando Miracle, Minnesota Lynx
(12 teams in 2015)	2000	Indiana Fever, Seattle Storm, Miami Sol, Portland Fire
	2006	Chicago Sky
	2008	Atlanta Dream

Note: 'Expansion' clubs are defined as those clubs joining a league as a start-up entity. This list therefore excludes 'new' clubs created by merger (Brisbane Lions, AFL, 1997) or relocation (Baltimore Ravens, NFL, 1996; New Orleans Hornets/Pelicans, NBA, 2002) and includes those clubs that have acquired or been assigned the historical records of a predecessor and thus not recognized as an 'expansion' club in official league records (Charlotte Bobcats/Hornets, NBA, 2004; Cleveland Browns, NFL, 1999).

Sources: afl.com.au, cfl.ca, mlb.com, nba.com, nhl.com, nfl.com, wnba.com.

Table 3.4   AFL, NBA and NFL expansion club performance

League	Club	Inaugural season	Regular season WPCT					Mean S1–S5
			S1	S2	S3	S4	S5	
AFL	Brisbane Bears	1987	0.273	0.318	0.364	0.182	0.136	0.255
	West Coast Eagles	1987	0.500	0.591	0.318	0.727	0.864	0.600
	Adelaide Crows	1991	0.455	0.500	0.600	0.432	0.409	0.479
	Fremantle Dockers	1995	0.364	0.318	0.455	0.318	0.227	0.336
	Port Adelaide	1997	0.477	0.432	0.545	0.341	0.727	0.505
	Gold Coast Suns	2011	0.136	0.136	0.364	0.455	–	0.273
	GWS Giants	2012	0.091	0.045	0.273	–	–	0.136
	Mean WPCT							*0.369*
NBA	Charlotte Hornets	1988–89	0.244	0.232	0.317	0.378	0.537	0.342
	Miami Heat	1988–89	0.183	0.220	0.293	0.463	0.439	0.320
	Minnesota Timberwolves	1989–90	0.268	0.354	0.183	0.232	0.244	0.256
	Orlando Magic	1989–90	0.220	0.378	0.256	0.500	0.610	0.393
	Vancouver Grizzlies	1995–96	0.183	0.171	0.232	0.160	0.268	0.203
	Toronto Raptors	1995–96	0.256	0.366	0.195	0.460	0.549	0.365
	Charlotte Bobcats	2004–05	0.220	0.317	0.402	0.390	0.427	0.351
	Mean WPCT							*0.318*
NFL	Carolina Panthers	1995	0.437	0.750	0.437	0.250	0.500	0.475
	Jacksonville Jaguars	1995	0.250	0.562	0.687	0.687	0.875	0.612
	Cleveland Browns	1999	0.125	0.187	0.438	0.562	0.312	0.325
	Houston Texans	2002	0.250	0.312	0.438	0.125	0.375	0.300
	Mean WPCT							*0.428*

Notes: Winning Percentage (WPCT); Finals/Playoffs (FI); 'Grand Final', the AFL Grand Final/NBA Conference Championship Series/NFL Conference Championship Game (GF); 'Premier', the winner of AFL Grand Final/NBA Conference Championship Series/NFL Conference Championship Game (PR); 'Champion', the winner of NBA Championship Series/NFL Super Bowl (CH).

Sources: afl.com.au, basketball-reference.com, nba.com, nfl.com, pro-football-reference. com.

AFL expansion clubs to those in the NBA and the NFL.[8] When the Gold Coast Suns and Greater Western Sydney (GWS) Giants are excluded from the analysis, the remaining five AFL expansion clubs compare favourably to both the NFL and NBA clubs on all reported performance criteria, even allowing for the fact that two of those AFL clubs each took nine years to reach their debut AFL Finals Series. For the Queensland-based Brisbane Bears in particular, the initial player recruitment concessions were ineffective and limited.

Ahead of their inaugural season, the Brisbane Bears enjoyed a playing list of 40 players from which to field only one team per week, and were

Regular season WPCT					Mean S6–S10	Mean S1–S10	Seasons to reach . . .				
S6	S7	S8	S9	S10			0.500	FI	GF	PR	CH
0.205	0.200	0.409	0.455	0.705	0.395	0.325	10	9	15	15	n.a.
0.705	0.600	0.727	0.636	0.682	0.670	0.635	1	2	5	6	n.a.
0.364	0.591	0.591	0.364	0.409	0.464	0.471	2	3	7	7	n.a.
0.364	0.091	0.409	0.636	0.500	0.400	0.368	9	9	19	–	n.a.
0.818	0.818	0.773	0.523	0.364	0.659	0.582	3	3	8	8	n.a.
–	–	–	–	–	–	0.273	–	–	–	–	n.a.
–	–	–	–	–	–	0.136	–	–	–	–	n.a.
					0.517	*0.399*					
0.500	0.610	0.500	0.659	0.622	0.578	0.460	5	5	–	–	–
0.512	0.390	0.512	0.744	0.671	0.566	0.443	6	4	9	18	18
0.256	0.317	0.488	0.549	0.500	0.422	0.339	9	8	15	–	–
0.695	0.732	0.549	0.500	0.660	0.627	0.510	4	5	6	–	–
0.280	0.280	0.341	0.610	0.549	0.412	0.307	9	9	18	–	–
0.573	0.512	0.293	0.402	0.402	0.436	0.401	5	5	–	–	–
0.537	0.415	0.106	0.256	0.524	0.368	0.359	6	6	–	–	–
					0.487	*0.403*					
0.437	0.062	0.438	0.688	0.438	0.413	0.444	2	2	2	9	–
0.437	0.375	0.375	0.312	0.562	0.412	0.512	2	2	2	–	–
0.250	0.375	0.250	0.625	0.250	0.350	0.337	4	4	–	–	–
0.500	0.500	0.563	0.375	0.625	0.513	0.406	6	10	–	–	–
					0.422	*0.425*					

assigned two players from each of the existing 12 VFL clubs (as nominated by those 12 clubs), the right to select six players before the 1986 National Draft, the first selection in each of the five rounds of the 1986 National Draft and an exclusive recruiting zone in the state of Queensland (Dabscheck, 1989; Pierik, 2011; Lovett, 2015). The special recruiting assistance afforded the Brisbane Bears was little better in future seasons, until a series of measures were introduced in the early 1990s to support the Brisbane Bears and a non-expansion club, the Sydney Swans (Booth, 1997). In comparison, the other four AFL expansion clubs of the 1987–97 era enjoyed much stronger recruiting concessions and the benefit of being located in 'traditional' Australian football states.[9]

The central feature of the labour market regulations governing the entry of the West Coast Eagles (1987) and Adelaide Crows (1991) was the granting of exclusive or first-option recruiting rights to players from the home states (Western Australia and South Australia, respectively) of the two expansion clubs. These rights included the opportunity to recruit current VFL players who were former residents of those states. Both clubs were excluded from the basic order of selection in the National Drafts held prior to their first two seasons in the VFL/AFL competition, although West Coast was able to exercise a number of pre-draft, additional or residential zone selections at the 1988–91 National Drafts. Unlike West Coast and Adelaide, the next two expansion clubs, Fremantle (1995, based in Western Australia) and Port Adelaide (1997, based in South Australia) were both granted a combination of National Draft selections preceding their debut seasons. This immediate National Draft participation was in addition to exclusive or first-right options to players from their home states, as well as rights to select a number of out-of-contract current AFL players (Lovett, 2015).

The raw data in Table 3.4 takes no account of the size or regulatory structure of each league, socio-economic differences in the markets of leagues and league clubs, the different team production functions of each sport, or the player recruitment concessions granted to each expansion club (see Quinn, 2008 for details of the NFL and NBA expansion drafts). The comparatively strong performance of the five AFL expansions clubs from the 1987–1997 era nevertheless begs the question – just how successful will the Gold Coast Suns and Greater Western Sydney Giants be in their first decade? The 'generous' (Clark and Warner, 2012; Quayle, 2014) player recruitment concessions granted to both clubs are summarized in Table 3.5 (Gold Coast Suns) and Table 3.6 (GWS Giants). Simulation of the impact of alternative packages of National Draft selections is modelled upon simplifications of these regulations.

THE SPORTS SYNTHESIS LEAGUE MANAGEMENT SIMULATION FRAMEWORK

Indicators, Reference Points and Performance Measures

In this subsection, formal definitions are introduced to translate the various league management objectives discussed above into elements of the Sports Synthesis simulation framework. These definitions and the simulation framework itself both draw heavily upon the decision theory used in marine resource modelling, which in turn has parallels in quantum mechanics and computer gaming, such as flight simulators (Sainsbury et al., 2000; Schnute and Haigh, 2006).

When managing complex dynamic systems, there are clearly states of the system that are desirable according to management objectives and states that are not. For example, extreme competitive imbalance and insolvent or unprofitable sporting leagues or clubs are clearly undesirable, as are

Table 3.5   AFL expansion club recruiting assistance, Gold Coast Suns, 2009–2014

Season and competition	Primary List + Rookie List players	National Draft selections	Pre-Season Draft and Rookie Draft selections	TPPC allowance	Recruitment zone and other recruitment assistance
2009 TAC Cup	–	–	–	–	QLD & NT ZONE PLAYERS – GCS may offer up to 20 contracts for 2009 and 2010 seasons to players eligible for the 2008 or 2009 National Drafts. Players must be QLD (in 2008 or 2009) or NT (in 2009) residents and may be included on the 2011 Primary List or 2011 Rookie List with player consent.
2010 VFL	–	–	2010 Rookie Draft selections: R1: 1, 2, 3, 4, 5	–	2010 ROOKIE DRAFT – Players selected in 2010 Rookie Draft who decline a contract offer may be traded prior to 2010 National Draft. 17-YEAR-OLD PLAYERS – GCS may nominate up to 12 x 17-year-old players (born 1/1/92–30/4/92) for a three-year contract (2010–12). Nominated players may either (i) accept contract offer and be added to 2011 Primary List; (ii) decline contract offer and be traded prior to 2010 National Draft; (iii) decline contract offer and be added to 2011 Primary List; or (iv) be waived by GCS and be eligible for the 2010 National Draft.

Table 3.5 (continued)

Season and competition	Primary List + Rookie List players	National Draft selections	Pre-Season Draft and Rookie Draft selections	TPPC allowance	Recruitment zone and other recruitment assistance
2011 AFL	48 Primary List + 9 Rookie List players	2010 National Draft selections: R1: 1, 2, 3, 5, 7, 9, 11, 13, 15 R2+: First selection of each round	Pre-draft uncontracted player selections prior to R1 of 2011 Pre-Season Draft First selection of each round of 2011 Rookie Draft and of each QLD Priority Round; GCS to alternate QLD Priority Round selections with Brisbane Lions	$1,000,000	QLD & NT ZONE PLAYERS – GCS may add 5 x QLD residents and 3 x NT residents (who have not previously been on an AFL club List) to 2011 Primary List; such players may be traded prior to 2010 National Draft. UNLISTED PLAYERS – GCS may add up to 10 x currently unlisted players to 2011 Primary List who have either been nominated for the National Draft or previously listed by an AFL club; such players may be traded prior to 2010 National Draft. UNCONTRACTED PLAYERS – Prior to 2010 National Draft, at the 2010 National Draft or prior to the 2011 Pre-Season Draft, GCS may add up to 16 uncontracted current AFL players to 2011 Primary List (maximum one per AFL club without the consent of that club). Any AFL clubs losing uncontracted players to be awarded compensation selections exercisable at any National Draft b/w 2010–14.

2012 AFL	46 Primary List + 9 Rookie List players	Standard 2011National Draft selections	Standard 2012 Pre-Season Draft and 2012 Rookie Draft selections	$800,000	QLD ZONE PLAYERS – GCS may add 5 x QLD residents (who have not previously been on an AFL club list) to 2012 Primary List; such players may be traded prior to 2011 National Draft.
2013 AFL	42 Primary List + 9 Rookie List players	Standard 2012 National Draft selections	Standard 2013 Pre-Season Draft and 2013 Rookie Draft selections	$600,000	QLD ZONE PLAYERS – GCS may add 5 x QLD residents (who have not previously been on an AFL club list) to 2013 Primary List; such players may be traded prior to 2012 National Draft.
2014 AFL	40 Primary List + 9 Rookie List players	Standard 2013 National Draft selections	Standard 2014 Pre-Season Draft and 2014 Rookie Draft selections	$400,000	–

Note: Gold Coast Suns (GCS), Northern Territory (NT), Queensland (QLD). In 2009, Gold Coast fielded a team of young players in the Victorian-based TAC Cup, a competition for players aged under 18. The TAC Cup clubs are not otherwise affiliated with AFL clubs. In 2010, Gold Coast fielded a team of young and open-aged players in the Victorian-based VFL, a second-tier open-aged competition that includes teams fielding reserve players from the Victorian-based AFL clubs. Historically, the National Draft has been dated for the year it is held, though the next season after each National Draft is contested in the following calendar year.

Source: AFL (2014a) and Lovett (2010).

Table 3.6 AFL expansion club recruiting assistance, Greater Western Sydney Giants, 2011–2018

Season and competition	Primary List + Rookie List players	National Draft selections	Pre-Season Draft and Rookie Draft selections	TPPC allowance	Other recruitment assistance
2010 TAC Cup	–	–	–	–	NSW ZONE PLAYERS – GWS may offer up to 20 contracts for 2010 and 2011 seasons to players eligible for the 2009 or 2010 National Drafts. Players must be residents of designated regions of NSW and may be included on the 2012 Primary List or 2012 Rookie List with player consent.
2011 VFL	–	–	2011 Rookie Draft selections: R1: 1, 2, 3, 4, 5, 6, 7, 8	–	2011 ROOKIE DRAFT – Players selected in 2011 Rookie Draft who decline a contract offer may be traded prior to 2011 National Draft.
17-YEAR-OLD PLAYERS – GWS may nominate up to 12 x 17-year-old players (born 1/1/93–30/4/93) for a three-year contract (2011–13). Nominated players may either (i) accept contract offer and be added to 2012 Primary List; (ii) decline contract offer and be traded prior to 2011 National Draft; (iii) decline contract offer and be added to 2012 Primary List; or (iv) be waived by GWS and be eligible for the 2011 National Draft.

| 2012 AFL | 44–50 Primary List + 9 Rookie List players | 2011 National Draft selections: R1: 1, 2, 3, 5, 7, 9, 11, 13, 15 R2+: First selection of each round | Pre-draft uncontracted player selections prior to R1 of 2012 Pre-Season Draft First selection of each round of 2012 Rookie Draft and each NSW Priority Round; GWS to alternate NSW Priority Round selections with Sydney Swans | $640,000–$1,000,000 | 17-YEAR-OLD PLAYER TRADING – GWS may trade the right to select up to 4 (in total) x 17-year-old players, either born 1/1/94–30/4/94 ahead of the 2011 National Draft or born 1/1/95–30/4/95 ahead of the 2012 National Draft. NSW & NT ZONE PLAYERS – GWS may add up to 16 (in total, ahead of the 2011–13 National Drafts) x residents of designated NSW regions and any number of NT residents (who have not previously been on an AFL club list) to 2012 Primary List; such players may be traded prior to 2012 National Draft. UNLISTED PLAYERS – GWS may add up to 10 (in total, ahead of the 2011 & 2012 National Drafts) x currently unlisted players to 2012 Primary List who have either been nominated for the National Draft or previously listed by an AFL club; such players may be traded prior to 2011 National Draft. UNCONTRACTED PLAYERS – Prior to 2011 National Draft, at the 2011 National Draft, prior to 2012 Pre-Season Draft or after 2012 Pre-Season Draft, GWS may add up to 16 uncontracted current AFL players to 2012 Primary List (none from GCS, maximum one per AFL club without the consent of that club). Any AFL clubs |

Table 3.6 (continued)

Season and competition	Primary List + Rookie List players	National Draft selections	Pre-Season Draft and Rookie Draft selections	TPPC allowance	Other recruitment assistance
2012 AFL					losing uncontracted players to be awarded compensation selections exercisable at any National Draft b/w 2011–15.
2013 AFL	44–50 Primary List + 9 Rookie List players	Standard 2012 National Draft selections	Standard 2013 Pre-Season Draft and 2013 Rookie Draft selections	$640,000– $1,000,000	17-YEAR-OLD PLAYER TRADING – GWS may trade the right to select the balance of up to 4 x 17-year-old players ahead of the 2012 National Draft.
					NSW & NT ZONE PLAYERS – GWS may add up to 16 (in total, ahead of the 2011–13 National Drafts) x residents of designated NSW regions and any number of NT residents (who have not previously been on an AFL club list) to 2013 Primary List; such players may be traded prior to 2013 National Draft.
					UNLISTED PLAYERS – GWS may add up to 10 (in total, ahead of the 2011 & 2012 National Drafts) x currently unlisted players to 2013 Primary List who have either been nominated for the National Draft or previously listed by an AFL club; such players may be traded prior to 2012 National Draft.

	Primary/Rookie List	National Draft	Pre-Season/Rookie Draft	Salary	Other
2014 AFL	44–50 Primary List + 9 Rookie List players	Standard 2013 National Draft selections	Standard 2014 Pre-Season Draft and 2014 Rookie Draft selections	$640,000–$1,000,000	UNCONTRACTED PLAYERS – Prior to 2011 National Draft, at the 2011 National Draft, prior to 2012 Pre-Season Draft or after 2012 Pre-Season Draft, GWS may add up to 16 uncontracted current AFL players to 2013 Primary List (none from GCS, maximum one per AFL club without the consent of that club). Any AFL clubs losing uncontracted players to be awarded compensation selections exercisable at any National Draft b/w 2011–15.
2015 AFL	44–48 Primary List + 9 Rookie List players	Standard 2014 National Draft selections	Standard 2015 Pre-Season Draft and 2015 Rookie Draft selections	$640,000–$880,000	NSW & NT ZONE PLAYERS – GWS may add up to 16 (in total, ahead of the 2011–13 National Drafts) x residents of designated NSW regions and any number of NT residents (who have not previously been on an AFL club list) to 2014 Primary List; such players may be traded prior to 2014 National Draft.
					–

Table 3.6 (continued)

Season and competition	Primary List + Rookie List players	National Draft selections	Pre-Season Draft and Rookie Draft selections	TPPC allowance	Other recruitment assistance
2016 AFL	42–46 Primary List + 9 Rookie List players	Standard 2015 National Draft selections	Standard 2016 Pre-Season Draft and 2016 Rookie Draft selections	$520,000–$760,000	–
2017 AFL	40–44 Primary List + 9 Rookie List players	Standard 2016 National Draft selections	Standard 2017 Pre-Season Draft and 2017 Rookie Draft selections	$400,000–$640,000	–
2018 AFL	38–42 Primary List + 9 Rookie List players	Standard 2017 National Draft selections	Standard 2018 Pre-Season Draft and 2018 Rookie Draft selections	$200,000–$520,000	–

Note: Gold Coast Suns (GCS), Greater Western Sydney (GWS), New South Wales (NSW), Northern Territory (NT). In 2010, Greater Western Sydney fielded a team of young players in the Victorian-based TAC Cup. In 2011, Greater Western Sydney fielded a team in the Victorian-based VFL. Also see note to Table 3.5.

Source: AFL (2014a) and Lovett (2010).

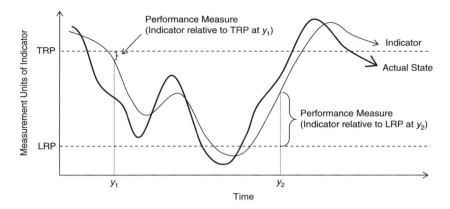

Notes: A representation of the time trajectory of an indicator in a single simulation and its relationship with the TRP, LRP and two performance measures (at times y_1 and y_2). Also shown is an example of the unknown actual system state that the indicator is attempting to measure (bold line). In this case, there is a lag between the true system state and the point at which management observes the indicator, and the indicator has a dampened response in comparison to the true system state.

Figure 3.1   An indicator time trajectory and its relationship with reference points and performance measures in a single simulation

collapsed fisheries or over-harvested forests (Walters and Maguire, 1996; AFL, 2014c; Késenne, 2014). Performance indicators are used to exactly measure, or estimate, the system state and are the foundation of management decision-making (Sainsbury et al., 2000). Indicators are expected to change in response to both management decisions and uncontrollable (internal and external) influences (see Figure 3.1). Examples of on-field or sporting performance indicators of course include competitive balance statistics, club rankings on the league ladder and the number of club wins per season. Off-field business performance indicators include club profitability and the number of club members or supporters as mentioned above. A target reference point (TRP) defines a value of the indicator representing a desirable state of the system. A limit reference point (LRP) defines an unacceptable system state (Punt et al., 2001; Prager et al., 2003). All reference points for an indicator are defined in the same units and represent the formalization of management objectives for the purposes of strategy and policy-making and subsequent policy evaluation.

Performance measures are the link between the indicator and the reference points and allow interpretation of the indicator for decision-making (again, see Figure 3.1). Performance measures can be identified as trends (for example, for an expansion club, an increasing league ladder ranking is good), quantitative measures of distance from the target or limit (for example, for a league manager, the expansion club may be ranked five positions lower on the league ladder than desired), a ratio of the indicator to the appropriate target or limit reference point (for example, expansion club revenue may be 20 per cent below the budget projection) or simply a statement of the indicator relative to the reference points (for example, for a league manager, the competition has less competitive balance than the TRP).

Using the performance measures as a guide, management decisions are therefore intended to achieve the management objectives by moving the system towards the TRP. For example, in 1993, the AFL set management objectives of ensuring a range of ten wins per season between the best and worst clubs, and for the worst club to win no fewer than one-quarter of matches per season. With these target reference points and other management objectives in mind (including the effectiveness of the strategy and the avoidance of perverse incentive effects), the AFL reformed the 'special assistance' regulations (which assigned additional (National) Draft selections to poorly performed clubs) twice in four years (1994 and 1997) in the 1990s alone (Borland et al., 2009; Tuck and Whitten, 2013).

Management actions are undertaken at particular decision points in a single simulation (or in the real world, which in effect, is a single simulation). The 'within-simulation' performance measures and subsequent actions should be considered on time-scales suitable to the nature of the system, the importance of the issue in question and the capacity of the manager to collect and evaluate valid and reliable data. For a professional sporting league, critical time-scales may be suggested by the length of the CBA between league/clubs and player association, by the length of the agreements with broadcast rights holders, government agencies and other financiers or by the term of participation agreements/licences between league managers and league clubs. In practice, the critical time-scales for a league manager may therefore range from one season to a decade of sporting competition.

Management Strategies and the Simulation and Evaluation Frameworks

The examination of alternative options for management via Monte Carlo simulation is called Management Strategy Evaluation (MSE) in the fields of natural resource decision analysis (Bunnefeld et al., 2011; Punt et al., 2014). This approach formally recognizes that the quality of management decision-making is contingent upon the uncertainty of the system and the ability to obtain data to inform managers (Polacheck et al., 1999). The key features of MSE are:

(a) uncertainty is specified and assessed for its influence on management outcomes
(b) it allows for experimentation across multiple management strategies (current and alternatives) and system structures in circumstances where real-world manipulation is problematic (financially, ethically)
(c) optimal solutions are not necessarily sought, rather the identification of feasible options with an explicit outline of the inherent trade-offs between competing objectives
(d) the framework should promote learning of the system dynamics, for both decision-makers and other stakeholders providing input to the formulation of the simulation model, the management objectives, performance indicators, target points and performance measures (Bunnefeld et al., 2011).

As with simulation models of natural resources, trade-offs should become clear when framing the objectives, performance indicators, reference points and measures in a league simulation. For the managers of natural resource systems, choices must be made between utilization and conservation of that resource (for example, fish or forests). For a league manager, conflicting objectives include the desire to provide special recruiting assistance to expansion clubs or poorly performed clubs with the desire to avoid (or minimize) perverse incentives for a club to deliberately 'tank' or under-perform (Tuck and Whitten, 2012). The trade-off between competitive balance and profit maximization in a league with clubs located in different sized markets is also well understood, both in practice and in the existing Walrasian equilibrium league modelling literature.

The first step in the MSE process requires that a scenario is chosen for evaluation; that is, a particular model parameterization of the system (the sporting league, natural resource and so on). A management strategy (such as the choice of labour market and revenue-sharing regulations of a sporting league, or catch and size limits in a fishery) is then chosen for modelling from among a set of identified options (Figure 3.2). We define a management strategy to include (1) data collection, to provide relevant information on the state of the system; (2) analysis of that data to specify suitable indicators, reference points and performance measures; and (3) regulatory choices. For example, the management strategy may be to provide an expansion club with a series of special assistance player draft selections in the foundation years of the club. A further management strategy might also be, for example, the automatic and pre-defined (one-off or longer-term) modification of the basic order of player draft selection

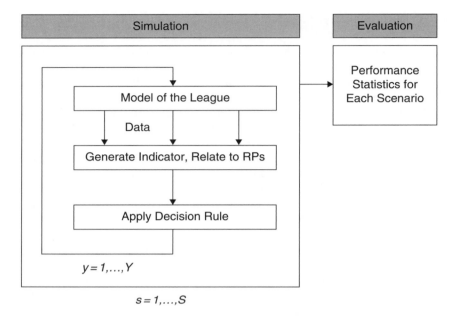

Notes: A management strategy (including data collection, indicators, reference points (RPs) and decision rules) and a league system parameterization are chosen, together forming a scenario. Each scenario is simulated over *Y* years and *S* simulations, and performance statistics are recorded. Once all scenarios are complete the management strategies can be evaluated against the performance statistics.

Figure 3.2   The general framework of the Management Strategy Evaluation simulation

where club performance or league-wide competitive balance falls outside the value of the LRP. Multiple runs of the simulation are then conducted for the chosen management strategy.

The performance measures and evaluation statistics generated by each simulation are then recorded for the chosen management strategy. Evaluation statistics include descriptive results such as the maximum, minimum, mean and variance of each indicator across the era simulated. A further important evaluation statistic is the probability of an indicator moving above or below the relevant TRP and LRP. Once all management strategies of interest have been simulated, comparison of these alternative management strategies may proceed with reference to both the quantum of the relevant evaluation statistic as well as the probability of different outcomes.

Due to the uncertain dynamics of a complex system, multiple future realities are possible. As such, management strategies are sought that are robust to system uncertainty. This requires stochastic simulations for a chosen scenario and the subsequent evaluation of management performance across multiple scenarios (Figure 3.2). The simulation process can highlight weaknesses or biases in current or possible management strategies, as well as identify the weaknesses of indicators of the system state (such as an inappropriately formulated measure of competitive balance, see Owen and King, 2015). However, in the example we describe below, there is no error between the actual system state and the indicator (club rankings on the league ladder). Instead, we introduce uncertainty to the system via the player and club production functions used to model annual club playing strengths. These estimates of club playing strength are used to calculate the annual league ladder rankings of clubs in season y and thereby determine the basic order of player draft selection ahead of season $y + 1$. Extensions of this basic approach to simulation of the club and league production functions are discussed below in the final section.

SIMULATING LEAGUE EXPANSION

A Dynamic Model of an AFL-like League

To demonstrate the utility of reference points and the simulation framework, we use the example of a sports league introducing a new club into a well-established competition. The sports league is based upon an AFL-like league and the simulation modelling framework used to model the league, Sports Synthesis, has been described in Tuck and Whitten (2012, 2013) and is not repeated in detail. Here we define the simulation structure with reference to the framework described in the previous subsection.

Assume a win-maximizing league of L clubs operating under a reverse-order player draft system to assign players to clubs at the end of each season (or year). An $(L + 1)$th club, L_{new}, joins the league in year $y = Y_{est}$ making a total of $L^+ = L + 1$ clubs. For the purposes of this exercise, we run each simulation for a total of $Y = 140$ years, and set $Y_{est} = 41$. The first 40 years are simulated with the initial L clubs alone to eliminate any effects of the initial conditions. In this manner, the new club is established at a time when league and draft dynamics are representative of a well-established competition.

The new club, L_{new}, employs P players, and is provided with a number of draft selections, P_{new}, in the year prior to their first in the league, $y = Y_{est} - 1$. These draft selections displace the selections the original L clubs would have obtained according to the 'basic' order of draft selection. The remaining $P_{est} = P - P_{new}$ players are established players whose age and draft selections are selected at random from subsets of ages and draft selections. These subsets can be modified depending on the desired initial strength of the new club. While more formal rules could be implemented, such as the acquisition of players from other clubs, for simplicity and illustrative purposes, each of the P_{est} established players is provided an age and draft selection taken randomly from an input range, namely ages [4, 10] and draft selections [1, 90]. The sequence of P_{new} draft selections is defined by the vector $\underline{P}_{seq} = (d_1, d_2, d_3, \ldots, d_{P_{new}})$ where d_i represents the ith draft selection for the new club. With this formulation of the members of the new club, both (a) the number of concessional draft selections to the new club, P_{new} and (b) the vector sequence of draft selections, $\underline{P}_{seq}$, are alternative management strategies that can be tested against operational management objectives.

As a management objective, the league manager is unlikely to want the new club to be weak over an extended period of time, as this will not help establish a supporter base, or promote financial stability through the sale of club memberships (season and match tickets and sponsorships). Equally, a new club that quickly dominates the league will not please the existing clubs (or supporters of those clubs). Supporters of existing clubs may lament the recruitment and transfer of too many good quality players from the existing clubs to the new club if P_{est} is large. Similarly, supporters of existing clubs may lament the loss of draft selections to the new club if the vector of draft selections $\underline{P}_{seq}$ is perceived to be 'too generous' (Clark and Warner, 2012; Quayle, 2014). In both cases, concerns may be raised about the perceived legitimacy and fairness of the labour market regulations imposed by the league manager. In order to manage these trade-offs, clear objectives for the new club should be articulated. As discussed above, management objectives may relate to some measure of league competitive balance or the 'success' (ranking) of the new club, within an agreed time period, Y_{new} (Table 3.4). As real-world dynamic systems are often stochastic, the management objectives should be framed as a statement of probability of the form,

$$P \text{ (Indicator} > \text{ERP, by year } Y_{new}) > \text{Pr} \qquad (3.1)$$

where ERP is an evaluation reference point (for example, target or limit). Note that the direction of the inequalities (or equalities) will be specific to the objective and the reference points. For example, managers may want a low probability of being less than a limit ERP, and/or a high probability of being greater than a target ERP. All modelling, calculations of reference points and other statistics, and simulation exercises were performed using the statistical computing and programming language R (R Core Team, 2014, Version 3.1.2).

The Simulation Procedure

The dynamic model for the AFL-like league for years up to the year the new club is established, Y_{est}, follows the steps below (Tuck and Whitten, 2013).

1. Choose an initial set of $P = 40$ players for each of the L clubs at random, with each player having a draft number (between 1 and $5L$) and 'age' (seasons since debut; between 1 and 15).
2. A player's productivity (ability) is a function of their draft number and age, and a random variable (with greater uncertainty regarding production as draft number increases; the draft choice error, DCE, defined by parameters σ_{min} and σ_{max} (Tuck and Whitten, 2013)).
3. Team productivity is assumed to be the sum over the team size, $p = 18$, of the best players in the team list.
4. Team productivity of all teams is then compared and ranked. The team with the greatest team productivity is the premier (or champion). Individual games are not modelled in this example.
5. Players add a further year to their age, with a consequent change in their productivity.
6. Players (five or more) are removed from each club either through retirement (years played greater than $a_{max} = 15$) or delisting (they have the lowest productivity on the club list).
7. Clubs enter the draft and gain new players, with their productivity a function of draft selection and choice error.
8. Return to step (3).

In the year prior to the new club joining the league, $y = Y_{est} - 1$, the draft is altered according to the management strategy criteria, P_{new} and $\underline{P}_{seq}$. The new club, L_{new}, receives the sequence of draft selections, $\underline{P}_{seq}$, and the L original clubs receive the free or remaining draft selections in reverse order to their finishing position in that year. The new club then enters the competition in year, Y_{est}, with a full complement of 40 players. The simulation then follows the steps above from step (3), until the final simulation year Y.

At the end of each year, the team finishing position and productivity are recorded (as data for use as indicators).

The player productivity function at age a is assumed to be the truncated (at maximum age) density function of the lognormal distribution (Tuck and Whitten, 2013). A linear decline in productivity with draft number d is assumed. The uncertainty associated with player productivity follows a lognormal distribution, with uncertainty increasing with draft number. We do not estimate the parameters of the productivity function, but instead explore model sensitivity to varying degrees of draft choice error. Alternative functional forms for player productivity could be used, and tested as part of the parameterization of the model for a particular scenario.

Management Objectives and Evaluation Statistics

For a particular management strategy, a total of $S = 100$ simulations are conducted. Once these simulations are complete, evaluation statistics related to the management objectives are calculated. For the example presented here, we consider the probability that the new club's ranking R_{new} is Rth or better within Y_{new} years. This probability must be greater than Pr to have satisfied the management objective. Here the indicator is the new club's ranking and the target evaluation reference point is the new club's rank being R or better. The general evaluation statistic is then

1. $P(R_{new} \geq R$, by year $Y_{new})$

Other evaluation statistics considered are:

2. W_{orig} = the average number of premierships won by the L original clubs from years Y_{est} to Y.
3. W_{new} = the average number of premierships won by the new club L_{new}, from years Y_{est} to Y.
4. The annual average coefficient of variation (cv) of the team productivities, $U^{y,l}$ across all teams, l, for a particular year y,

$$\overline{CV_y} = \frac{1}{S} \sum_{s=1}^{S} cv_s(U^{y,1}, \ldots, U^{y,L^+})$$

5. From establishment of the new club, the mean over the initial 20 years and all simulations S of the coefficient of variation (cv) of the club productivities across all teams for a particular year,

$$\overline{CV}_{20} = \frac{1}{S.20} \sum_{s=1}^{S} \sum_{y=Y_{est}}^{Y_{est}+19} cv_s(U^{y,1},\ldots,U^{y,L^+}).$$

The first evaluation statistic is directly related to the management objectives of the league, namely the desire to have a 'reasonably' competitive new club. The second and third evaluation statistics provide a comparison between the success of the new club and the original clubs following the establishment of the new club. The fourth and fifth statistics provide a measure of competitive balance across the league following the establishment of the new club. The fourth measure tracks the annual competitive balance averaged across all simulations. For a particular management strategy ($\underline{P}_{seq}$), this will provide a measure of how long the new club takes to assimilate, as eventually this measure will stabilize after an initial perturbation on introduction of the new club. A similar measure could be used as an indicator for management. Namely, if competitive balance across the league is a management objective, consideration of the time-series of the cv of team productivities could be attached to a decision rule, with additional assistance provided if competitive balance is unsatisfactory.

We consider the following evaluation statistics with examples of associated management probabilities:

(a) $P(R_{new} \leq 8, \text{ by year } 5) > 0.75$
(b) $P(R_{new} \leq 4, \text{ by year } 10) > 0.5$
(c) $P(R_{new} > L^+ - 4, \text{ at year } 5) < 0.1$

The first two statistics attempt to ensure a successful club by having a high probability of success in the first five years (making finals) and an even chance of making the best four teams at any time within the first ten years of their existence. The final evaluation statistic relates performance to a limit evaluation reference point, such that the club should have a low probability of being amongst the bottom four clubs by their fifth year.

Management Strategies for Evaluation

The variables of central interest in our simulation modelling are player draft selections granted to expansion clubs joining a closed league. As seen above, the AFL has provided considerable recruiting assistance to the two most recent AFL expansion clubs, with the granting of additional National Draft selections only one element of a comprehensive package of regulations intended to aid the formation and on-field competitiveness of the Gold Coast Suns and GWS Giants. These regulations motivate our analysis, but simulation requires us to simplify this comprehensive set of AFL regulations to a mere set of player draft selections to be exercised by an expansion club.

In this simulation, both the data informing the decision rules and indicator are measured without error. We assume the league managers accept the club rankings (which in this simulation are a proxy for league ladder rankings) are an accurate measure of the system state. The decision rules in the simulation are (a) the allocation of player draft selections to the expansion club ($\underline{P}_{seq}$) which modify the basic order of draft selection of the players in the first draft in which the expansion club participates and (b) the basic order of draft selection in year y, which we define as the reverse order of club rankings in year $y - 1$.

It is clear that many alternative allocations of draft selections to the expansion club ($\underline{P}_{seq}$) may satisfy the objectives of the league manager. However, the choice among these alternative allocations is contingent upon other management objectives and constraints beyond the current scope of the simulation framework (for example, financial constraints, legal constraints, consumer demand for the expansion club and existing clubs). Within the context of the simulation, the management objectives, indicators and reference points are defined in terms of club (league ladder) rankings and league competitive balance.

Other league management strategies could also be tested using the Sports Synthesis framework. For example, the sustained poor on-field performance of a club may motivate a league manager to provide other 'special assistance' draft selections to modify the basic order of draft selection to the benefit of a poorly performed club (see Tuck and Whitten, 2012, 2013 for such examples and Borland et al., 2009 for empirical analysis of the alleged perverse incentive effects of such regulations in the AFL). This would be akin to setting a within-simulation limit reference point that triggers a decision rule. We do not test such management strategies here.

Using the National Draft selections afforded to five AFL expansion clubs as inspiration, Table 3.7 summarizes the simplified sets of player draft selections granted to the expansion club in various simulation runs.[10] In each simulation scenario, the vector of draft selections summarized in Table 3.7 are given to the new club in its first year. The remaining selections in that year are spread among existing clubs following the basic reverse-order draft selection process. Also included is a hypothetical example, whereby the expansion club is provided with the first draft selection in each round. The hypothetical example has only six concessional draft selections, and so the bulk of this team will be composed of established players ($P_{est} = 34$).

Table 3.7   Simulated allocations of draft selections to expansion club

Scenario	P_{new}	Draft selections allocated to expansion club ($\underline{P}_{seq}$)	Clubs in draft (L^+)	Simulation of VFL/ AFL expansion club
A	13	1, 2, 3, 5, 7, 9, 11, 13, 15 | 27 | 45 | 63 | 81	18	GWS Giants
B	13	1, 2, 3, 5, 7, 9, 11, 13, 15 | 26 | 43 | 60 | 77	17	Gold Coast Suns
C	10	1, 2, 3, 4, 5 | 21 | 37 | 53 | 69 | 85	16	Port Adelaide Power
D	12	1, 2 | 18, 19 | 35, 36 | 52, 53 | 69, 70 | 86, 87	16	Fremantle Dockers
E	11	1, 2, 3, 4, 5, 6, 7 | 20 | 33 | 46 | 59	13	Brisbane Bears
F	6	1 | 19 | 37 | 55 | 73 | 91	18	Hypothetical

Note: Vertical lines between numbered draft selections indicate the end of a round of the player draft. For simplicity, a league expanding from 12 to 13 clubs is simulated in Scenario E (Brisbane Bears). In 1987, both the Brisbane Bears and West Coast Eagles joined the VFL competition, however the West Coast Eagles did not immediately participate in the National Draft.

RESULTS

The Sports Synthesis modelling framework is able to generate evaluation statistics relating to the expansion club's league ladder ranking and the level of competitive balance across the league. Managers of the league and the expansion club are both likely to seek a high probability of success for the new club within a relatively short timeframe. League managers may also have preferences for the maintenance of competitive balance at a relatively stable level over the years following the establishment of the new club.

The draft selections (and other regulatory assistance with player recruitment) provided to an expansion club can greatly influence the probability of on-field success for that club. While the league expansion and associated draft selection scenarios in each simulation are a deliberate simplification of actual events, the simulation results plainly highlight the importance of careful design of labour market regulations in line with clearly stated management objectives.

Tables 3.8 and 3.9 show values of the evaluation statistics across each of the concessional draft selections (as defined in Table 3.7) for medium and high draft choice error (that is, the relative confidence in choosing quality players in the draft). The draft selections of Scenarios A, B and E (those akin to GWS Giants, the Gold Coast Suns and the Brisbane Bears) show a high probability of success within ten years of their establishment

Table 3.8   *Draft selections (scenarios) against evaluation statistics for medium draft choice error, $(\sigma_{min}, \sigma_{max}) = (0.05, 0.5)$*

Scenario	$P(R_{new} \leq 8,$ by year 5)	$P(R_{new} \leq 4,$ by year 10)	$P(R_{new} > (L^+ - 4),$ at year 5)	W_{orig}	W_{new}	$\overline{CV}_{20}$
A	0.99	1.00	0.00	0.052	0.122	0.041
B	0.98	0.99	0.00	0.055	0.124	0.040
C	0.89	0.94	0.02	0.060	0.095	0.039
D	0.75	0.89	0.22	0.062	0.075	0.037
E	0.99	1.00	0.00	0.073	0.129	0.041
F	0.55	0.61	0.46	0.056	0.056	0.037

Table 3.9   *Draft selections (scenarios) against evaluation statistics for high draft choice error, $(\sigma_{min}, \sigma_{max}) = (0.2, 0.8)$*

Scenario	$P(R_{new} \leq 8,$ by year 5)	$P(R_{new} \leq 4,$ by year 10)	$P(R_{new} > (L^+ - 4),$ at year 5)	W_{orig}	W_{new}	$\overline{CV}_{20}$
A	0.90	0.93	0.03	0.054	0.089	0.065
B	0.87	0.91	0.08	0.057	0.096	0.064
C	0.76	0.83	0.14	0.061	0.079	0.061
D	0.57	0.65	0.22	0.063	0.060	0.061
E	0.90	0.91	0.09	0.075	0.110	0.064
F	0.39	0.51	0.44	0.055	0.056	0.060

(Tables 3.8 and 3.9). This is in contrast to Scenarios D and F (those akin to the Fremantle Dockers and the hypothetical example) that, while initially stronger in team productivity, have much reduced probabilities of success. The draft selections provided under Scenarios A, B and E include a number of early selections (first round draft selections; Table 3.7). As a consequence, these clubs are relatively weak in the years that follow establishment due to a preponderance of very young players. The clubs' initial poor performance also enables additional high draft selections to be secured under the reverse-order draft system. However, with time, the clubs rapidly grow in team productivity as the high draft selections mature and become higher-quality players. By their fifth year they have moved up the rankings and have reached the best eight teams in the league with almost certainty. Over the 100-year time horizon considered (following establishment), the clubs under Scenarios A, B and E also win approximately twice as many premierships as the original L clubs.

The evaluation statistic relating to competitive balance (the mean coefficient of variation of team productivity for the first 20 years following establishment, $\overline{CV}_{20}$ shows higher values under Scenarios A, B and E. This is due to the markedly poorer initial team productivity and subsequent rapid increase in team productivity of the expansion clubs under these scenarios. Clubs having initial team productivity similar to the original clubs, not surprisingly, lead to more stable annual competitive balance measures (but less success).

These results are clearly dependent, inter alia, on assumptions regarding the form of the player and team productivity functions (Tuck and Whitten, 2013). If the DCE associated with player productivity is increased, leading to more uncertainty regarding the quality of players obtained in the draft, then probabilities of success reduce across all scenarios and evaluation statistics. This is because obtaining high draft selections will no longer guarantee a club access to high-quality players and the consequent reduction in team productivity reduces the probability of winning. The competitive balance measure, $\overline{CV}_{20}$ has also increased markedly, as the range in team productivity between the better and poorer sides increases. Poorer sides are no longer as assured of obtaining good players with high draft selections and, through bad luck or misplaced judgements of player ability in the draft, may remain a poor side for longer than they would have with lower DCE.

Consideration of the proposed evaluation statistics and associated management probabilities:

(a) $P(R_{new} \leq 8, \text{ by year 5}) > 0.75$
(b) $P(R_{new} \leq 4, \text{ by year 10}) > 0.5$
(c) $P(R_{new} > L^{+}-4, \text{ at year 5}) < 0.1$

shows that Scenarios A, B, C and E satisfy all of these conditions under medium DCE (Table 3.8). Scenarios D and F do not meet the requirements of evaluation statistics (a) and (c), while statistic (b) is satisfied for all scenarios. With high DCE similar results are found (Table 3.9), except that Scenario C now does not satisfy evaluation statistic (c) and only marginally satisfies (a). Scenario F is only marginally able to satisfy statistic (b).

The results displayed in Tables 3.8 and 3.9 show the range of possible outcomes for new clubs entering a league under alternative management scenarios, namely, with differing first year draft allocations. Scenarios B (Gold Coast Suns) and D (Fremantle Dockers) have considerably different draft allocations and consequent dynamics. Considering these scenarios in more detail, when a new club enters a league with a highly favorable set of first year draft allocations, such as in Scenario B (cf. Gold Coast Suns entry to the AFL in 2011) it will be expected to gain strength and increase its ranking greatly in the first three to five seasons as its many highly rated

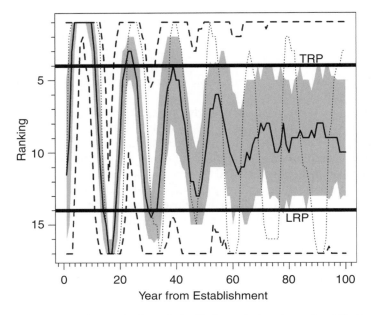

Notes: For draft selections under Scenario B, this figure displays the median (thin black line) and 50th (grey shading) and 95th percentiles (long dashed lines) of the ranking of the new club for each year from its establishment. The thick horizontal lines are the 4th and 14th ranking points, respectively, and are shown as potential target (TRP) and limit (LRP) reference points. The thin dashed line is an example (one realization) of a single simulation.

Figure 3.3   *The annual median and 50th and 95th percentiles of the ranking of the new club (medium draft choice error, Scenario B)*

young players reach their peak productivity (Figure 3.3). The same new club may stay highly ranked for several years (Figure 3.4). This type of trajectory is often followed by a similarly rapid decrease in ranking, as a large number of key and highly productive players age and pass their peak years of performance (Figure 3.3). Once a new club has begun this cyclic pattern of success followed by lower rankings, it is likely to continue for many years in a similarly cyclic pattern, owing to the nature of the reverse-order draft system. When a new club receives a large number of first round draft selections in its first year, existing clubs miss out on those same selections. This can cause a change to the competitive balance of a league. Figure 3.5 shows how the coefficient of variation among club productivities, as a measure of competitive balance for a given league, can increase following the introduction of a new club. This change is due to the initial relatively poor performance of the new club, followed by exceptionally good perform-

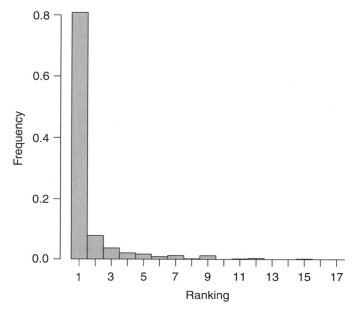

Figure 3.4   *The frequency of rankings for the new club from five years and up to and including ten years since establishment (medium draft choice error; Scenario B)*

ance as the high draft selection players mature. When a new club enters a league and receives a more mediated set of draft allocations (for example, Scenario D) this effect is much less noticeable (Figures 3.6 to 3.8), as the new club quickly enters a cyclic pattern more reminiscent of an 'average club' (Figure 3.6). A new club of this type has a much lower probability of finishing in the upper levels of the league rankings in its first ten years, but from a large set of simulation trials, can regularly be expected to finish in the upper half of the league rankings (Figure 3.7).

Increased DCE, as mentioned, leads to a dampening of the cycles experienced by the new club (Figure 3.9) and a more rapid transition to attaining the characteristics of the other clubs (with respect to age and draft selection structure). However, there remains a high likelihood of success, and subsequent poor performance, in the first 20 years of existence (Figures 3.9 and 3.10). The annual competitive balance statistic is also much broader than with lower DCE, indicating that clubs may experience greater fluctuation in team productivity and the league will, occasionally, see greater disparity between the better and worse performing clubs (Figure 3.11).

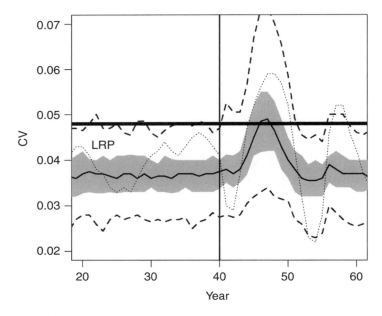

Notes: For draft selections under Scenario B, shown are the median (thin black line), 50th (grey shading) and 95th percentiles (dashed line) of the cv of team productivities. The thin dashed line is an example (one realization) of a single simulation. The thick line is shown as a potential limit reference point (LRP).

Figure 3.5   The annual cv of team productivities from 20 years before to 20 years after the establishment of the new club (medium draft choice error, Scenario B)

Simulation exercises of this type allow likely outcomes to be judged against predetermined management objectives. For example, comparing Scenario B and D (Figures 3.3 and 3.6, respectively), a new club that receives highly favorable first year draft allocations is far more likely to reach a pre-defined target reference point (in this case, to rank at number four or higher) in the first 20 years. However, that same club is also highly likely to fall below the limit reference point during the same time period. A new club that has a player structure that is similar to the existing clubs (Scenarios D and F) is much less likely to move above or below the target and limit reference points (Figure 3.6), and has a less dramatic cycle of success and failure in its first 20 years.

The suggested reference points illustrated in the figures (thick lines) have not been associated with management actions in the simulations conducted. However, in future refinements of the Sports Synthesis model,

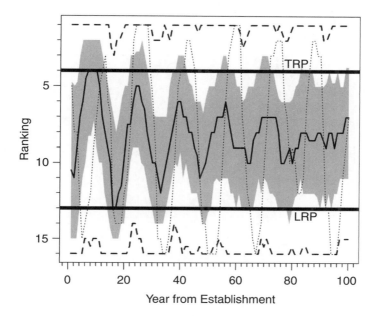

Notes: For draft selections under Scenario D, this figure displays the median (thin black line) and 50th (grey shading) and 95th percentiles (dashed lines) of the ranking of the new club for each year from its establishment. The thick horizontal lines are the 4th and 13th ranking points, respectively, and are shown as potential target (TRP) and limit (LRP) reference points. The thin dashed line is an example (one realization) of a single simulation.

Figure 3.6 *The annual median and 50th and 95th percentiles of the ranking of the new club (medium draft choice error; Scenario D)*

feedback management strategies could be included, whereby breaches of limit reference points could lead to management intervention (for example, in the form of additional draft selections to poor performing clubs). Feedback management strategies could then be tested against evaluation statistics to see if management outcomes, such as those displayed in Tables 3.8 and 3.9, display evidence of improvement.

DISCUSSION

Simulation of complex system dynamics via the MSE framework has become popular in single-species fisheries and cetacean management, with more recent application to marine ecosystems, threatened species

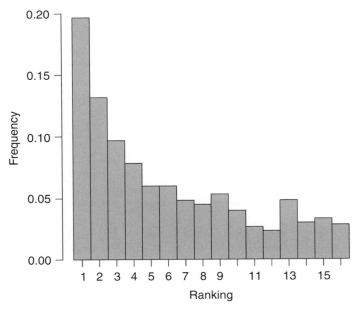

Figure 3.7   *The frequency of rankings for the new club from five years and up to and including ten years since establishment (medium draft choice error; Scenario D)*

management and terrestrial conservation (Sainsbury et al., 2000; Bunnefeld et al., 2011; Tuck, 2011; Fulton et al., 2014). In contrast, there are few (or few known) practical applications of simulation in the context of professional sporting league management. A number of academic studies have adopted the simulation approach. The closest analogue to our approach is Owen and King's (2015) analysis of the sampling properties of the popular seasonal competitive balance indicator, the ratio of actual standard deviation of club WPCT to the 'idealized' standard deviation (RSD). Owen and King (2015) show RSD is highly sensitive to changes in both season length and the number of league clubs, whereas the above-explained Sports Synthesis simulation framework (Tuck and Whitten, 2013) holds these variables constant to allow evaluation of the impact of changes to the order of club selection in the player draft. Like the Sports Synthesis simulation though, Owen and King (2015) adopt a data-free simulation method, meaning the model itself is not calibrated to historical conditions.[11] This offers a 'clean' approach from which league managers can derive benchmark results for comparative analysis. As a tool of normative

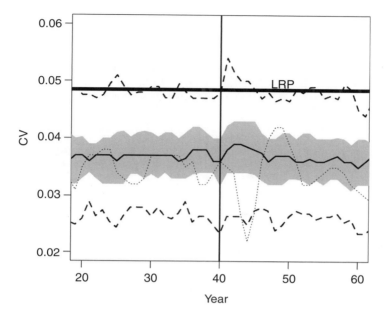

Notes: For draft selections under Scenario D, shown are the median (thin black line), 50th (grey shading) and 95th percentiles (dashed line) of the cv of team productivities. The thin dashed line is an example (one realization) of a single simulation. The thick line is shown as a potential limit reference point (LRP).

Figure 3.8   *The annual cv of team productivities from 20 years before to 20 years after the establishment of the new club (medium draft choice error; Scenario D)*

analysis, the output of the Sports Synthesis framework may therefore supplement, or even replace, the 'ideal type' results generated by a Walrasian equilibrium model of a league with a free agency labour market and no revenue-sharing between clubs (or between clubs and the league manager).

For this chapter, we have used the example of the expansion of the AFL competition to highlight how alternative management strategies can be evaluated via simulation. The Sports Synthesis framework allows comparison of the potential effect of the National Draft selections granted to recent AFL expansion clubs, including the Gold Coast Suns and Greater Western Sydney Giants. While the presented model is AFL-like in structure, the results should not be interpreted as a reliable predictor of future success or otherwise of the AFL expansion clubs. The models of this chapter have been developed for demonstration purposes only, and

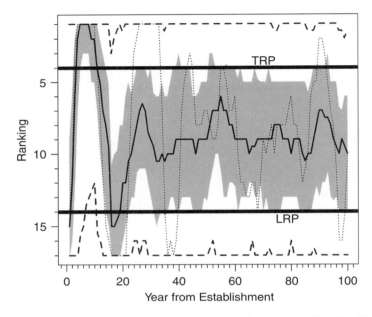

Notes: For draft selections under Scenario B, this figure displays the median (thin black line) and 50th (grey shading) and 95th percentiles (dashed lines) of the ranking of the new club for each year from its establishment. The thick horizontal lines are the 4th and 14th ranking points, respectively, and are shown as potential target (TRP) and limit (LRP) reference points. The thin dashed line is an example (one realization) of a single simulation.

Figure 3.9   The annual median and 50th and 95th percentiles of the ranking of the new club (high draft choice error; Scenario B)

show how a simulation model (and an MSE framework) could be used by managers of sporting leagues to compare alternative concessional draft selection strategies for the establishment of a new club, prior to that club entering the competition.

Sports Synthesis, like other simulation modelling tools, is not designed to make accurate predictions about the performance of a given club in a given year. Instead, it quantifies the range of possible outcomes of league dynamics, for any given club within that league, and for any given alternative management scenario. The strength of this approach is that it allows managers to make quantifiable and unbiased management decisions, based upon a set of predetermined objectives (ideally agreed upon by multiple stakeholders). Furthermore, simulations of alternative management strategies can provide useful insights into the likely outcomes of choices among sometimes disparate management options. As such, simulation

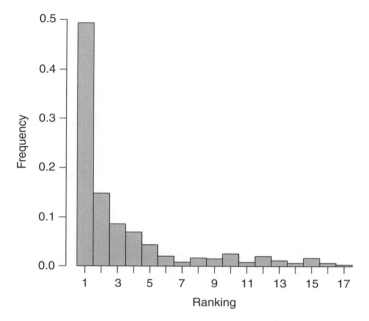

*Figure 3.10   The frequency of rankings for the new club from five years
            and up to and including ten years since establishment (high
            draft choice error; Scenario B)*

modelling tools can be used by league managers both to help determine a suitable course of action during times of league management intervention and, importantly, to better understand the dynamics of their leagues.

Another advantage of simulation is its ability to explicitly deal with uncertainties in the system; whether through the structural assumptions of the system (including assumptions about the randomness of individual player productivity, team productivity and the outcome of sporting contests), the dynamics of the league as a system of *n* clubs, the data used to inform the system state, or the implementation of alternative management strategies (labour market regulations). By clearly recognizing and discussing these uncertainties and creating plausible system hypotheses, current and alternative regulatory options can be simulated and tested for their robustness. Simulation of only a limited number of system structures can lead to poor regulatory choices. As such, a key feature of simulation is its ability to anticipate when management strategies may not achieve the intended objective, and highlight necessary improvements in data collection and the choice of indicators and reference points, as well as the need

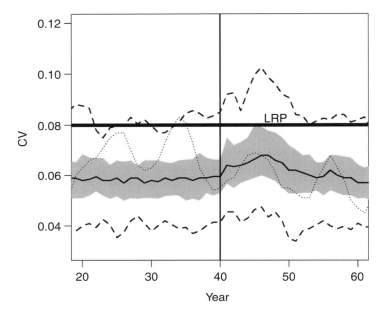

Notes: For draft selections under Scenario B, shown are the median (thin black line), 50th (grey shading) and 95th percentiles (dashed line) of the cv of team productivities. The thin dashed line is an example (one realization) of a single simulation. The thick line is shown as a potential limit reference point (LRP).

Figure 3.11   *The annual cv of team productivities from 20 years before to 20 years after the establishment of the new club (high draft choice error, Scenario B)*

for alternative management strategies (in this case, alternative player draft regulations). These advantages also distinguish simulation from conventional descriptive or regression analysis of time-series competitive balance indicators. Simulation provides an additional dimension of analysis by formally modelling the causal relationship between club performance, competitive balance and labour market regulation.

The simulation of sports leagues, as with other dynamic systems, may be limited by the large-scale complexities, cost and parameterizations required to fully capture plausible system dynamics (Bunnefeld et al., 2011). For example, Sports Synthesis is currently limited to evaluation of the effect of the order of selection in a player draft for new players, given a set number of players per club and the number of league clubs. Other labour market regulations or economic regulations such as revenue-sharing are not simulated. Economic considerations including, inter alia, a club salary cap and production functions modelling the relationships between club on- and off-field performance, consumer demand and the pricing of sporting contests may all be introduced in future iterations, subject to the availability of necessary informative data. A further next step in the development of Sports Synthesis is the calibration of the model with historical data. Recent developments in both sports analytics and 'big data' (Silver, 2012; Alamar, 2013) are being supported by increasing investments in the collection of on-field (sporting performance) and off-field (financial and business performance) data in the AFL and the sports industry at large. Even though the understanding of AFL player and AFL club production functions is still in its relative infancy, a decade or more of raw data is now available for a wide range of variables. These include on-field player performance statistics and standardized approaches to AFL club reporting of player injury statistics and off-field financial and marketing performance. Access to such data would allow for a comprehensive calibration of the Sports Synthesis simulation framework as it is further developed.

Irrespective of the legal implications, the structure of player drafts remains of interest to league managers. In 2015, the AFL announced a new policy for the determination of the 'price' to be paid in the form of foregone National Draft selections by an AFL club seeking to recruit a player via the 'Father-Son Rule' (AFL, 2015). The AFL also regularly penalizes AFL clubs for breach of the *AFL Rules* by prohibiting the club from exercising National Draft selections; as with the removal of the Round 1 and 2 selections of the Essendon Football Club at both the 2013 and 2014 National Drafts (for breaches related to an anti-doping investigation) (AFL, 2013b). Other clubs to have been penalized via the removal of National Draft selections include Adelaide, Carlton and West Coast (Lovett, 2015). Meanwhile, league managers and club coaches alike in Australia's second-largest professional league, the National Rugby League (NRL), continue to fuel speculation about the introduction of a player draft (Koch, 2015; NRL, 2015). In North America, debate continues about the inclusion of international players in the MLB Draft (Morosi, 2015; Rosenthal, 2015), or change to the NBA Draft lottery system (Krawczynski, 2014; Feldman, 2015), even though reform of either draft currently seems unlikely. All five examples highlight contemporary issues where simulation may provide timely and relevant information to league managers faced with difficult matters of economic design and regulatory policy. Given the outcomes of league management decisions will always be susceptible to uncertainties, and that managers can be faced with a wide range of alternative policy options, we recommend the use of simulation tools like Sports Synthesis to enable objective, defensible and robust decisions.

NOTES

1. Booth (1997), Macdonald (2012) and Lovett (2015) provide additional institutional detail of the AFL labour market. For the current regulations, see AFL (2014a) and AFL and AFLPA (2012).
2. The VFL/AFL has also adopted two other types of player draft. The two-round reverse-order Interstate Draft was conducted following the 1981 and 1982 seasons, whereby the 12 VFL clubs drafted players from outside the state of Victoria. Between 1990 and 1993, the AFL conducted the reverse-order Mid-Season Draft, but only 163 players were drafted in four years.
3. Subject to meeting the qualification criteria, individuals must nominate themselves to be eligible for selection in any of the National, Pre-Season or Rookie Drafts. As a general rule, players must be a minimum of 18 years old, though the minimum age and the cut-off date for the minimum age qualification have regularly changed over the years.
4. On average, 74 players per annum were selected in the National Drafts held in the first decade of this century. The entry of Gold Coast and Greater Western Sydney dramatically increased this number from the 2010 National Draft onwards. On average, 62 players per annum have been selected in the Rookie Drafts held this century. Rookie List players earn less than Primary List players and may only be selected to play in an AFL Premiership Season or AFL Finals Series game if so nominated by their club in the pre-season to be an 'eligible Rookie', or, if during the season, the Rookie is temporarily or permanently upgraded to replace a Primary List player with a long-term injury or who has retired. Clubs now largely bypass the Pre-Season Draft (only 115 players in total had been selected in the Pre-Season Drafts between 2000 and 2015), in favour of selecting players in the National and Rookie Drafts.
5. Players delisted by an AFL club are unrestricted free agents. All listed players with at least ten years of continuous service to one club are also unrestricted free agents. Listed players with at least eight years of service are split into two categories. Those who are in the top 25 per cent of salaries at their club are restricted free agents, whereby their current club has the right to match a competing offer; requiring a restricted free agent to either remain at the club or enter the draft. All other players with at least eight years of service are unrestricted free agents. In the first three years of this system, 41 free agents (including nine restricted free agents) have moved between AFL clubs.
6. In *Buckley v Tutty*, the High Court of Australia identified a defence to an action claiming a labour market regulation to be an unreasonable restraint of trade: 'It is a legitimate objective of the league and of the [league] district clubs to ensure that the teams fielded in the competitions are as strong and well matched as possible, for in that way the support of the public will be attracted and maintained, and players will be afforded the best opportunity of developing and displaying their skill' (*Buckley v Tutty* (1971) 125 CLR 353, 377).
7. This statement was made in a case that, upon appeal, successfully challenged the Internal Draft of the New South Wales Rugby League (NSWRL). As a mechanism for the movement of players between league clubs, the NSWRL Internal Draft was similar to the AFL Pre-Season Draft. It was implemented in 1990 in furtherance of League Competition Rules drafted with the object of ensuring that 'the teams fielded in the [NSWRL] Competition are as strong and competitive as possible . . . [between] evenly matched and financially viable Clubs' (NSWRL Limited 1990, cited in *Adamson v New South Wales Rugby League* (1991) 31 FCR 242, 250).
8. The NFL and NBA are selected for comparison as the economic design of the NFL in particular has heavily influenced AFL regulatory policy (AFL Commission, 1999); whereas the NBA represents an outlying case, where the marginal improvement in club performance of one extra player may be extreme.
9. Australian football is the most popular sport in Victoria, South Australia (home of expansions clubs, the Adelaide Crows and Port Adelaide Power), Western Australia (home of expansions clubs, the West Coast Eagles and Fremantle Dockers) and

Tasmania, and is also popular in the Australian Capital Territory, the Northern Territory, the Riverina region of southern New South Wales and pockets of southeastern Queensland. In Queensland, New South Wales and the Australian Capital Territory, rugby league is the most popular code of football and, on balance, Australian football is of secondary or tertiary public interest.

10. With reference to the previous subsection 3.3 and Tables 3.5 and 3.6, the simplifications we have adopted ignore (1) the rights of an expansion club to recruit out-of-contract players from existing clubs as effective free agents; (2) the draft selections granted to existing clubs as 'compensation' for the loss of an out-of-contract player to the expansion club; (3) the (first-option or exclusive) rights of an expansion club to 'pre-list' players from a defined geographic/residency zone or other talent pool ahead of a player draft; (4) the (first-option or exclusive) rights of an expansion club to 'pre-list' young players ahead of the 'normal' year of draft eligibility for those players; (5) the rights of existing clubs to 'pre-list' players from defined geographic/residency zones or other (age-based) talent pools (as a trade-off negotiated by the league manager to placate existing clubs at the time of league expansion); (6) the trading of players (including pre-listed players) and draft selections (including special recruiting rights) between an expansion club and existing clubs; (7) the extra number of players an expansion club may employ during the foundation years of the club; and (8) the right of the expansion club to make additional player payments above the standard salary cap applying to the player salary expenditure by existing clubs. Further assumptions could also be made about the talent profile of the pool of players (the number, absolute quality and relative quality of players) from which the expansion club and the existing clubs are able to draft players.

11. Simulation can be used where there are contrasting degrees of available data, from data-rich to data-poor (Carruthers et al., 2014). Where data is unavailable, the collection of valid and reliable data is time- or cost-prohibitive, or where parameter values are simply not known with any certainty, data-free simulation can still highlight inadequacies in the statistical properties of indicators and provide valuable insights into likely system behaviours (Owen and King, 2015). The Sports Synthesis simulation is data-free in that it does not use data to 'condition' or parameterize the player productivity function. Instead, broad assumptions are made about the system dynamics, using best estimates of the player and team productivity functions, as well as relevant parameters borrowed from other similar fields.

REFERENCES

Adams, C. (2006), 'Estimating the value of "going for it" (when no one does)', SSRN *Working Paper Series*, available at http://ssrn.com/abstract=950987 (accessed 28 January 2015).

Adamson v New South Wales Rugby League (1991) 27 FCR 535.

Adamson v New South Wales Rugby League (1991) 31 FCR 242.

Alamar, B.C. (2013), *Sports Analytics: A Guide for Coaches, Managers, and Other Decision-makers*, New York: Columbia University Press.

Andreff, W. (2014), 'Building blocks for a disequilibrium model of a European team sports league', *International Journal of Sport Finance*, **9**, 20–38.

AFL (Australian Football League) (1993), *Draft Rules Re-structure*, Jolimont, Victoria: Australian Football League.

AFL (Australian Football League) (2008), *112th Annual Report 2008*, Docklands, Victoria: Australian Football League.

AFL (Australian Football League) (2012), *116th Annual Report 2012*, Docklands, Victoria: Australian Football League.

AFL (Australian Football League) (2013a), *117th Annual Report 2013*, Docklands, Victoria: Australian Football League.

AFL (Australian Football League) (2013b), *List of Sanctions Against Essendon and its Officials*, available at http://www.afl.com.au/news/2013-08-27/list-of-charges-against-essendon-and-its-officials (accessed 20 February 2015).

AFL (Australian Football League) (2014a), *AFL Rules: December 2014*, Docklands, Victoria: Australian Football League.

AFL (Australian Football League) (2014b), *118th Annual Report 2014*, Docklands, Victoria: Australian Football League.

AFL (Australian Football League) (2014c), *AFL Statement: Competitive Balance Policy*, 4 June, available at http://www.afl.com.au/news/2014-06-04/afl-statement-competitive-balance-policy (accessed 28 January 2015).

AFL (Australian Football League) (2015), *Bidding System Review – F/S and Academy Supporting Exhibits: January 2015*, Docklands, Victoria: Australian Football League.

AFL and AFLPA (Australian Football League and Australian Football League Players' Association Inc.) (2012), *Collective Bargaining Agreement 2012–2016*, Melbourne, Victoria.

AFL (Australian Football League) Commission (1999), *Competitiveness on the Field and Uncertainty of Outcomes: Equalisation Strategies at the AFL*, Jolimont, Victoria.

Bedford, A. and A.J. Schembri (2006), 'A probability based approach for the allocation of player draft selections in Australian rules football', *Journal of Sports Science and Medicine*, **5**, 509–16.

Berri, D.J., M.B. Schmidt and S.L. Brook (2007), *The Wages of Wins: Taking Measure of the Many Myths in Modern Sport*, Stanford, CA: Stanford University Press.

Booth, D.R. (2000), 'Labour market intervention, revenue sharing and competitive balance in the Victorian Football League/Australian Football League, 1987–1998', PhD Thesis, Department of Economics, Monash University.

Booth, R. (1997), 'History of player recruitment, transfer and payment rules in the Victorian and Australian Football League', *ASSH Bulletin*, **26**, 13–33.

Borland, J. (2006), 'Economic design and professional sporting competitions', *Australian Economic Review*, **39**(4), 435–41.

Borland, J. and R. Macdonald (2003), 'Demand for sport', *Oxford Review of Economic Policy*, **19**(4), 478–502.

Borland, J., M. Chicu and R.D. Macdonald (2009), 'Do teams always lose to win? Performance incentives and the player draft in the Australian Football League', *Journal of Sports Economics*, **10**(5), 451–84.

Buckley v Tutty (1971) 125 CLR 353.

Budzinski, O. and T. Pawlowski (2014), 'The behavioural economics of competitive balance: implications for league policy and championship management', Ilmenau Economics Discussion Papers, No. 89.

Bunnefeld, N., E. Hoshino and E.J. Milner-Gulland (2011), 'Management strategy evaluation: a powerful tool for conservation?', *Trends in Ecology and Evolution*, **26**(9), 441–7.

Caddy, J.F. (1984), 'An alternative to equilibrium theory for management of fisheries', in *Proceedings of the Papers Presented at the Expert Consultation on the Regulation of Fishing Effort, Fishing Mortality*, Rome, 17–26 January, 1983, pp. 63–75. FAO Fisheries Report 289, Suppl. 2 (English), p. 214.

Carruthers, T.R., A.E. Punt, C.J. Walters et al. (2014), 'Evaluating methods for setting catch limits in data-limited fisheries', *Fisheries Research*, **153**, 48–68.

Clark, J. and M. Warner (2012), 'Rivals tip juggernaut as Greater Western Sydney amasses top draft picks', *Herald Sun* (Melbourne), 10 October.

Coase, R.H. (1960), 'The problem of social cost', *Journal of Law and Economics*, **3**, 1–44.

Coleman, B.J. (2012), 'Identifying the "players" in sports analytics research', *Interfaces*, **42**(2), 109–18.

Dabscheck, B. (1989), 'Abolishing transfer fees: the Victorian Football League's new employment rules', *Sporting Traditions*, **6**(1), 66–87.

Dabscheck, B. and H. Opie (2003), 'Legal regulation of sporting labour markets', *Australian Journal of Labour Law*, **16**, 1–25.

Davies, C. (2005), 'The AFL's Holy Grail: the quest for an even competition', *James Cook University Law Review*, **12**, 65–92.

Davies, C. (2006), 'Draft systems in professional team sports and the restraint of trade doctrine: is the AFL draft distinguishable from the NSWRL draft?', *Australian and New Zealand Sports Law Journal*, **1**(1), 80–102.

Drayer, J. and D. Rascher (2010), 'Simulation in sport finance', *Simulation & Gaming*, **41**(2), 231–7.

Einolf, K.W. (2005), 'EconFantasy.com: where fantasy becomes reality in an economics-of-sports simulation', *Journal of Sports Economics*, **6**(3), 338–9.

El-Hodiri, M. and J. Quirk (1971), 'An economic model of a professional sports league', *Journal of Political Economy*, **79**(6), 1302–19.

Fairweather, J. (2010), *Review of the Australian Water Polo Inc. National Water Polo League*, Canberra: Australian Sports Commission.

Feldman, D. (2015), 'Re-inventing the wheel: Mike Zarren presents modified NBA-draft-lottery-reform proposals', 27 February, available at http://probasket-balltalk.nbcsports.com/2015/02/27/re-inventing-the-wheel-mike-zarren-presents-modified-nba-draft-lottery-reform-proposals/ (accessed 5 March 2015).

Flato, G., J. Marotzke, B. Abiodun et al. (2013), 'Evaluation of climate models', in T.F. Stocker, D. Qin, G.-K. Plattner, M. Tignor, S.K. Allen, J. Boschung, A. Nauels, Y. Xia, V. Bex and P.M. Midgley (eds), *Climate Change 2013: The Physical Science Basis. Contribution of Working Group I to the Fifth Assessment Report of the Intergovernmental Panel on Climate Change*, Cambridge: Cambridge University Press, pp. 741–866.

Fort, R. D. and J. Quirk (1995), 'Cross-subsidization, incentives and outcomes in professional team sports leagues', *Journal of Economic Literature*, **33**(3), 1265–99.

Fry, M.J., A.W. Lundberg and J.W. Ohlmann (2007), 'A player selection heuristic for a sports league draft', *Journal of Quantitative Analysis in Sports*, **3**(2), article 5.

Fulton, E.A., A.D.M. Smith, D.C. Smith and P. Johnson (2014), 'An integrated approach is needed for ecosystem based fisheries management: insights from ecosystem-level management strategy evaluation', *PLoS ONE*, **9**(1), doi:10.1371/journal.pone.0084242.

Gahan, P. and R.D. Macdonald (2001), 'Collective bargaining simulation: the Federal Football League versus the National Association of Professional Footballers', *Sport Management Review*, **4**(1), 89–114.

García, J. and P. Rodríguez (2009), 'Sports attendance: a survey of the literature 1973–2007', *Rivista di Diritto ed Economia dello Sport*, **5**(2), 111–51.

Grier K.B. and R.D. Tollison (1994), 'The rookie draft and competitive balance: the case of professional football', *Journal of Economic Behavior and Organization*, **25**, 293–8.

Haigh, J. (2009), 'Uses and limitations of mathematics in sport', *IMA Journal of Management Mathematics*, **20**(2), 97–108.

Hilborn, R. and C.J. Walters (1992), *Quantitative Fisheries Stock Assessment: Choice, Dynamics and Uncertainty*, New York: Chapman and Hall.

Humphreys, B.R. and N.M. Watanabe (2012), 'Competitive balance', in L.H. Kahane and S. Shmanske (eds), *Handbook of Sports Economics. Volume 1: The Economics of Sports*, Oxford: Oxford University Press, pp. 18–37.

Jahangirian, M., T. Eldabi, A. Naseer, L.K. Stergioulas and T. Young (2010), 'Simulation in manufacturing and business: a review', *European Journal of Operational Research*, **203**(1), 1–13.

Kahane, L. (2006), 'The reverse-order-of-finish draft in sports', in W. Andreff and S. Szymanski (eds), *Handbook on the Economics of Sport*, Cheltenham, UK and Northampton, MA, USA: Edward Elgar, pp. 643–5.

Késenne, S. (2014), *The Economic Theory of Professional Team Sports: An Analytical Treatment*, 2nd edn, Cheltenham, UK and Northampton, MA, USA: Edward Elgar.

Koch, D. (2015), 'Wayne Bennett urges Commission to reconsider an external draft', *The Australian* (Sydney), 13 February.

Krawczynski, J. (2014), 'NBA owners vote down changes to lottery system', 22 October, available at http://www.nba.com/2014/news/10/22/lottery-reform-vote.ap/ (accessed 5 March 2015).

Lahvička, J. (2013), 'The impact of playoffs on seasonal uncertainty in the Czech ice hockey Extraliga', *Journal of Sports Economics*, doi: 10.1177/1527002513509109.

Levin, R.C., G.J. Mitchell, P.A., Volcker and G.F. Will (2000), *The Report of the Independent Members of the Commissioner's Blue Ribbon Panel on Baseball Economics, July 2000*, New York: Major League Baseball.

Lewis, M. (2004), *Moneyball: The Art of Winning an Unfair Game*, New York: W.W. Norton & Company.

Lovett, M. (ed.) (2010), *AFL Record Season Guide 2010*, Docklands, Victoria: Australian Football League.

Lovett, M. (ed.) (2011), *AFL Record Season Guide 2011*, Docklands, Victoria: Australian Football League.

Lovett, M. (ed.) (2012), *AFL Record Season Guide 2012*, Docklands, Victoria: Australian Football League.

Lovett, M. (ed.) (2013), *AFL Record Season Guide 2013*, Docklands, Victoria: Australian Football League.

Lovett, M. (ed.) (2014), *AFL Record Season Guide 2014*, Docklands, Victoria: Australian Football League.

Lovett, M. (ed.) (2015), *AFL Record Season Guide 2015*, Docklands, Victoria: Australian Football League.

Macdonald, R.D. (2012), '"Player shares of revenue", collective bargaining and the Australian Football League: a comment on Dabscheck', *Labour & Industry*, **22**(4), 447–64.

Macdonald, R.D. and A.C.T. Smith (2015), 'Sports league design from behind the veil of ignorance', Unpublished manuscript, University of Melbourne and RMIT University.

Maxcy, J. (2012), 'Economics of the NFL player entry draft system', in K.G. Quinn (ed.), *The Economics of the National Football League*, New York: Springer, pp. 173–86.

McKeown, J.T. (2011), 'The economics of competitive balance: sports antitrust claims after *American Needle*', *Marquette Sports Law Review*, **21**(2), 517–50.

Morosi, J.P. (2015), 'Players' union head not ready to endorse commissioner's idea of worldwide draft, 1 March, available at http://www.foxsports.com/mlb/story/mlb-players-union-not-endorsing-worldwide-draft-tony-clark-030115 (accessed 5 March 2015).

Mun, J. (2010), *Modeling Risk: Applying Monte Carlo Risk Simulation, Strategic Real Options, Stochastic Forecasting, and Portfolio Optimization*, New York: John Wiley & Sons.

Neale, W.C. (1964), 'The peculiar economics of professional sports: a contribution to the theory of the firm in sporting competition and in market competition', *Quarterly Journal of Economics*, **78**(1), 1–14.

NRL (National Rugby League) (2015), *NRL Appoints Richardson to Strategy Role*, 21 January, available at http://www.nrl.com/nrl-appoints-richardson-to-strategy-role/tabid/10874/newsid/83471/default.aspx (accessed 20 March 2015).

O'Shaughnessy, D. (2010), 'On the value of AFL player draft picks', in A. Bedford (ed.), *Proceedings of the 10th Australasian Conference on Mathematics and Computers in Sport*, Canberra, Australian Capital Territory: Mathsport, pp. 113–20.

Owen, P.D. and N. King (2015), 'Competitive balance measures in sports leagues: the effects of variation in season length', *Economic Inquiry*, **53**(1), 731–44.

Pettigrew, S. (2014), 'How the west will be won: using Monte Carlo simulations to estimate the effects of NHL realignment', *Journal of Quantitative Analysis in Sports*, **10**(3), 345–56.

Pierik, J. (2011), 'Suns can win and bear it', *The Age* (Melbourne), 1 April.

Polacheck, T., N.L. Klaer, C. Millar and A.L. Preece (1999), 'An initial evaluation of management strategies for southern bluefin tuna', *ICES Journal of Marine Science*, **56**, 811–26.

Prager, M.H., C.E. Porch, K.W. Shertzer and J.F. Caddy (2003), 'Targets and limits for management of fisheries: a simple probability-based approach', *North American Journal of Fisheries Management*, **23**, 349–61.

Price, J., B.P. Soebbing, D. Berri and B.R. Humphreys (2010), 'Tournament incentives, league policy, and NBA team performance revisited', *Journal of Sports Economics*, **11**(2), 117–35.

Punt, A.E., R. Campbell and A.D.M. Smith (2001), 'Evaluating empirical indicators and reference points for fisheries management: application to the Broadbill Swordfish Fishery off Eastern Australia', *Marine and Freshwater Research*, **52**, 819–32.

Punt, A.E., D.S. Butterworth, C.L. de Moor, J.A.A. De Oliveira and M. Haddon (2014), 'Management strategy evaluation: best practices', *Fish and Fisheries*, doi: 10.1111/faf.12104.

Puterman, M.L. and Q. Wang (2011), 'Optimal dynamic clustering through relegation and promotion: how to design a competitive sports league', *Journal of Quantitative Analysis in Sports*, **7**(2), article 7.

Quayle, E. (2014), 'How the Suns and Giants got the best of both worlds', *The Age* (Melbourne), 16 May.

Quinn, K.G. (2008), 'Player drafts in the major North American sports leagues', in B.R. Humphreys and D. Howard (eds), *The Business of Sports. Volume 3: Bridging Research & Practice*, Westport, CT: Praeger, pp. 191–217.

R Core Team (2014), *R: A Language and Environment for Statistical Computing, Vienna: R Foundation for Statistical Computing*, available at http://www.R--project.org/ (accessed 20 March 2015).

Richardson, D.H. (2000), 'Pay, performance, and competitive balance in the National Hockey League', *Eastern Economic Journal*, **26**(4), 393–417.

Rockerbie, D.W. (2014), 'Exploring interleague parity in North America: the NBA anomaly', *Journal of Sports Economics*, doi: 10.1177/1527002514529795.

Rosenthal, K. (2015), 'Commissioner Manfred talks pace, players, plans in new role', 28 January, available at http://www.foxsports.com/mlb/story/rob-manfred-mlb-baseball-commissioner-talks-pace-players-and-plans-012815 (accessed 5 March 2015).

Rottenberg, S. (1956), 'The baseball player's labor market', *Journal of Political Economy*, **64**(3), 242–58.

Rottenberg, S. (2000), 'Resource allocation and income distribution in professional team sports', *Journal of Sports Economics*, **1**(1), 11–20.

Ryan, P. and N. Bowen (2015), 'Million-dollar club shrinks again as more players share the wealth', 22 January, available at http://www.afl.com.au/news/2015-01-22/1m-club-shrinks-again (accessed 28 January 2015).

Sainsbury, K.J., A.E. Punt and A.D.M. Smith (2000), 'Design of operational management strategies for achieving fishery ecosystem objectives', *ICES Journal of Marine Science*, **57**, 731–41.

Sargent, J. and A. Bedford (2010), 'Improving Australian Football League player performance forecasts using optimized nonlinear smoothing', *International Journal of Forecasting*, **26**, 489–97.

Schnute, J.T. and R. Haigh (2006), 'Reference points and management strategies: lessons from quantum mechanics', *ICES Journal of Marine Science*, **63**, 4–11.

Sheehan, K. (2010), 'Gold Coast 2011: building the list', in Champion Data (ed.), *AFL Prospectus: The Essential Number Cruncher for Season 2010*, Southbank, Melbourne, Champion Data, pp. 367–9.

Siegfried, J.J. (1995), 'Sports player drafts and reserve system', *Cato Journal*, **14**, 443–52.

Silver, N. (2012), *The Signal and the Noise: The Art and Science of Prediction*, London: Penguin Books.

Szymanski, S. (2003), 'The economic design of sporting contests', *Journal of Economic Literature*, **41**(4), 1137–87.

Szymanski, S. (2010), 'Teaching competition in professional sports leagues', *Journal of Economic Education*, **41**(2), 150–68.

Taylor, B.A. and J.G. Trogdon (2002), 'Losing to win: tournament incentives in the National Basketball Association', *Journal of Labor Economics*, **20**(1), 23–41.

Tuck, G.N. (2011), 'Are bycatch rates sufficient as the principal fishery performance measure and method of assessment for seabirds?', *Aquatic Conservation*, **21**(5), 412–22.

Tuck, G.N. and A.R. Whitten (2012), 'Who's driving the tank? A dynamic non-equilibrium simulation model to test alternative amateur draft systems for major sporting leagues', in A. Bedford and A. Schembri (eds), *Proceedings of the 11th Australasian Conference on Mathematics and Computers in Sport*, Canberra, Australian Capital Territory: MathSport, pp. 8–19.

Tuck, G.N. and A.R. Whitten (2013), 'Lead us not into tanktation: a simulation modelling approach to gain insights into incentives for sporting teams to tank', *PLoS ONE*, **8**(11), doi: 10.1371/journal.pone.0080798.

Tuck, G.N. and A.R. Whitten (2014), 'Windows of opportunity: using a simulation model to explore the duration of success of sporting teams', *Proceedings of the 12th Australasian Conference on Mathematics and Computers in Sport*, Canberra, Australian Capital Territory: MathSport, p. 75.

Walters, C. and J. Maguire (1996), 'Lessons for stock assessment from the northern cod collapse', *Reviews in Fish Biology and Fisheries*, **6**, 125–37.

Welfe, W. (2013), *Macroeconomic Models*, New York: Springer.

Wright, M.B. (2009), '50 years of OR in sport', *Journal of the Operational Research Society*, **60**, S161–S168.

Wright, M. (2014), 'OR analysis of sporting rules: a survey', *European Journal of Operational Research*, **232**(1), 1–8.

Websites

Australian Football League   afl.com.au
Canadian Football League   cfl.ca
Major League Baseball   mlb.com
National Basketball Association   nba.com
National Football League   nfl.com
National Hockey League   nhl.com
Women's National Basketball Association   wnba.com
basketball-reference.com
pro-football-reference.com

4. The metrics of competitive imbalance

Jean-Pascal Gayant and Nicolas Le Pape

INTRODUCTION

The issue of competitive imbalance in professional sport leagues is one of the most central topics in the field of the economics of sport. It is traditionally considered that in a perfectly balanced league, each team would have the same probability of winning; there would be a great degree of uncertainty over the outcome of a championship. Conversely, an unbalanced competition is supposed to diminish interest on the part of the spectator, consequently decreasing demand for sports contests and also confidence in the legitimacy of competition (Neale, 1964; Daly, 1992; Zimbalist, 2003; Késenne, 2006). The relationship between the attractiveness of a league and its level of competitive imbalance is probably quite complex: Szymanski (2001, 2007) has observed that in some cases, the majority of the fans seem to prefer that a dominant team beats all opponents, like Manchester United in the English Premier League (EPL) during the 1990s, and that despite its growing imbalance since 1995, the attractiveness of the EPL has not declined. Szymanski (2001, pp. 72–3) explains that the traditional argument about competitive balance has to be qualified: since 'some teams draw on larger (or more devoted) fan bases, then the success of these teams will yield greater total utility than the success of teams with small fan bases'. As a consequence, considering the attractiveness of a league, 'perfect balance is not generally desirable'. In recent models, authors now define a league welfare function and try to assess the degree of imbalance that maximizes welfare (see, for instance, Dietl et al., 2009). Either one is concerned about the effective level of competitive imbalance in a league or one endeavours to define the socially desirable level of imbalance; in either case, one has to measure the level of imbalance accurately.

The first measure of competitive imbalance in a league that emerged in the literature was the standard deviation of the number (or percentage) of wins. So that frequent changes in the size of the leagues and/or changes in the schedules of championships might be taken into account, Quirk and

Fort (1992) and Fort and Quirk (1995) suggested that a relative standard deviation should be used, being the ratio of the actual standard deviation to an idealized one – for a league in which each team would have the same chance of winning. This measure was supposed to facilitate inter-seasonal comparisons of competitive imbalance. In the same way, Depken (1999) proposed measuring the imbalance using a corrected Hirschman-Herfindahl index (HHI), defined as the gap between the actual Herfindahl index and an idealized one. Using a Herfindahl index makes an explicit reference to issues in industrial organization (in particular, measures of market concentration) by making an analogy between the market share of a firm and the percentage of points gained by a team, despite the fact that no team can reach a monopoly position (except for the extreme case of a two-team league, no contestant may obtain a market share equals to 100 per cent). Implicitly, a low value for the Herfindahl index can be viewed as an indication of a desirable situation by a league manager in the same way that an antitrust authority would consider a market structure. However, measuring competitive imbalance with a Herfindahl index or with a standard deviation is essentially the same, because both measures are cardinally equivalent.

Where sports involve games that may end in ties (soccer, handball, rugby, hockey – some years ago) the measure of competitive imbalance becomes more complicated (as noted by Cain and Haddock, 2006) since the design of the point award system may diminish the quality of the measure. Indeed, any measure of competitive imbalance has to be based on absolute or relative points; however, depending on the number of ties registered during the season, the total number of points awarded may vary, and hence the weight associated with any one win. Because of this instability in the weighting process, the most essential properties that a measure should satisfy may not be fulfilled. This phenomenon is a crucial issue in the assessment of competitive imbalance: when the existing point award generates structural instability, either the measure will be improper, but based on the real *ex ante* point allocation system or the measure may be adequate as an index, but based on a 'non-existing' point award system. This is the source of an irresolvable trade-off: either dealing with a real *ex ante* system that provides the actual incentives for teams but gives a biased index of imbalance or dealing with an *ex post* system that betrays the substance of incentives but provides an unbiased measure. In this chapter, we adopt the second perspective.

Measuring competitive imbalance in a league is, in many respects, similar to measuring income inequality in a community (Quirk and Fort, 1992; Utt and Fort, 2002; Borooah and Mangan, 2012). We therefore examine whether using a Gini index will provide an adequate measure of competitive imbalance. More precisely, we study the sensitivity of the Gini index to the substitution of one subset of consecutively ranked teams under perfect competitive imbalance by another subset of teams under perfect competitive balance. We show that (1) the more teams there are suffering from competitive balance, the smaller the Gini index and (2) the Gini index is insensitive to the positioning of the block of teams under competitive balance. Finally, we study the case of the substitution of two blocks of teams under competitive balance. When comparing the level of imbalance (measured by the Gini index) between a unique block and two blocks of equal size, we note that for the same number of teams under competitive balance, the imbalance appears to be greater when there are two blocks in the distribution. This may be inappropriate or counterintuitive in the case of an open league (with promotion and relegation); indeed, a championship in which there is a great rivalry at the top and at the bottom can be considered more attractive (or less 'imbalanced') than a championship in which there is great rivalry in the middle of the distribution. Therefore, we suggest using a generalized Gini index. An index of this kind is built on a generalized equivalent number of points calculated on an S-shaped function.

FORMALIZATION

Let us consider a league consisting of $n \in \mathbb{N}$ teams and let us denote by p_i ($i \in \{1, \ldots, n\}$) the number of points obtained by the ith team at the end of the contest,[1] in a one home-one away championship.[2] Absolute points p_i are ranked in increasing order, that is, $p_1 \leq p_2 \leq \ldots \leq p_n$ and the vector of absolute points is denoted $p = (p_1, p_2, \ldots, p_n)$.[3] In such a championship each team plays $2(n - 1)$ games and the total number of games played is $n(n - 1)$. We choose to base the measure of the league imbalance on the distribution of points rather than on the distribution of wins; hence, our results are also suitable for sports where ties can happen. Suppose that, for every game that it plays, a team is awarded z_w points for a win, z_t points for a tie and z_l points for losing ($z_w > z_t > z_l$). Then

$$\sum_{i=1}^{n} p_i = n(n - 1)(z_w + z_l) + T(2z_t - z_w - z_l) = P_{z_w, z_t, z_1}(n)$$

where T refers to the aggregate number of ties in the championship ($0 \leq T \leq 2n(n - 1)$). In sports where ties cannot happen, the total number of points is constant (assuming the number of competing teams does not vary), that is, independent of the way the points are distributed among the teams. Moreover, in the case where $z_l = 0$, the design of the point award system has no impact on the distribution of relative points.[4] Conversely, in sports where ties happen (like soccer, rugby or handball), the total number of points varies[5] with T and the distribution of relative points is unstable, except if $2z_t = z_w + z_l$. The question of the stability of the distribution of relative points is fundamental when measuring the imbalance of a league. Indeed, with an unstable distribution, an index of imbalance may not reach its minimum value for the most balanced distribution and its maximum value for the most imbalanced distribution.[6] Such a situation would be a major failure for any inequality/imbalance index. In the next section, having clarified the characteristics of the least and the most imbalanced distribution, we will show, by using an example, that if $2z_t \neq (z_w + z_l)$, then any index may violate the property that the measure will reach its maximal value for the most imbalanced distribution.

DESIGN OF THE POINT AWARD SYSTEM AND MEASUREMENT OF COMPETITIVE IMBALANCE

As Borooah and Mangan (2012, p. 1094) summarize: 'In a perfectly balanced competition, each team would have an equal chance of winning each match and, therefore, of winning the championship or the league.' Under a regular schedule, such a situation would lead to the hypothetical Perfect Competitive Balance (*PCB*) configuration where each team wins $(n - 1)$ games and loses $(n - 1)$ games. Finally, the total points of the ith team at the end of the championship are then[7] $p_i^{PCB} = (z_w + z_l)(n - 1)$. In the less imbalanced distribution, all the teams have then exactly the same number of points.

The idea of Perfect Competitive Imbalance (*PCI*) is also very intuitive, but has rarely been formalized. Here the weakest team has no chance of winning against all others; the second weakest is going to win against the weakest and to lose against all others with certainty, and so on up to the strongest team that will win every game with certainty. Such a hypothetical configuration has been characterized by Horowitz (1997), Fort and Quirk (1997), Utt and Fort (2002) and Borooah and Mangan (2012). Under a regular schedule, *PCI* can then be specified as follows.

The 1st team loses its $[2 \times (n - 1)]$ games, the 2nd team wins 2 games (the 2 games against the previous team) and loses $[2 \times (n - 2)]$ games, the 3rd team wins 4 games (the 4 games against the 2 previous teams) and loses $[2 \times (n - 3)]$ games, . . ., the nth team wins its $[2 \times (n - 1)]$ games. Finally, the total points of ith team at the end of the championship are:

$$p_i^{PCI} = 2z_w(i-1) + 2z_l(n-i)$$

The *PCB* and *PCI* configurations are the two polar configurations, respectively the least and the most imbalanced ones, so that for all $n \in \mathbb{N}$, for all $p \in \mathbb{N}^n$, any imbalance index $I_{IMB}(p)$ must satisfy:

$$I_{IMB}(p^{PCB}) \leq I_{IMB}(p) \leq I_{IMB}(p^{PCI})$$

Let us now show in an example that if $2z_t \neq (z_w + z_l)$, the standard deviation (as well as all traditional indices) may violate this inequality.[8] This example is based on the characterization of a hypothetical (*H*) configuration concerning a league with an even number of teams. Let us divide the league into two subsets of $\frac{n}{2}$ teams and characterize the teams belonging to the first subset by the indices $i \in \{1, \ldots, \frac{n}{2}\}$, and the teams belonging to the second subset by the indices $i \in \{\frac{n}{2} + 1, \ldots, n\}$. Suppose that:

- Each team of the first subset ties twice against each of the $(\frac{n}{2} - 1)$ other teams of the same subset, and loses twice against the $\frac{n}{2}$ teams of the other subset. As a result, $\forall i \in \{1, \ldots, \frac{n}{2}\} : p_i^H = (n-2)z_t + nz_l$
- Each team of the second subset wins twice against the $\frac{n}{2}$ teams of the other subset, wins once and loses once against each of the $(\frac{n}{2} - 1)$ others teams of the same subset. As a result, $\forall i \in \{\frac{n}{2} + 1, \ldots, n\} :$ $p_i^H = (\frac{3n}{2} - 1)z_w + (\frac{n}{2} - 1)z_l$

Let us now recall that the standard deviation of the distribution of relative points (or market share) is:

$$\sigma^2(S) = \frac{1}{n} \sum_{i=1}^{n} (s_i - \bar{s})^2$$

where $\bar{s} = \frac{1}{n} \sum_{i=1}^{n} s_i$ and $s_i = \frac{p_i}{P_{z_w,z_t,z_l}(n)}$

Under the current point award system in European and North American soccer leagues, wherein $z_w = 3$, $z_t = 1$ and $z_l = 0$, the standard deviation in configurations *H* and *PCI* is:

$$\sigma^2(S^H) = \frac{49n^2 - 28n + 4}{n^2(11n - 10)^2}$$

and

$$\sigma^2(S^{PCI}) = \frac{(n+1)}{3n^2(n-1)}$$

Consequently, as soon as $n \geq 2$,

Table 4.1 *Distributions of points when n = 20 under the (3 ; 1 ; 0) and (2 ; 1 ; 0) systems*

Team	3 points for a win		2 points for a win	
	Config. *PCI*	Config. *H*	Config. *PCI*	Config. *H*
1	0	18	0	18
2	6	18	4	18
3	12	18	8	18
4	18	18	12	18
5	24	18	16	18
6	30	18	20	18
7	36	18	24	18
8	42	18	28	18
9	48	18	32	18
10	54	18	36	18
11	60	87	40	58
12	66	87	44	58
13	72	87	48	58
14	78	87	52	58
15	84	87	56	58
16	90	87	60	58
17	96	87	64	58
18	102	87	68	58
19	108	87	72	58
20	114	87	76	58

$$\sigma^2(S^H) - \sigma^2(S^{PCI}) = \frac{2(n-2)^2(13n-14)}{3n^2(n-1)(11n-10)^2} > 0$$

or

$$I_{IMB}(p\mathrm{H}) > I_{IMB}(p^{\mathrm{PCI}})$$

This result is a major problem. We can illustrate this undesirable phenomenon with an example. In Table 4.1, we compare the distributions of points under the actual (3 ; 1 ; 0) system and under the (2 ; 1 ; 0) system – which fulfils the $2z_t = (z_w + z_l)$ condition – for $n = 20$ (as in four of the five major European soccer leagues).

Whereas $\sigma^2(S^H) = 0.00304 < 0.00325 = \sigma^2(S^{PCI})$ when using the 'satisfying' (2 ; 1 ; 0) system, we find that $\sigma^2(S^H) = 0.00340 > 0.00325 = \sigma^2(S^{PCI})$ when the inappropriate (3 ; 1 ; 0) system is used.

More generally, the choice of a point award system in which the total number of points awarded depends on the actual number of ties is inappropriate for calculating any index of imbalance. Indeed, the more ties that occur, the less the total of points registered when the design of points does not respect the condition $2z_t = (z_w + z_l)$. Then a tie (or a win, or a loss) does not have the same relative weight in the calculus of the index, depending on whether – or not – a high proportion of ties has been recorded. As a consequence, the value taken by any index of imbalance in an intermediate configuration can be strictly greater than the value this index takes in the most imbalanced configuration.

We must then presume that $2z_t = (z_w + z_l)$ to measure competitive imbalance properly. This will be the case for the remainder of this chapter. As a consequence, any real distribution of points should be recalculated on this basis to properly assess the level of imbalance. As underlined in the introduction, this provides an unbiased measure, but one that does not conform to the real point award system and its corresponding incentive properties.

A second point of concern is the need to take proper account of changes in the size of the league.

MEASUREMENT OF COMPETITIVE IMBALANCE AND CHANGES IN THE SIZE OF LEAGUES

To deal with changes in the size of leagues, Quirk and Fort (1992), Fort and Quirk (1995) and Depken (1999) proposed using corrected indices: a corrected standard error in the works of Fort and Quirk, a corrected Hirschman-Herfindahl index in the paper by Depken.

Fort and Quirk suggest using a relative standard deviation, which is the ratio of the actual standard deviation to an idealized one. Fort and Quirk define an idealized distribution as a distribution of wins in a league (where no tie can happen) in which 'each team is of equal playing strength': if $\tilde{X}$ denotes the random variable that indicates the number of games that a team, playing m matches, wins in a season, the expected value of $\tilde{X}$ is $0.5m$ (because the probability of winning any game is 0.5, and the games are implicitly supposed to be independent). It is easy to calculate that the idealized variance of $\tilde{X}$ equals $\sigma_{Id}^2(\tilde{X}) = 0.25m$, and then that the Idealized Standard Deviation (*ISD*) is $\sigma_{Id}(\tilde{X}) = 0.5\sqrt{m}$. For convenience, one can also work with the random value $\tilde{W}$, which indicates the percentage of wins. Obviously, $\tilde{W} = \frac{\tilde{X}}{m}$ and the *ISD* becomes $\sigma_{Id}(\tilde{W}) = \frac{0.5}{\sqrt{m}}$. Fort and Quirk suggest using the ratio $RSE = \frac{ASD}{ISD}$ where *ASD* designates the actual standard deviation of the percentage of wins. If $\sigma(\tilde{W})$ denotes the actual standard deviation, the relative standard deviation is:

$$RSE = \frac{\sigma(\tilde{W})\sqrt{m}}{0.5} \qquad (4.1)$$

An alternative way of taking account of possible changes in the size of the league is to use a corrected Hirschman-Herfindahl index. Depken (1999) proposes calculating the difference between the actual value of the Herfindahl index and an idealized one. By analogy, in an idealized industry (or an industry in which no firm dominates its competitors in terms of market share) all firms have the same market share $\frac{1}{n}$, implying that a Herfindahl index also equals $\frac{1}{n}$. The corrected index is obtained in the following way:

$$dHHI = HHI - \frac{1}{n} \qquad (4.2)$$

where $HHI = \sum_{i=1}^{n} s_i^2$.

Lenten (2008) or Pawlowski et al. (2010) prefer to work with the ratio of the actual value of HHI to its idealized value, which is obviously the minimal value. This ratio is:

$$HICB = \frac{Actual\ HHI}{Idealized\ HHI} = \frac{HHI}{\frac{1}{n}} = nHHI \qquad (4.3)$$

Link between the Relative Standard Error and *dHHI*

It is possible to establish the formal link between RSE and $dHHI$. Let us now show that:

$$RSE = \sqrt{m.n.dHHI} \qquad (4.4)$$

Proof:
The variance of market shares satisfies:

$$\sigma^2(S) = \frac{1}{n} \sum_{i=1}^{n} (s_i - \bar{s})^2$$

where: $\bar{s} = \dfrac{\sum_{i=1}^{n} s_i}{n} = \dfrac{\sum_{i=1}^{n} \frac{p_i}{\sum_{i=1}^{n} p_i}}{n} = \dfrac{\frac{1}{n}\sum_{i=1}^{n} p_i}{\sum_{i=1}^{n} p_i} = \dfrac{1}{n}$

Consequently: $n\sigma^2(S) = \sum_{i=1}^{n} \left(s_i - \frac{1}{n}\right)^2$

It follows that: $n\sigma^2(S) = \sum_{i=1}^{n}\left(s_i^2 - \frac{2s_i}{n} + \frac{1}{n^2}\right) = \sum_{i=1}^{n}s_i^2 - \frac{2}{n}\sum_{i=1}^{n}s_i + \frac{n}{n^2}$

Yet, by construction, $\sum_{i=1}^{n}s_i = 1$

Then $n\sigma^2(S) = \sum_{i=1}^{n}s_i^2 - \frac{1}{n}$

Consequently: $n\sigma^2(S) = HHI - \frac{1}{n} = dHHI$.

Now we need to express the relationship between the variance of the market shares and the variance of the percentage of wins. Let x_i and w_i respectively denote the number and the percentage of team i wins (in a league where no tie can happen). Under the condition that $z_l = 0$, $p_i = z_w$ x_i. As each team plays m games, $\sum_{i=1}^{n}p_i = m\frac{n}{2}z_w$, $s_i = \frac{p_i}{\sum_{i=1}^{n}p_i} = \frac{z_w x_i}{m\frac{n}{2}z_w} = \frac{2x_i}{nm} = \frac{2w_i}{n}$. Then $\sigma^2(S) = \frac{4}{n^2}\sigma^2(\tilde{W})$. As $n\sigma^2(S) = dHHI$, $\sigma^2(\tilde{W}) = \frac{n}{4}dHHI$.

Now, as $RSE^2 = \frac{\sigma(\tilde{W})m}{0.25}$, it follows that $RSE^2 = m.n.dHHI$ or $RSE = \sqrt{m.n.dHHI}$.

Remark 1: Under a regular schedule such as the one described in the previous section, each team plays $2(n-1)$ games so that:

$$RSE = \sqrt{2n(n-1)dHHI} \qquad (4.5)$$

Remark 2: In his paper Depken (1999) prefers to work with the variable that measures the number of team i wins. The relations he demonstrates relate to the link between $\sigma^2(S)$ and $\sigma^2(\tilde{X})$. In particular, he shows that $\sigma^2(\tilde{X}) = \frac{m^2n}{4}(HHI - \frac{1}{n})$.

Remark 3: The variance $\sigma^2(S)$ is deterministic while the variances $\sigma^2(\tilde{W})$ or $\sigma^2(\tilde{X})$ are probabilistic. Whereas Fort and Quirk briefly specify the characteristics of the underlying random process (in any game, the two competing teams have the same chance of winning), Depken does not. By analogy with the measurement of concentration in an industry, one does not need to characterize a priori a random process. When considering the case of sports where ties can happen, a complete characterization of a random process is much more complicated. To our knowledge, this has never been completely done.

The interesting work done by Fort and Quirk and Depken (correcting the index to deal with the changes of its minimal value) needs to be extended: in the same way that the minimal value of the index changes when the size of the league is modified, its maximal value also changes. This intuition was not clear before Horowitz (1997), Fort and Quirk (1997) and Utt and Fort (2002) specified 'the most unequal distribution'. However, it seems essential to take into account the variability of the upper bound as well as that of the lower bound. This work has been done by Owen et al. (2007) and Adjemian et al. (2012). As in Owen et al. (2007), let us start by calculating the maximal value of the Hirschman-Herfindahl index. For the sake of simplicity, we will choose a particular point award system that fulfils the condition $2z_t = (z_w + z_l)$: from now on we assume that $z_w = 2$, $z_t = 1$ and $z_l = 0$. The maximal value that the Hirschman-Herfindahl index takes is:

$$HHI_{max} = \frac{2(2n-1)}{3n(n-1)} \tag{4.6}$$

Proof:
The maximal value of any imbalance index is reached in the *PCI* hypothetical configuration. Let us recall that $\forall i \in \{1, \ldots, n\}$, $p_i^{PCI} = 2z_w(i-1) + 2z_l (n-i)$. As we assume that $z_w = 2$, $z_t = 1$ and $z_l = 0$, then $p_i^{PCI} = 4(i-1)$ and $\forall i \in \{1, \ldots, n\}$, $s_i^{PCI} = \frac{4(i-1)}{\sum_{i=1}^{n} p_i} = \frac{4(i-1)}{2n(n-1)} = \frac{2(i-1)}{n(n-1)}$, where s_i^{PCI} designates the market share of the ith team in the *PCI* configuration:

$$HHI_{max} = \sum_{i=1}^{n} (s_i^{PCI}) = \sum_{i=1}^{n} \left[\frac{2(i-1)}{n(n-1)}\right]^2 = \frac{4}{n^2(n-1)^2} \sum_{i=1}^{n} (i-1)^2$$

$$= \frac{4}{n^2(n-1)^2} \sum_{i=1}^{n} (i^2 - 2i + 1)$$

As $\sum_{i=1}^{n} i = \frac{1}{2}n(n+1)$ and $\sum_{i=1}^{n} i^2 = \frac{1}{6}n(n+1)(2n+1)$,

$$\sum_{i=1}^{n} (i^2 - 2i + 1) = \sum_{i=1}^{n} i^2 - 2\sum_{i=1}^{n} i + n = \frac{1}{6}n(n+1)(2n+1)$$

$$- 2 \times \frac{1}{2}n(n+1) + n = \frac{n}{6}[(n+1)(2n+1) - 6(n+1) + 6]$$

$$\sum_{i=1}^{n} (i^2 - 2i + 1) = \frac{n}{6}[(n+1)(2n+1) - 6n] = \frac{n}{6}(2n^2 + 3n + 1 - 6n)$$

$$= \frac{n}{6}(2n^2 - 3n + 1) = \frac{n}{6}(n-1)(2n-1)$$

Then $HHI_{max} = \dfrac{4n(n-1)(2n-1)}{6n^2(n-1)^2} = \dfrac{2(2n-1)}{3n(n-1)}.$

Owen et al. (2007) then define a normalized *HHI* as the ratio of *dHHI* to the difference between the maximal and the minimal value of the Hirschman-Herfindahl index. They denote this normalized index as *HHI**

(Adjemian et al., 2012 call this index the Herfindahl Ratio of Competitive Balance (*HRCB*)).

$$HRCB = HHI^* = \frac{HHI - HHI_{\min}}{HHI_{\max} - HHI_{\min}} \tag{4.7}$$

where HHI_{min} denotes the minimum value of the Hirschman-Herfindahl index.

Indeed, according to Hall and Tideman (1967), any concentration measure must satisfy a set of desirable axioms; in particular (axiom vi), a concentration index should be between zero and one.

It appears that:

$$HRCB = HHI^* = 3\,\frac{(n-1)}{(n+1)}\,(nHHI - 1) \tag{4.8}$$

Proof:
In a league with n teams, $HHI_{min} = \frac{1}{n}$. Then,

$$HRCB = HHI^* = \frac{HHI - HHI_{\min}}{HHI_{\max} - HHI_{\min}} = \frac{HHI - \frac{1}{n}}{\frac{2(2n-1)}{3n(n-1)} - \frac{1}{n}}$$

$$= \frac{\frac{nHHI}{n} - \frac{1}{n}}{\frac{2(2n-1)}{3n(n-1)} - \frac{3(n-1)}{3n(n-1)}}$$

$$HRCB = \frac{3n(n-1)(nHHI-1)}{n(4n-2-3n+3)} = 3\,\frac{(n-1)}{(n+1)}(nHHI-1)$$

Following the same line of reasoning, Gayant and Le Pape (2012) assess the value of a normalized index that is not predicted upon the measurement of the Hirschman-Herfindahl index but upon the measurement of the standard deviation. They construct a Competitive Balance Ratio (*CBR*) as:

$$CBR = \frac{\sigma^2(S) - \sigma^2_{\min}(S)}{\sigma^2_{\max}(S) - \sigma^2_{\min}(S)} \tag{4.9}$$

where $\sigma^2_{\min}(S)$ and $\sigma^2_{\max}(S)$ respectively denote the minimum and the maximum value of the variance of the market share of teams. The Competitive Balance Ratio is:

$$CBR = 3\,\frac{(n-1)}{(n+1)}\,n^2\sigma^2(S) \tag{4.10}$$

Proof:

The minimum value of the variance of market shares is $\sigma^2_{\min}(S) = 0$. Besides, we have calculated previously that $n\sigma^2(S) = HHI - \frac{1}{n}$ and that $HHI_{max} = \frac{2(2n-1)}{3n(n-1)}$. It follows then:

$$\sigma^2_{\max}(S) = \frac{HHI_{max}}{n} - \frac{1}{n^2} = \frac{2(2n-1)}{3n^2(n-1)} - \frac{1}{n^2} = \frac{2(2n-1)}{3n^2(n-1)} - \frac{1}{n^2}$$

$$= \frac{2(2n-1)}{3n^2(n-1)} - \frac{3(n-1)}{3n^2(n-1)} = \frac{4n - 3n - 2 + 3}{3n^2(n-1)}$$

$$\sigma^2_{\max}(S) = \frac{(n+1)}{3n^2(n-1)}$$

Finally,

$$CBR = \frac{\sigma^2(S) - \sigma^2_{\min}(S)}{\sigma^2_{\max}(S) - \sigma^2_{\min}(S)} = \frac{\sigma^2(S)}{\sigma^2_{\max}(S)} = \frac{\sigma^2(S)}{\dfrac{(n+1)}{3n^2(n-1)}} = 3\frac{(n-1)}{(n+1)}n^2\sigma^2(S)$$

Link between *HRCB* and *CBR*

Remarkably, the two normalizations lead to the same index of competitive imbalance:

$$CBR = HRCB \tag{4.11}$$

Proof:

Knowing that $n\sigma^2(S) = HHI - \frac{1}{n}$, we can rewrite Equation (4.10) as:

$$CBR = 3n\frac{(n-1)}{(n+1)}n\sigma^2(S) = 3n\frac{(n-1)}{(n+1)}\left(HHI - \frac{1}{n}\right)$$

$$= 3\frac{(n-1)}{(n+1)}(nHHI - 1) = HRCB$$

This elegant result strengthens the validity of the normalization process. It also shows clearly that there is intrinsically no difference between calculating a variance or a Hirschman-Herfindahl index when measuring the level of competitive imbalance in a league. Let us now illustrate the magnitude of the normalization process by constructing Iso Competitive (Im)Balance curves.

The Iso Competitive (Im)Balance Curves (Gayant and Le Pape, 2012)

Following Davies (1979), who defines iso concentration curves, Gayant and Le Pape (2012) propose drawing Iso Competitive (Im)Balance curves

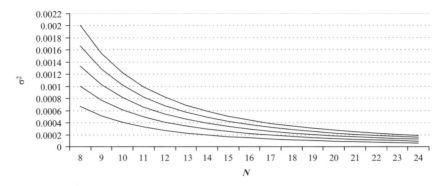

Figure 4.1   Iso Competitive (Im)Balance curves

for different sizes of leagues. Starting either from the measurement of the variance or from the measurement of the Hirschman-Herfindahl index, the key idea is to visualize all the values of the elementary index ($\sigma^2(S)$ or *HHI*) corresponding to a given level of Competitive (Im)Balance, depending on the number of teams in the league.

Let *C* denote a given level of (Im)Balance, *C* being a constant term varying between zero and one. The equation of any Iso Competitive Balance curve is *CBR = C*. We can then easily express the value of the index $\sigma^2(S)$ as depending on the number of teams *n*. Indeed,

$$CBR = C$$

$$\Leftrightarrow 3\,\frac{(n-1)}{(n+1)}\,n^2\sigma^2(S) = C$$

$$\Leftrightarrow \sigma^2(S) = \frac{(n+1)\,C}{3n^2(n-1)} \tag{4.12}$$

The Iso Competitive (Im)Balance curves for values of *C* between 0.1 and 0.3 are drawn in Figure 4.1.

The normalized index described in this section is a suitable tool for assessing the level of dispersion/concentration of teams in a league, even in sports where ties can happen and/or even when the size of the league changes. Now, using the analogy between measuring competitive imbalance in a league and measuring income inequality in a community, it also seems relevant to study the ability of a Gini index to measure the level of competitive imbalance.

GINI INDEX AND COMPETITIVE IMBALANCE

The Gini index is one of the most popular inequality indices; because it is easy to calculate, and it can be seen graphically from the plot of the Lorenz curve. The Gini index is a measure of how far a given distribution (of incomes) is from a perfectly egalitarian distribution, where all individuals would have the same income. The Gini index is based on calculating an equivalent income y_e, that is, the level of income such that, if any individual would earn it, the level of inequality in the community would be exactly the same as it is now. In the field of sports, we will calculate an equivalent number of points p_e and measure the gap between p_e and the number of points obtained by any team in a perfectly egalitarian distribution. The *PCB* configuration is indeed just such a perfectly egalitarian distribution, where all teams have the same number of points $\bar{p}$ (where $\bar{p} = \frac{1}{n} \sum_{i=1}^{n} p_i$). The Gini index is then:

$$I_{Gini} = 1 - \frac{p_e}{\bar{p}} \qquad (4.13)$$

where

$$p_e = \frac{\sum_{i=1}^{n} (2(n-i)+1)p_i}{n} \qquad (4.14)$$

When replacing p_e by its value in (4.13), we have:

$$I_{Gini} = 1 - \frac{\sum_{i=1}^{n} (2(n-i)+1)p_i}{n\frac{1}{n}\sum_{i=1}^{n} p_i} = 1 - \frac{(2n+1)\sum_{i=1}^{n} p_i - 2\sum_{i=1}^{n} ip_i}{n\sum_{i=1}^{n} p_i}$$

$$= \frac{n}{n} - \frac{2n+1}{n} + \frac{2\sum_{i=1}^{n} ip_i}{n\sum_{i=1}^{n} p_i}$$

Finally, the Gini index is:

$$I_{Gini} = \frac{2\sum_{i=1}^{n} ip_i}{n\sum_{i=1}^{n} p_i} - \frac{n+1}{n} \qquad (4.15)$$

And since in our framework $z_w = 2$, $z_t = 1$, $z_l = 0$ and since then $\sum_{i=1}^{n} p_i = 2n(n-1)$ (and consequently $\bar{p} = 2(n-1)$):

$$I_{Gini} = \frac{\sum\limits_{i=1}^{n} ip_i}{n^2(n-1)} - \frac{n+1}{n} \tag{4.16}$$

Let us now calculate the minimal and the maximal value of the Gini index in the case of Competitive Imbalance measurement.

Its minimal value, which is reached under *PCB*, is:

$$I_{Gini}^{PCB} = 0 \tag{4.17}$$

Proof:
As under *PCB*, $\forall\, i \in \{1, \ldots, n\}$, $p_i^{PCB} = 2(n-1)$,

$$p_e^{PCB} = \frac{\sum\limits_{i=1}^{n}(2(n-i)+1)p_i^{PCB}}{n^2} = \frac{\sum\limits_{i=1}^{n}(2(n-i)+1) \times 2(n-1)}{n^2}$$

$$= \frac{2(n-1) \times \left(2n^2 + n - 2\sum\limits_{i=1}^{n} i\right)}{n^2}$$

As $\sum\limits_{i=1}^{n} i = \dfrac{1}{2}n(n+1)$,

$$p_e^{PCB} = \frac{2(n-1) \times \left[2n^2 + n - 2 \times \dfrac{1}{2}n(n+1)\right]}{n^2}$$

$$= \frac{2(n-1) \times (2n^2 + n - n^2 - n)}{n^2} = \frac{2(n-1)n^2}{n^2} = 2(n-1) = \bar{p}$$

Then $I_{Gini}^{PCB} = 1 - \dfrac{\bar{p}}{\bar{p}} = 0$.

Its maximal value, which is reached under *PCI*, is:

$$I_{Gini}^{PCI} = \frac{n+1}{3n} \tag{4.17}$$

Proof:
As under *PCI*, $\forall\, i \in \{1, \ldots, n\}$, $p_i^{PCI} = 4(i-1)$,

$$p_e^{PCI} = \frac{\sum\limits_{i=1}^{n}(2(n-i)+1)p_i^{PCI}}{n^2} = \frac{\sum\limits_{i=1}^{n}(2(n-i)+1) \times 4(i-1)}{n^2}$$

$$= \frac{\sum\limits_{i=1}^{n}(8ni - 8n - 8i^2 + 12i - 4)}{n^2}$$

$$p_e^{PCI} = \frac{8n \sum_{i=1}^{n} i - 8n^2 - 8 \sum_{i=1}^{n} i^2 + 12 \sum_{i=1}^{n} i - 4n}{n^2}$$

As $\sum_{i=1}^{n} i = \frac{1}{2} n(n+1)$ and $\sum i^2 = \frac{1}{6} n(n+1)(2n+1)$,

$$p_e^{PCI} = \frac{4n^2(n+1) - 8n^2 - \dfrac{4}{3} n(n+1)(2n+1) + 6n(n+1) - 4n}{n^2}$$

$$p_e^{PCI} = \frac{4n(n+1) - \dfrac{4}{3}(n+1)(2n+1) - 8n + 6(n+1) - 4}{n}$$

$$p_e^{PCI} = \frac{4n^2 + 4n - \dfrac{8}{3}n^2 - 4n - \dfrac{4}{3} - 8n + 6n + 6 - 4}{n}$$

$$p_e^{PCI} = \frac{\dfrac{4}{3}n^2 - 2n + \dfrac{2}{3}}{n} = \frac{4n^2 - 6n + 2}{3n} = \frac{2(n-1)(2n-1)}{3n}$$

Then,

$$I_{Gini}^{PCI} = 1 - \frac{p_e^{PCI}}{\bar{p}} = 1 - \frac{\dfrac{2(n-1)(2n-1)}{3n}}{2(n-1)} = 1 - \frac{2n-1}{3n} = \frac{3n}{3n} - \frac{2n-1}{3n}$$

And finally, $I_{Gini}^{PCI} = \dfrac{n+1}{3n}$.

We will now show that the Gini index satisfies some of the fundamental properties that a 'good' imbalance index should satisfy. To character-ize these properties, we need to construct hypothetical configurations of point distributions. To this purpose, we will substitute one or more 'blocks' of consecutively ranked teams in the *PCI* distribution by the same number of 'blocks' of teams under *PCB*. Let us first describe the principle of substituting one block of teams under *PCI* by one block of teams under *PCB*.

Let us start with a hypothetical *n* teams – *PCI* configuration and let us consider that a subset of *b* consecutively ranked teams ($2 \le b \le n - 1$) are now on an equal footing, and that they still lose or win against all the ($n - b$) other teams. As a result, in this one home-one away schedule, each team of the subset will win ($b - 1$) games and lose ($b - 1$) games when playing against ($b - 1$) other teams of the subgroup. Everything happens as

Table 4.2 *Distribution of points after the substitution of one block of* b
teams under PCI *by one block of* b *teams under* PCB

Team (i)	Points (pi)	Blocks
1	0	h teams under *PCI*
2	4	
. . .		
h	$4(h - 1)$	
$h + 1$	$4h + 2(b - 1)$	b teams under *PCB*
$h + 2$	$4h+2(b - 1)$	
. . .	$4h + 2(b - 1)$	
$h + b$	$4h + 2(b - 1)$	
$h + b + 1$	$4(h + b)$	$(n - h - b)$ teams under *PCI*
$h + b + 2$	$4(h + b + 1)$	
. . .		
$n - 1$	$4(n - 2)$	
n	$4(n - 1)$	

if a block of b teams initially under *PCI* (in the distribution where all the n
teams are under *PCI*) would be replaced by a block of b teams under *PCB*.

Let us suppose that the block of b teams is inserted after h teams ($1 \leq$
$h \leq n - 3$). The 1st to the hth teams and the $(h + b + 1)^{th}$ to the nth teams
are still under *PCI*. The distribution of points becomes:

$$p_i = 4(i - 1) \text{ if } i \in \{1, \ldots, h\} \text{ or } i \in \{h + b + 1, \ldots, n\}$$
$$\& \, p_i = 4h + 2(b - 1) \text{ if } i \in \{h + 1, \ldots, h + b\}$$

Such a hypothetical configuration is intermediate between the two polar
cases: *PCI* and *PCB*. As a result, one expects that, for any Imbalance index

$$I_{IMB}(p^{PCB}) < I_{IMB}(p^{1PCB \, Block}) < I_{IMB}(p^{PCI}) \tag{4.17}$$

where $p^{1PCB \, Block}$ designates the intermediate distribution of points
described above.

From an axiomatic point of view, any imbalance/inequality index that
fulfils the principle of transfers should satisfy inequality (4.17). Let now
recall the statement of this central axiom.

Principle of Transfers

For all $n \in \mathbb{N}$, for all $p = (p_1, \ldots, p_i, \ldots, p_j, \ldots, p_n) \in \mathbb{N}^n$ and all positive
real number Δ, if $p_i < p_i + \Delta \leq p_j - \Delta < p_j$, then:

$$I_{IMB}(p_1, \ldots, p_i + \Delta, \ldots, p_j - \Delta, \ldots, p_n) < I_{IMB}(p_1, \ldots, p_i, \ldots, p_j, \ldots, p_n)$$

The principle of transfers means that any progressive transfer between two teams, that is, from a higher ranked team to a lower ranked team and which does not change their relative standings, will decrease imbalance. The substitution of a block of b teams – initially under PCI – by b teams under PCB is a transformation that only leads to progressive transfers. Stated exactly, the $(h + b)^{\text{th}}$ team 'gives' 2 points to each of the $(b - 1)$ lower ranked teams, the $(h + b - 1)^{\text{th}}$ team 'gives' 2 points to each of the $(b - 2)$ lower ranked teams (and 'receives' 2 points from the previous team), ..., the $(h + 2)^{\text{th}}$ team 'gives' 2 points to the $(h + 1)^{\text{th}}$ team (and 'receives' $2(b - 2)$ points from the $(b - 2)$ higher ranked teams), and finally the $(h + 1)^{\text{th}}$ team 'receives' $2(b - 1)$ points from the $(b - 1)$ higher ranked teams.

In other words, the transition from the PCI distribution to a '1 Block of b teams under PCB' distribution is obtained only by enforcing progressive transfers. As a consequence, the Gini index, which satisfies the principle of transfers, will necessarily satisfy the inequality:

$$I_{IMB}(p^{1 PCB \, Block}) < I_{IMB}(p^{PCI})$$

Furthermore, the transition from a '1 Block of b teams under PCB' distribution towards the PCB distribution can also only be obtained by enforcing progressive transfers. Indeed, if we consider the particular case where $b = n - 1$, it is straightforward to note that:

- If the nth team is team 1, the transition towards the PCB distribution is obtained by the 'gift' of 2 points to team 1 by each of the $(n - 1)$ higher ranked teams.
- If the nth team is team n, the transition towards the PCB distribution is obtained by the 'gift' of 2 points to each of the $(n - 1)$ lower ranked teams by team n.

Then the Gini index also necessarily satisfies:

$$I_{IMB}(p^{PCB}) < I_{IMB}(p^{1 PCB \, Block})$$

We will now calculate the value of the Gini index for the '1 Block of b teams under PCB' distribution and infer some properties. For such a distribution of points, it appears that:

$$I_{Gini}{}^{1 PCB \, Block} = \frac{1}{3n^2(n - 1)} \left[n(n^2 - 1) - b(b^2 - 1) \right] \qquad (4.18)$$

Proof:

By definition, the Gini index is: $I_{Gini} = \dfrac{2\displaystyle\sum_{i=1}^{n} i \times p_i}{n\displaystyle\sum_{i=1}^{n} p_i} - \dfrac{n+1}{n}$

Let first consider the numerator of the index:

$$\sum_{i=1}^{n} i \times p_i = \sum_{i=1}^{h} i \times p_i + \sum_{i=h+1}^{h+b} i \times p_i + \sum_{i=h+b+1}^{n} i \times p_i = \sum_{i=1}^{h} 4i(i-1)$$

$$+ \sum_{i=h+1}^{h+b} (4h + 2(b-1))i + \sum_{i=h+b+1}^{n} 4i(i-1) \quad \sum_{i=1}^{h} i \times p_i = 4\sum_{i=1}^{h} i^2 - 4\sum_{i=1}^{h} i$$

Since: $4\displaystyle\sum_{i=1}^{h} i = 2h(h+1)$ and $4\displaystyle\sum_{i=1}^{h} i^2 = \dfrac{2}{3}h(h+1)(2h+1)$

Then,

$$\sum_{i=1}^{h} i \times p_i = 4\sum_{i=1}^{h} i^2 - 4\sum_{i=1}^{h} i = \frac{2}{3}h(h+1)(2h+1) - 2h(h+1) = \frac{4h}{3}(h^2 - 1)$$

$$\sum_{i=h+1}^{h+b} i \times p_i = \sum_{i=h+1}^{h+b} (4h + 2(b-1))i = (4h + 2(b-1))$$

$$\sum_{i=h+1}^{h+b} i = 2(2h + (b-1))\sum_{j=1}^{b} (j+h) = 2(2h + (b-1))\left(\left(\sum_{j=1}^{b} j\right) + hb\right)$$

$$\sum_{i=h+1}^{h+b} i \times p_i = (2h + (b-1))(b(b+1) + 2hb)$$

$$= b(2h + b - 1)(2h + b + 1)$$

$$\sum_{i=h+b+1}^{n} i \times p_i = 4\sum_{i=h+b+1}^{n} i(i-1) = 4\left(\sum_{i=h+b+1}^{n} i^2 - \sum_{i=h+b+1}^{n} i\right)$$

$$= 4\left(\sum_{j=1}^{n-h-b} (j+h+b)^2 - \sum_{j=1}^{n-h-b} (j+h+b)\right)$$

$$\sum_{i=h+b+1}^{n} i \times p_i = 4\left[\sum_{j=1}^{n-h-b} (j)^2 + \sum_{j=1}^{n-h-b} (h+b)^2 + 2\sum_{j=1}^{n-h-b} (h+b)j\right.$$

$$\left. - \sum_{j=1}^{n-h-b} j - \sum_{j=1}^{n-h-b} (h+b)\right]$$

$$\sum_{i=h+b+1}^{n} i \times p_i = 4\left[\sum_{j=1}^{n-h-b} (j)^2 + (n-h-b)(h+b)^2 - (n-h-b)(h+b)\right.$$

$$+ (2(h + b) - 1) \sum_{j=1}^{n-h-b} j \Bigg]$$

$$\sum_{i=h+b+1}^{n} i \times p_i = 4 \sum_{j=1}^{n-h-b} (j)^2 + 4(n - h - b)(h + b)(h + b - 1)$$

$$+ 4(2(h + b) - 1) \sum_{j=1}^{n-h-b} j$$

Now, $4 \sum_{j=1}^{n-h-b} (j)^2 = \dfrac{2}{3}(n - h - b)(n - h - b + 1)(2(n - h - b) + 1)$

And $4(2(h + b) - 1) \sum_{j=1}^{n-h-b} j = 2(2(h + b) - 1)(n - h - b)(n - h - b + 1)$

Then,

$$\sum_{i=h+b+1}^{n} i \times p_i = \dfrac{2}{3}(n - h - b)(n - h - b + 1)(2(n - h - b) + 1)$$

$$+ 4(n - h - b)(h + b)(h + b - 1)$$

$$+ 2(2(h + b) - 1)(n - h - b)(n - h - b + 1)$$

$$\sum_{i=h+b+1}^{n} i \times p_i = \dfrac{4}{3}(n - h - b)\Bigg[\dfrac{1}{2}(n - h - b + 1)(2(n - h - b) + 1)$$

$$+ 3(h + b)(h + b - 1) + \dfrac{3}{2}(2(h + b) - 1)(n - h - b + 1)\Bigg]$$

By simplifying, the term becomes:

$$\dfrac{1}{2}(n - h - b + 1)(2(n - h - b) + 1) + 3(h + b)(h + b - 1)$$

$$+ \dfrac{3}{2}(2(h + b) - 1)(n - h - b + 1) = n^2 + (b + h)n + (b + h)^2 - 1$$

And consequently:

$$\sum_{i=h+b+1}^{n} i \times p_i = \dfrac{4}{3}(n - h - b)(n^2 + (b + h)n + (b + h)^2 - 1)$$

Finally:

$$\sum_{i=1}^{n} i \times p_i = \sum_{i=1}^{h} i \times p_i + \sum_{i=h+1}^{h+b} i \times p_i + \sum_{i=h+b+1}^{n} i \times p_i = \dfrac{4h}{3}(h^2 - 1)$$

$$+ b(2h + b - 1)(2h + b + 1) + \dfrac{4}{3}(n - h - b)$$

$$(n^2 + (b + h)n + (b + h)^2 - 1)$$

Since: $\dfrac{4h}{3}\,(h^2-1)+\dfrac{4}{3}\,(n-h-b)\,(n^2+(b+h)n+(b+h)^2-1)$

$$=\dfrac{4}{3}\,(n(n^2-1)-b(3h(h+b)+b^2-1))$$

And $b(2h+b-1)\,(2h+b+1)=b(4h^2+4hb+b^2-1)$
$$=b(4h(h+b)+b^2-1)$$

Then:

$$\sum_{i=1}^{n}i\times p_i=\dfrac{4}{3}\,n(n^2-1)-4b(h(h+b)-\dfrac{4}{3}\,b(b^2-1)$$
$$+\,b(4h(h+b)+b^2-1)=\dfrac{1}{3}\,(4n(n^2-1)-b(b^2-1))$$

Let us now consider the denominator of the index. Since, by construction $\sum_{i=1}^{n}p_i=2n(n-1)$, the Gini index is equal to:

$$I_{Gini}=\dfrac{1}{n^2(n-1)}\sum_{i=1}^{n}i\times p_i-\dfrac{n+1}{n}=\dfrac{1}{3n^2(n-1)}\,(4n(n^2-1)$$
$$-\,b(b^2-1))-\dfrac{n+1}{n}$$

That is:

$$I_{Gini}^{1PCBBlock}=\dfrac{1}{3n^2(n-1)}\,(n(n^2-1)-b(b^2-1))$$

It therefore appears that proposition (4.17) holds. Indeed, on the one hand,

$$I_{Gini}^{PCI}-I_{Gini}^{1PCBBlock}=\dfrac{n+1}{3n}-\dfrac{1}{3n^2(n-1)}\,[n(n^2-1)-b(b^2-1)]$$
$$=\dfrac{n(n-1)\,(n+1)-n(n^2-1)+b(b^2-1)}{3n^2(n-1)}$$

$$I_{Gini}^{PCI}-I_{Gini}^{1PCBBlock}=\dfrac{b(b^2-1)}{3n^2(n-1)}$$

As $b\geq 2$, $I_{Gini}^{PCI}-I_{Gini}^{1PCBBlock}>0$, then $I_{Gini}^{PCI}>I_{Gini}^{1PCBBlock}$.
And, on the other hand, as $b\leq n-1$, $n(n^2-1)>b(b^2-1)$, then $I_{Gini}^{1PCBBlock}>0\Leftrightarrow I_{Gini}^{1PCBBlock}>I_{Gini}^{PCB}$.
Furthermore, two additional properties may be inferred.

Proposition 1: The more teams in the block of teams under PCB, *the smaller is the level of competitive imbalance measured by the Gini index.*

Proof:

As $b \geq 2$, $\dfrac{\partial I_{Gini}^{1PCBBlock}}{\partial b} = \dfrac{1 - 3b^2}{3n^2(n-1)} < 0$, then the Gini index decreases when b increases.

Proposition 2: The level of competitive imbalance, measured by the Gini index, is insensitive to the position of the block of teams under PCB in the distribution.

Proof:

The proof is trivial because IGini$^{1PCB\ Block}$ does not depend on the value of h.

Let us now consider the case of the substitution of two blocks of teams.

Substitution of Two Blocks of Teams under *PCI* by Two Blocks of Teams under *PCB*

Let b_1 and b_2 respectively denote the number of teams in the two blocks that are henceforth under *PCB*. b_1 and b_2 are such that $b_1 \geq 2$, $b_2 \geq 2$ and $4 \leq b_1 + b_2 < n$. The first block of b_1 teams is inserted after h_1 teams ($1 \leq h_1$). As a consequence, the teams of this first block are located between teams $h_1 + 1$ and $h_1 + b_1$. The second block of b_2 teams is inserted after $h_1 + b_1 + h_2$ teams ($1 \leq h_2$). The teams of the second block (of size b_2) are located between $h_1 + b_1 + h_2 + 1$ and $h_1 + b_1 + h_2 + b_2$. The condition $1 \leq h_2$ permits a clear distinction to be made between one or two blocks of teams (at least one team has to be intercalated between the two blocks).

The distribution of points becomes:

$$p_i = 4(i - 1) \text{ if } i \in \{1, \ldots, h_1\} \text{ or } i \in \{h_1 + b_1 + 1, \ldots, h_1 + b_1 + h_2\}$$
$$\text{or } i \in \{h_1 + b_1 + h_2 + b_2 + 1, \ldots, n\},$$

$$p_i = 4h_1 + 2(b_1 - 1) \text{ if } i \in \{h_1 + 1, \ldots, h_1 + b_1\}$$

$$\text{and } p_i = 4(h_1 + b_1 + h_2) + 2(b_2 - 1) \text{ if } i \in \{h_1 + b_1 + h_2 + 1, \ldots, h_1 + b_1 + h_2 + b_2\}$$

Let now calculate the value of the Gini index for a '2 Blocks of b_1 and b_2 teams under *PCB*' distribution and infer some properties. Using the same line of reasoning as before, it can be shown that:

$$I_{Gini}^{2PCB\ Blocks} = \frac{1}{3n^2(n-1)} [n(n^2 - 1) - b_1(b_1^2 - 1) - b_2(b_2^2 - 1)] \quad (4.19)$$

Table 4.3 Distribution of points after the substitution of two blocks of b_1 and b_2 teams under PCI by two blocks of b_1 and b_2 teams under PCB

Team (i)	Points (pi)	Blocks
1	0	h_1 teams under *PCI*
2	4	
. . .	. . .	
h_1	$4(h_1 - 1)$	
$h_1 + 1$	$4h_1 + 2(b_1 - 1)$	b_1 teams under *PCB*
$h_1 + 2$	$4h_1 + 2(b_1 - 1)$	
. . .	$4h_1 + 2(b_1 - 1)$	
$h_1 + b_1$	$4h_1 + 2(b_1 - 1)$	
$h_1 + b_1 + 1$	$4(h_1 + b_1)$	h_2 teams under *PCI*
$h_1 + b_1 + 2$	$4(h_1 + b_1 + 1)$	
. . .	. . .	
$h_1 + b_1 + h_2$	$4(h_1 + b_1 + h_2 - 1)$	
$h_1 + b_1 + h_2 + 1$	$4(h_1 + b_1 + h_2) - 2(b_2 - 1)$	b_2 teams under *PCB*
$h_1 + b_1 + h_2 + 2$	$4(h_1 + b_1 + h_2) - 2(b_2 - 1)$	
. . .	$4(h_1 + b_1 + h_2) - 2(b_2 - 1)$	
$h_1 + b_1 + h_2 + b_2$	$4(h_1 + b_1 + h_2) - 2(b_2 - 1)$	
$h_1 + b_1 + h_2 + b_2 + 1$	$4(h_1 + b_1 + h_2 + b_2)$	$n - (h_1 + b_1 + h_2 + b_2)$
$h_1 + b_1 + h_2 + b_2 + 2$	$4(h_1 + b_1 + h_2 + b_2 + 1)$	teams under *PCI*
. . .	. . .	
$n - 1$	$4(n - 2)$	
N	$4(n - 1)$	

We can immediately notice that the value of the Gini index does not depend on the position of the two blocks in the distribution. Furthermore, there is an interesting property that can be inferred. If we focus on the particular case where the two blocks are of the same size, it is possible to directly compare the Gini index for a distribution including one block of b teams under *PCB* and the Gini index for a distribution including two blocks of $\frac{b}{2}$ teams under *PCB*.

Proposition 3: *The level of competitive imbalance measured by the Gini index is smaller when the teams under PCB are gathered into one block than it is when they are divided into two blocks of equal size.*

Proof:
Let us calculate the difference $I_{Gini}^{2PCB\ Blocks} - I_{Gini}^{1PCB\ Block}$ when $b_1 = b_2 = \frac{b}{2}$

$$I_{Gini}{}^{2PCB\ Blocks} - I_{Gini}{}^{1PCB\ Block} = \frac{1}{3n^2(n-1)}$$

$$\left[n(n^2 - 1) - \frac{b}{2}\left(\frac{b_2}{4} - 1\right) - \frac{b}{2}\left(\frac{b_2}{4} - 1\right) - n(n^2 - 1) + b(b^2 - 1) \right]$$

$$I_{Gini}{}^{2PCB\ Blocks} - I_{Gini}{}^{1PCB\ Block} = \frac{1}{3n^2(n-1)}\left(-\frac{b_3}{8} + \frac{b}{2} - \frac{b_3}{8} + \frac{b}{2} + b^3 - b \right)$$

$$I_{Gini}{}^{2PCB\ Blocks} - I_{Gini}{}^{1PCB\ Block} = \frac{b^3}{4n^2(n-1)} > 0$$

Proposition 3 may be seen as intuitive for the measurement of imbalance in a closed league, but is somewhat counterintuitive when one is measuring imbalance in an open league. Indeed, if we compare a distribution including a unique block of b teams (under PCB) located in the middle of the distribution with a distribution including two blocks of $\frac{b}{2}$ teams, one located at the top and one located at the bottom, the second distribution will be seen as more imbalanced than the first, whereas the spectator would probably have preferred to attend the second championship. A high level of rivalry among the top and the bottom teams is undoubtedly more attractive than a high level of rivalry concentrated in the middle of the distribution. For that reason, Gayant and Le Pape (2015) argue that a generalized Gini index would be preferable. To generalize the index, they suggest calculating an equivalent number of points with a generalized formula. In fact, the equivalent number of points p_e as in Equation (4.14) may be considered as a particular case of a more general concept (see Blackorby and Donaldson, 1978; Dorfman, 1979; Yaari, 1987). The term p_e can be seen as the particular value of a generalized equivalent number of points $p_{e\phi}$ in the quadratic case. Indeed the generalized equivalent number of points is:

$$p_{e\phi} = \sum_{i=1}^{n-1} p_i \left[\phi\left(\frac{n+1-i}{n}\right) - \phi\left(\frac{n-i}{n}\right) \right] + p_n \phi\left(\frac{1}{n}\right) \qquad (4.20)$$

and the equivalent number of points p_e is its particular case when $\forall\ q \in [0\ ;\ 1]$, $\phi(q) = q^2$.

Gayant and Le Pape (2015) argue that the transformation function ϕ may be chosen to give more weight to what happens either at the top or at the bottom of the distribution, and not only at the bottom (as the simple Gini index does). As a consequence, it would be preferable to use an S-shaped function, either of the form:

$$\phi(q) = \frac{q^\beta}{[q^\beta + (1-q)^\beta]^{\frac{1}{\beta}}} \qquad \text{(Wu and Gonzalez, 1996)}$$

or of the form:

$$\phi(q) = \exp[-\beta(-\log(q))^{\alpha}] \text{ (Prelec, 1998)}$$

However, the generalized index that may be constructed cannot simply be calculated as $1 - \frac{p_{e\phi}}{\bar{p}}$ because the generalized equivalent number of points is no longer necessarily less than $\bar{p}$. It can be shown that $p_{e\phi\min} = p_{e\phi PCB}$ and that $p_{e\phi\max} = p_{e\phi PCI}$ (where $p_{e\phi\min}$ and $p_{e\phi\max}$ respectively denote the minimum and the maximum value that the generalized equivalent number of points may take): this allows a generalized index to be calculated as:

$$\frac{p_{e\phi} - p_{e\phi\min}}{p_{e\phi\max} - p_{e\phi\min}} \tag{4.21}$$

CONCLUSION

There is an analogy between measuring competitive imbalance in a league and measuring income inequality in a community, but this analogy is not perfect. It seems desirable to provide a specific axiomatic basis to the elaboration of any competitive imbalance index. The key question is quite clearly the attractiveness of the league. In addition to the principle of transfers, some additional specific axioms should be stated in order to express the intuition of how attractive the championship turned out to have been in terms of the characteristics of the final distribution of points. Such axioms could differ when considering closed leagues or open leagues. Besides, the possible existence of play-offs or of irregular schedules may require the statement of additional specific axioms. Ultimately, the existence of a more supported team may also be taken into account, and would need to be integrated with the axiomatic foundations.

NOTES

1. The final ranking only gives a limited view of how attractive the competition was throughout the contest. Some authors advocate measuring imbalance on a daily basis or even throughout each game (see, for instance, Andreff and Scelles, 2014). Further developments of our approach can be generalized to a daily measurement.
2. We consider a championship with a unique governing body and organized according to the simplest regular schedule, as in the European sporting leagues. We also suppose that there is no bonus or malus points system.
3. Note that from the point of view of the ranking table, the 1st team is the lowest ranked team and the nth team is the highest ranked team.
4. The vector of relative points is $s = (s_1, s_2, \ldots, s_n)$ where for all $i \in \{1, \ldots, n\}$, $s_i = \frac{p_i}{P_{z_n, z_i, z_1}(n)}$. Any imbalance index is implicitly or explicitly built on the vector of relative points.

5. Unless $T = \{0\}$ or $T = \{2n(n-1)\}$.
6. Such is the case in the main European soccer leagues and in North American Major League Soccer where $z_w = 3$, $z_t = 1$ and $z_l = 0$.
7. In sports where ties can happen, the same final distribution of points may be reached if all games end in a tie. Indeed, in such a case, $p_i = 2z_t(n-1)$ and under the condition $2z_t = z_w + z_l$, $p_i = p_i^{PCB}$. However, from the point of view of attractiveness, these configurations are not similar.
8. This example is also presented in Adjemian et al. (2015).

REFERENCES

Adjemian, S., J.P. Gayant and N. Le Pape (2012), 'A generalised index of competitive balance in professional sports leagues', GAINS Working Paper 12.01, Université du Maine, Le Mans, France.

Adjemian, S., J.P. Gayant and N. Le Pape (2015), 'Comments on "measuring parity": the role of the principle of transfers', mimeo, Université du Maine, Le Mans, France.

Andreff, W. and N. Scelles (2014), 'Walter C. Neale 50 years after: beyond competitive balance, the league standing effect tested with French football data', *Journal of Sports Economics*, http://jse.sagepub.com/content/early/2014/11/04/15270025 14556621, 5 November.

Blackorby, C. and D. Donaldson (1978), 'Measures of relative equality and their meaning in terms of social welfare', *Journal of Economic Theory*, **18**, 59–80.

Borooah, V.K. and J. Mangan (2012), 'Measuring competitive balance in sports using generalized entropy with an application to English Premier League football', *Applied Economics*, **44**, 1093–102.

Cain, L.P. and D.D. Haddock (2006), 'Measuring parity: tying into idealized standard deviation', *Journal of Sports Economics*, **7**, 330–38.

Daly, G. (1992), 'The baseball player's labor market revisited', in P.M. Sommers (ed.), *Diamonds are Forever: The Business of Baseball*, Washington, DC: The Brookings Institution, pp. 11–28.

Davies, S. (1979), 'Choosing between concentration indices: the iso concentration curves', *Economica*, **46**, 67–75.

Depken, C.A. (1999), 'Free-agency and the competitiveness of Major League Baseball', *Review of Industrial Organization*, **14**, 205–17.

Dietl, H.M., M. Lang and S. Werner (2009), 'Social welfare in sports leagues with profit-maximizing and/or win-maximizing clubs', *Southern Economic Journal*, **76**(2), 375–96.

Dorfman, R. (1979), 'A formula for the Gini coefficient', *Review of Economics and Statistics*, **61**, 146–9.

Fort, R. and J. Quirk (1995), 'Cross-subsidization, incentives and outcomes in professional team sports leagues', *Journal of Economic Literature*, **33**, 1265–99.

Fort, R. and J. Quirk (1997), 'Introducing a competitive economic environment into professional sports', in W. Hendricks (ed.), *Advances in the Economics of Sports*, Vol. 2, Greenwich, CT: JAI Press, pp. 3–26.

Gayant, J.P. and N. Le Pape (2012), 'How to account for changes in the size of sports leagues: the iso competitive balance curves', *Economics Bulletin*, **32**, 1715–23.

Gayant, J.P. and N. Le Pape (2015), 'Mesure de la *competitive balance* dans les ligues de sports professionnels: faut-il distinguer les ligues fermées des ligues avec promotion et relégation?', *Revue Economique*, **66**, 427–48.

Hall, M. and N. Tideman (1967), 'Measures of concentration', *Journal of the American Statistical Association*, **62**, 162–8.

Horowitz, I. (1997), 'The increasing competitive balance in Major League Baseball', *Review of Industrial Organization*, **12**, 373–87.

Késenne, S. (2006), 'The win maximization model reconsidered: flexible talent supply and efficiency wages', *Journal of Sport Economics*, **7**, 416–27.

Lenten, L.J.A. (2008), 'Unbalanced schedules and the estimation of competitive balance in the Scottish Premier League', *Scottish Journal of Political Economy*, **55**, 488–508.

Neale, W.C. (1964), 'The peculiar economics of professional sports: a contribution to the theory of the firm in sporting competition and in market competition', *Quarterly Journal of Economics*, **78**, 1–14.

Owen, P.D., M. Ryan and C.R. Weatherston (2007), 'Measuring competitive balance in professional team sports using the Herfindahl-Hirschman index', *Review of Industrial Organization*, **31**, 289–302.

Pawlowski, T., C. Breuer and A. Hovemann (2010), 'Top clubs' performance and the competitive situation in European domestic football competitions', *Journal of Sports Economics*, **11**, 186–202.

Prelec, D. (1998), 'The probability weighting function', *Econometrica*, **66**, 497–527.

Quirk, J. and R.D. Fort (1992), *Pay Dirt, The Business of Professional Team Sports*, Princeton, NJ: Princeton University Press.

Szymanski, S. (2001), 'Income inequality, competitive balance and attractiveness of team sports: some evidence and a natural experiment from English soccer', *Economic Journal*, **111**, 69–84.

Szymanski, S. (2007), 'The Champions League and the Coase theorem', *Scottish Journal of Political Economy*, **54**, 355–73.

Utt, J. and R. Fort (2002), 'Pitfall to measuring competitive balance with Gini coefficients', *Journal of Sports Economics*, **3**(4), 367–73.

Wu, G. and R. Gonzalez (1996), 'Curvature of the probability weighting function', *Management Science*, **42**, 1676–90.

Yaari, M. (1987), 'The dual theory of choice under risk', *Econometrica*, **55**(1), 95–115.

Zimbalist, A.S. (2003), 'Reply: competitive balance conundrums. Response to Fort and Maxcy's comment', *Journal of Sport Economics*, **4**, 161–3.

5. Disequilibrium on the sports programmes market: the gender imbalance in TV coverage and TV viewership of the 2012 Olympic Games

Daam Van Reeth

INTRODUCTION

The Olympic Games is the biggest sports event in the world. With the addition of women's boxing, the 2012 Olympic Games in London became the first Games where women competed in every sport on the Olympic programme. The presence of parallel competitions for men and women is one of the appealing features of the Games. Many studies have therefore used the case of the Olympic Games to analyse gender balance in media coverage of sport. We refer, for instance, to research by Tuggle and Owen (1999), Capranica and Aversa (2002), Higgs et al. (2003), Billings (2008), Greer et al. (2009) and Billings et al. (2010). Generally, these studies conclude that although gender balance has improved importantly over time, male athletes are still favoured by the media. Moreover, the introduction of new events and sports for female athletes did not result in a net gain in clock time. Indeed, it appears that women are not shown with any greater frequency, only in a wider range of sports than before (Billings, 2008, p. 439).

The aforementioned studies as well as almost all other studies on gender balance in sports coverage focus exclusively on the supply side of the media market by measuring how much time TV channels or how much space newspapers dedicate to the coverage of competitions of both sexes. Our study is different and original in its approach because it also uses data on TV audiences, the demand side of the market. This creates an opportunity to check for evidence of disequilibrium between the supply of Olympic TV broadcasts (input market), on the one hand, and the TV demand revealed by sports consumers (output market), on the other hand. More precisely, by using TV audience data we are able to analyse if the observed preference of TV channels for broadcasts of male Olympic competitions is properly reflected in the preferences of TV viewers.

The chapter is structured as follows. In the following section we briefly discuss the relationship between sports and television and illustrate why they fit together very well. Next, we show how gender balance at the Olympics has evolved over time. The existing empirical research in this field is also summarized. Then we explain how our dataset was created and present the relevant data on Dutch Olympic TV coverage of the London 2012 Games. After tackling our main research question, we compare the actual Dutch TV audiences for Olympic broadcasts of male and female events with the broadcasters' choice for these competitions to find out if the right balance between the two is present. We then check if differences between the choices and preferences of TV broadcasters and TV audiences are related to the nature of the sport that is broadcast, before finally concluding.

THE RELATIONSHIP BETWEEN SPORTS AND TELEVISION

The relationship between sport and TV is organized around two markets. The first market is the one between the sports events organizers and the broadcasters. On this broadcasting rights market broadcasters (the demand side) try to acquire rights for broadcasts of events or leagues that are supplied by the event organizer (the supply side). In fact, soon after the start of television, sport federations and TV broadcasters discovered there were mutual gains in broadcasting sports. Broadcasters were looking towards the future of this novel medium and aired sports as a means of stimulating demand for television. Sport federations and event organizers quickly understood how live broadcasts could be useful in connecting to new audiences and serve as a vehicle for the promotion of sport. The 1936 Summer Olympics marked the first live television coverage of a sports event in world history. In total, 72 hours of live transmission went over the airwaves to special viewing booths, called 'Public Television Offices', in Berlin and Potsdam (http://www.TVhistory.TV). In London (1948), Helsinki (1952) and Melbourne (1956) live TV coverage of the Olympic Games was limited to viewers in the host nation only.

Things started to change when the International Olympic Committee (IOC) began selling broadcasting rights for the Olympic Games in line with rule 49 of the Olympic Charter: 'The IOC takes all necessary steps in order to ensure the fullest coverage by the different media and the widest possible audience in the world for the Olympic Games' (IOC, 2014, p. 20).

From the 1960s onwards, television broadcasts of the Olympic Games became the most significant factor in the communication of the Olympic ideals worldwide. In the past 50 years, coverage of the Games has been made available in an increasing number of markets throughout the world: from 21 countries or territories in 1960 (Rome) to over 100 since 1976 (Montreal) and over 200 since 1996 (Atlanta). According to the IOC (2014, p. 22), the London Games were broadcast in 220 territories. Over the same period, broadcasting rights for the Games rose from 1.2 million US dollars in 1960 to 2569 million US dollars in 2012 (IOC, 2014, p. 26).

This chapter, however, does not analyse the broadcasting rights market, but the sports programmes market, the place where broadcasters and TV viewers 'meet'. On this market, TV channels (now on the supply side) offer programmes of sports competitions to interested TV viewers (the demand side). Such live TV broadcasts of sports events are of great importance to TV broadcasters. In modern-day society, where consumers have a broad range of alternatives for spending their leisure time, sport has the power not only to attract TV viewers but also to retain them even outside TV prime time. More than 70 per cent of the free-to-air channels achieve a higher market share with sports programmes in comparison to the average performance of all genres combined. For instance, the market share of Canadian channel CBC rises to 29.9 per cent when it airs sports from 5 per cent for all its programming (IP & RTL Group, 2011). The ability of sport to create large audiences represents a major source of revenue to TV broadcasters, either directly by the sale of programmes (in the case of pay channels or pay-per-view programmes) or indirectly by the sale of advertising slots (Bolotny and Bourg, 2006, p. 112).

A top sports event guarantees high TV ratings because sport is among the best television can offer. TV viewers experience the action and the suspense of the game and the drama and tension it entails. They witness the joy as well as the anger of the players and the cheers and whistles of the spectators. But, unlike the characters in movies or soaps, the players are real people who put on a real fight and to whom the outcome is as uncertain as it is to the TV viewers. In sports broadcasts, good behaviour is not always rewarding and sometimes in the end 'the bad guy' or 'the mean girl' wins. All these sentiments mirror, at a more extreme level, the emotions people experience themselves in everyday life. Moreover, sports broadcasts are becoming increasingly visually attractive. Multiple cameras capture every aspect of a sports event. Close-up images and overview shots show the athlete's effort as well as the spectators' reactions while razor sharp replays allow TV viewers to study all action in detail. Through television, viewers at home can also enjoy to some extent the often colourful and joyful ambience the spectators create at the event. Such a transfer of happiness is absent from most other television broadcasts. Finally, much more than other TV programmes, sports broadcasts incite social watching. People join each other at home or in a bar not only to watch but also to discuss the game. Because the Olympic Games is the biggest sports event in the world and boosted by a good dose of patriotism, all of the above apply strongly for broadcasts of Olympic events.

GENDER BALANCE AT THE OLYMPICS

Shortly after organizing the men only Games in 1896, founder of the modern Olympic Games baron Pierre de Coubertin declared that 'Olympics with women would be incorrect, unpractical, uninteresting and unaesthetic.' Women's role was to applaud the actions of their men, explained de Coubertin (Independent, 2012). But despite the reticence of de Coubertin, already at the next Games (Paris, 1900) 22 women competed in five sports: tennis, sailing, croquet, equestrian sport and golf, although just golf and tennis included women only events (IOC, 2013, p. 1). More than a century later, the IOC is clearly committed to gender equality in sport. Rule 2, paragraph 7 of the Olympic Charter in force from 7 July 2007 states that one of the roles of the IOC is to encourage and support the promotion of women in sport at all levels and in all structures, with a view to implementing the principle of equality of men and women (IOC, 2013, p. 1).

Figure 5.1 illustrates the slow process of female representation at the Summer Olympics, both as a share of total participants and as a share

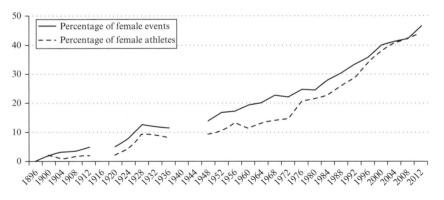

Source: Own calculations based on information from http://www.olympic.org.

Figure 5.1   *Share of female events and share of female participation at the Summer Olympics*

of total events. A steady growth over the years is visible but up until 1984 the share of female athletes at the Olympics did not exceed 25 per cent. It took in fact 60 years to increase the percentage share from 10 per cent (Amsterdam, 1928) to just over 25 per cent (Seoul, 1988). Things moved up a gear from the 1990s onwards. In the past 20 years the women's share of participants has grown from 26 per cent to 44 per cent. A similar evolution can be observed for the percentage share of female events at the Games. Note that the female events' share almost always exceeds the participants' share. This means that an average women's event at the Games includes fewer participants than the corresponding men's event. For instance, 16 nations were selected for the men's football competition at the 2012 Olympic Games while for the women's competition only 12 nations could qualify. It should be noted that in contrast to these observations and to the explicit gender paragraph in the Olympic Charter, even in 2014 less than 20 per cent of all the members of the IOC Board of Directors were women. It thus remains questionable whether the IOC clearly follows the 'practice what you preach' rule at its own executive level.

Figure 5.1 makes clear that the women's share at the Olympics became close to 50 per cent in 2012. Therefore, some media described the London Games as 'the women's games' (Independent, 2012). The 2012 Olympic Games were indeed historic from a gender point of view. For the very first time women competed in every sport on the Olympic programme (boxing was the last sport to allow women competitors) and about two-thirds of all sports had an equal number of male and female events. As a result, the share of female events reached an all-time high of 46.4 per cent. Furthermore, never before had every competing nation been represented by at least one female athlete. Saudi Arabia was the last country to give in to firm pressure from the IOC to include at least one woman in the team. The proportion of women participants at the London Games thus amounted to 44.2 per cent, also an all-time high. Moreover, some countries, like the United States, China, Russia, Japan, North Korea and Sweden, were, in fact, represented by more female than male athletes. While this was the first time ever this had happened to the US Olympic team, it was already the fourth time in Olympic history that the Chinese female delegation outnumbered the male delegation.

In the past couple of decades a number of studies have analysed the gender balance in TV coverage of the Summer Olympics. In Table 5.1 we present an overview and compare the women's TV share mentioned in each study with the women's event share for the corresponding Olympics. The latter number was based on information found in the IOC document 'Factsheet women in Olympic movement' (IOC, 2013). This share takes account of all events in which women can participate, including mixed

Table 5.1   Research findings on gender balance in TV coverage of the Summer Olympics

Reference	Olympics	Dataset	Women's TV share (%)	Women's event share (%)
Higgs & Weiller (1994)	1992	USA, prime time sample, 44 hours	44.0	33.5
Higgs et al. (2003)	1996	USA, prime time sample, 32.5 hours	54.2	35.8
Eastman & Billings (1999)	1996	USA, prime time sample, 34 hours	49.3	35.8
Tuggle & Owen (1999)	1996	USA, prime time all, 72 hours	47.4	35.8
Billings (2008)	2000	USA, prime time sample, 31 hours	47.5	40.0
Billings (2008)	2004	USA, prime time sample, 43 hours	47.7	41.5
Billings et al. (2010)	2008	USA, prime time all, 74.5 hours	45.8	42.1
Toohey (1997)	1988	Australia, all broadcasts, 198 hours	32.9	30.4
Toohey (1997)	1992	Australia, highlights only, 21 hours	29.7	33.5
Capranica & Aversa (2002)	2000	Italy, all broadcasts, 218.5 hours	28.9	40.0
Van Reeth (2014)	2012	Flanders, all broadcasts, 213 hours	46.3	46.4

sports (like equestrian sport) as well as mixed disciplines (like the mixed doubles in tennis). The share of women's only events therefore is still a bit smaller. While in 2012 women could compete in 46.4 per cent of all Olympic events, the share of women only events was 45.1 per cent.

The first group of studies focus on prime time Olympic coverage in the United States. Higgs and Weiller (1994) and Higgs et al. (2003) use randomized samples of the actual NBC coverage for the 1992 and 1996 Olympics and find that in 1992 women's events received 44 per cent of all media attention. Using the same methodology, a share of 54.2 per cent was found for 1996. It should be noted, though, that we had to compute this percentage ourselves from the data published in the paper because the authors do not report this share in their text. This percentage is exceptionally high and a direct result of the sampling technique used by the authors because for the same 1996 Olympics other researchers found an almost balanced

49.3 per cent share (Eastman and Billings, 1999) and 47.4 per cent share (Tuggle and Owen, 1999). Consequently, there is an almost 7 percentage point difference between multiple analyses for the same Games. In this respect, Billings (2008, p. 432) observed: 'as the number of Olympic clock studies grew, slight differences in male-female disparities were reported – not because of coding error as much as differing operational definitions of what should or should not be included in an overall analysis'. In a longitudinal analysis Billings (2008) and Billings et al. (2010) demonstrate that coverage of women's Olympic events remained stable between 2000 and 2008 with a 47.5 per cent, 47.7 per cent and 45.8 per cent share for the Sydney, Athens and Beijing Games, respectively. Overall, Table 5.1 makes it clear that women's Olympic events on NBC during prime time received a constant share of about 45 to 50 per cent of TV time between 1992 and 2008. Since the share of events open to women at the Games was still well below 40 per cent in the 1990s and 40 to 42 per cent between 2000 and 2008, it can be concluded that in the United States, at least during prime time, women definitely got more than their fair share of TV attention at the Olympics.

In an analysis of the Flemish TV coverage of the London Games, we found results similar to the findings for the United States. In the northern part of Belgium, women's events at the 2012 Olympics received 46.3 per cent of all television time (Van Reeth, 2014), which is perfectly balanced with the 46.4 per cent share of events open to women at the London Games.

We found information on gender balance in global TV coverage of the Summer Olympics for two more countries. In both Australia (Toohey, 1997) and Italy (Capranica and Aversa, 2002) women's events at the Olympics received a little less than a third of all TV broadcast time. The Australian analyses, however, refer to the 1988 and 1992 Olympic Games in which the female share of events was also still only about a third. The Australian broadcaster's choice of TV time dedicated to men's and women's events consequently mirrored rather well the actual gender balance at the Games at that time. This is not the case with Italy for the Sydney Games. While in 2000 the women's share at the Olympics was close to 40 per cent, women's competitions received only 28.9 per cent of all TV time on Italian television. Note that, in contrast to the case for the United States, the Flemish study, the Italian study and the 1998 Australian analysis do not focus on prime time coverage of the Games only, but include data on all TV broadcasts of the Olympics. Therefore, while the American studies only use 30 to 70 hours of broadcast time, for the other countries over 200 broadcast hours are analysed.

We admit that many more articles have been published on gender balance in media coverage of the Olympic Games. However, since our focus is on the gender balance in global TV coverage, we have not included in the discussion any papers on gender differences in the coverage of specific sports, like Licen and Billings (2012) on gymnastics or Greer et al. (2009) on track & field. Nor did we include any studies on gender balance for other media, like Jones (2013) on online coverage or Jones et al. (1999) and Hardin et al. (2002) on coverage in print media.

THE 2012 LONDON GAMES ON DUTCH TELEVISION

Olympic content is generated by the IOC through its media division Olympic Broadcast Services, which captures the signal from each Olympic event and delivers the signal to the broadcast partners to air over various media platforms throughout the world. From the full range of available material, each official broadcast partner may select the particular events to include in its Olympic programming. In this way, each broadcaster has the opportunity to choose those competitions and images that it determines to be of greatest interest to its home country audience (IOC, 2014, p. 25).

In the Netherlands, public channel NPO is the official Olympic media partner. One of its channels, NPO1, was exclusively and entirely reserved for TV broadcasts of the London Games. Live streams of events not broadcast were simultaneously provided on the NPO website but are not a part of our analysis. Since the Games took place in an adjacent time zone to the Netherlands, Olympic broadcasts started in the morning usually about 10 am and continued all day long until, depending on the live action, about midnight. The broadcasts of live and delayed Olympic competitions were interrupted only for regular news broadcasts, Olympic news programmes and a daily talk show. In total, the channel aired over 220 hours of Olympic programming.

We created our own dataset of Dutch Olympic TV broadcasts by monitoring on a daily basis the Dutch website www.kijkcijferonderzoek. nl. This website offers in great detail viewership information for all (bits of) programmes shown on Dutch TV channels. With respect to the Olympic Games, for instance, detailed information was provided at the specific competition level (for example, 100 metre butterfly men or pole vault women) instead of at the aggregate sport level (for example, swimming or track & field), enabling a detailed analysis of Olympic broadcasting. The initial dataset consisted of 1301 programme bits. Next the dataset was cleaned up by deleting talk shows, Olympic news broadcasts, reviews and erroneous data, resulting in a smaller dataset of 972 programme bits totalling about 145 hours of broadcasting. Another 32 broadcasts covered mixed sports competitions. Of the final 940 programme bits used in the analysis

*Table 5.2   Women's share in Olympic events, Dutch athletes and Dutch TV
           broadcasts by sport (2014)*

Sport	Olympic events		Dutch athletes		Dutch TV broadcasts		Dutch broadcast time	
	Total	% women	Total	% women	Total	% women	Total	% women
Track & field	47	48.9	23	47.8	296	42.8	1102	36.3
Gymnastics	14	42.9	2	50.0	235	42.4	669	39.9
Swimming	34	50.0	15	53.3	94	50.0	717	50.3
Judo	14	50.0	9	44.4	49	51.0	504	46.4
Cycling	14	50.0	21	47.6	48	41.7	921	44.4
Field hockey	2	50.0	32	50.0	47	53.2	1279	44.4
Rowing	14	42.9	32	40.6	34	47.1	197	48.2
Beach volleyball	2	50.0	6	66.7	22	54.5	471	35.0
Basketball	2	50.0	0	–	14	7.1	447	0.7
Tennis	4	50.0	2	0.0	12	16.7	244	19.3
All other sports	149	41.6	27	48.1	96	40.9	1524	46.4
Total	296	45.1	169	47.3	947	43.5	8075	40.3
Mixed events	8		19	15.8	32		601	

below, 409 (43.5 per cent) covered women's events while 531 (56.5 per cent)
covered men's events. But because broadcasts of women's events were
on average about 25 per cent shorter in duration than broadcasts of
men's events (12 minutes and 45 seconds versus 17 minutes), measured in
minutes the women's share is significantly lower. In fact, at the London
Olympics women's events received only 40.3 per cent of all broadcast
time on Dutch television. The share of broadcast time of women's events
in the Netherlands is thus clearly below the shares of over 45 per cent
recorded for the United States and Flanders (Table 5.1). A share of only
40.3 per cent is not in balance either with the 44.1 per cent share of female
athletes in the Dutch Olympic team (83 out of 188).

Table 5.2 presents a more detailed analysis of the gender balance in
Dutch Olympic TV broadcasts. For all sports with over ten broadcasts we
computed the women's share of four variables: (1) events on the Olympic
programme; (2) number of Dutch athletes; (3) number of Dutch broadcasts; and (4) Dutch broadcast time. Although in total number of broadcasts, track & field (296), gymnastics (235) and swimming (94) featured
the most on Dutch television, it was field hockey (21 hours), track & field
(almost 19 hours) and cycling (over 15 hours) that received the most time.
This is, of course, because field hockey games and cycling competitions
have a much longer duration than most track & field, gymnastics or swimming events. Broadcasting of women's basketball and women's tennis was

clearly unbalanced with shares well below 20 per cent while in these sports there are an equal number of men's and women's events on the Olympic programme. The lack of any Dutch female participants in these disciplines resulted in a strong focus on the male international superstars of these sports, like the US team in basketball and Roger Federer in tennis. For most sports, we observe that the actual women's share in broadcast time is some percentage points lower than the women's share in the number of broadcasts. For instance, women's track & field events had a 42.8 per cent share in the number of broadcasts but only a 36.3 per cent share in broadcast time. Only for swimming (50 per cent) and rowing (47–48 per cent) are both shares more or less equal. The most significant difference can be found for beach volleyball. More than half (54.5 per cent) of the beach volleyball broadcasts covered women's games while these games only accounted for about a third (35.0 per cent) of broadcast time for beach volleyball. Only in one sport does the opposite occur. Dutch television dedicated more broadcast time to women's cycling (44.4 per cent) than could be expected from its share in number of broadcasts (41.7 per cent).

DISEQUILIBRIUM ON THE SPORTS PROGRAMMES MARKET FOR OLYMPIC TV BROADCASTS

For most TV channels, broadcasting a mega sports event is a loss-making business. For instance, French TV channel TF1 made a net loss of over 50 million euros with its broadcasts of the 2014 World Cup in Brazil (L'Équipe, 2014). The total costs amounted to 135 million euros (130 million broadcasting rights and 5 million production costs) while the sale of advertising slots yielded 50 million euros and another 30 million euros was earned by reselling part of the broadcasting rights to pay channel BeIN. Similarly, French TV channels France 2 and France 3, the official broadcasters of the Tour de France, record a net loss of about 25 million euros with their broadcasts of the Tour de France (Toutelatélé, 2014). The total costs amount to 35 million euros (25 million broadcasting rights and 10 million production costs) while advertising revenues do not exceed 10 million euros. In the case of the Netherlands, Dutch Olympic broadcaster NPO is funded partly by private money and partly by contributions from the government. Consequently, the number of viewers is important not only for the sale of advertising slots but also in justifying the large sum of public money spent on buying the broadcasting rights and covering the production costs. We therefore assume that NPO, just like any other Olympic TV broadcaster, seeks to maximize the number of viewers.

We evaluate the choices made by the Dutch official broadcaster, presented above, by comparing them with the actual Dutch TV audiences for Olympic broadcasts of male and female events. The basic research question is: does the (broadcaster's) supply of women's/men's events properly match the (consumers') demand for women's/men's events. We assume consumers maximize personal utility by watching Olympic events. They pick the events they like to see and switch channels or turn off their television if a competition or event is shown that is of little or no interest to them. Therefore, in our analysis the demand for TV broadcasts of the Olympic Games is not a theoretical or hypothetical demand, but the real, observed demand as reflected in the TV ratings for Olympic broadcasts. In an equilibrium situation we expect that a TV broadcaster chooses the right amount of men's and women's events, that is, the amount that maximizes the combined viewing of both types of events.

To make a proper comparison, we use the concept of the average minute audience (AMA) for a sport. The sport-specific AMA measures the number of TV viewers for all broadcasts of a sport, averaged per minute. For instance, if there are two broadcasts of women's gymnastics competitions with a TV rating of 10.0 and 6.0, respectively, the AMA does not simply average both ratings (8.0). Instead, a weighted average, based on the duration of the programme, is computed. If the first broadcast lasted for 15 minutes and the second broadcast had a duration of 5 minutes, then the AMA would equal $(10.0 \times 15 + 6.0 \times 5)/20 = 9.0$. This procedure allows a much better comparison of sports comprising events of long duration (like field hockey games) with sports that have events of a much shorter duration (like many track & field events). Overall, for the 409 women's events broadcast on Dutch television we find an AMA of 8.27. This is 11.2 per cent higher than the AMA of 7.43 found for the 531 broadcasts of men's events. This telling difference hints at an important mismatch between the observed men's events-oriented supply of Dutch Olympic TV broadcasts and the demand revealed by the Dutch TV audience, which reflects a clear preference for women's events.

To further analyse the disequilibrium situation that arises on this market, we compute gender-based AMA ratings per sport and compare these ratings with the total broadcast time for each of these sports. The results are presented in Figure 5.2. The first part of the figure is a graphical representation of the information provided in the last two columns of Table 5.2. For the Olympic sports with over ten broadcasts on Dutch television, the total broadcast time for all men's and women's events is shown. For almost all sports, men's competitions received much more airtime on Dutch TV than women's competitions. Swimming and rowing are the only exceptions with a more or less balanced amount of TV time. Although some men's events have a longer duration than women's events and

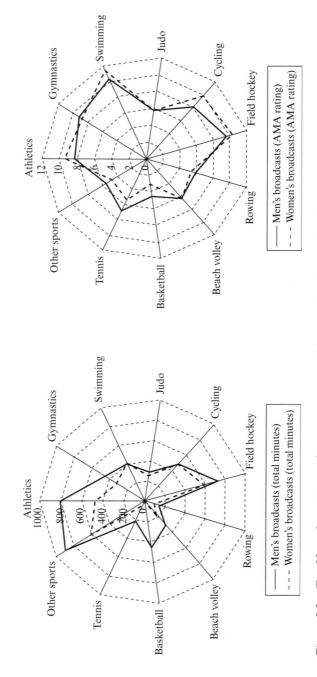

Figure 5.2   Total broadcast time and average minute audience ratings for men's and women's broadcasts

although in a number of sports (like gymnastics or rowing) the number of women's events is smaller than the number of men's events, these elements can never fully account for the observed differences in share of broadcast time. For instance, in gymnastics and track & field the women's share of broadcast time is still largely below what would be fair in comparison to the share of events. While in track & field 23 out of 47 events (47.8 per cent) are women's events, total broadcast time for women's competitions only equalled 36.3 per cent.

But the more interesting part of the analysis is the comparison between the choices of broadcasts and the gender-based average minute audience ratings for these sports shown in the second part of Figure 5.2. At first glance, the two parts of the figure already look fundamentally different. While for the broadcast time the line indicating the women's share is almost entirely enclosed by the men's line, for the average minute audience ratings another pattern emerges. For most sports, the line indicating the audience ratings for women's events is now close to or even crosses the line that reflects the audience ratings for men's events. For track & field, swimming, cycling and field hockey significantly higher TV ratings are recorded for broadcasts of women's competitions, while judo, rowing and beach volleyball show almost equal ratings. The interest in men's competitions is significantly higher for three sports only: basketball, tennis and, to a lesser extent, gymnastics.

From Figure 5.2 it becomes clear that there are some important differences between the preferences of Dutch TV viewers and the choices of Dutch Olympic TV broadcaster NPO. In five sports the mismatch is obvious. For track & field, women received only 36.3 per cent of broadcast time but the AMA rating for women's events was 1.28 higher than for men's events (9.39 versus 8.11).

For cycling, women received 44.4 per cent of broadcast time while the AMA rating for women's events equalled 10.07 versus only 8.16 for men's events. Also for field hockey women's games received 44.4 per cent of all broadcast time while the AMA rating equalled 10.29, which is 0.78 more than the AMA rating for men's games. While women's beach volleyball only received 35.0 per cent of all broadcast time, its AMA rating (6.09) was almost equal to the men's AMA rating (6.22). Finally, although women's swimming events received an equal amount of broadcast time compared to men's events, AMA ratings were the highest of all events and exceed men's swimming events by 1.11. For each of these five sports, an increased share of women's broadcasts would improve overall TV ratings significantly. For the other five sports, we think a better balance was present. Judo and rowing showed a satisfying gender balance with respect to the amount of broadcast time and both sports also recorded very similar AMA ratings for both genders. The larger share of men's broadcasts for gymnastics, tennis and basketball was also reflected in higher AMA ratings for the men's events over the women's broadcasts, indicating the Dutch broadcasters also made the right choice for these sports.

Of course, strong performances of Dutch athletes play an important role too. Since Dutch women won gold medals in cycling, swimming and field hockey, TV ratings for these sports are likely to be higher. Nevertheless, although there is a definite effect, for a number of reasons excellent women's performances cannot account for all of the differences we found. First, in our analysis we do not focus on TV ratings alone, but compare these ratings with the decisions on the supply of broadcasts. Sports with higher medal chances for Dutch female athletes, like cycling and swimming, also received relatively more airtime on Dutch television. Second, in sports where Dutch male athletes proved to be more successful than female athletes, like beach volleyball or track & field, TV ratings were significantly higher for women's broadcasts. Third, although only the women's team won the gold medal, both the Dutch men and the Dutch women's field hockey team reached the Olympic final and thus both performed at their best. TV ratings for women's field hockey games were nevertheless significantly higher than for men's games.

THE CHOICE BETWEEN 'PRETTY' AND 'POWERFUL'

A number of authors have analysed in detail some characteristics of the overall preference for male competitions in sports coverage. It has been observed by many that preferences for men's and women's events are often related to elements such as the nature of the sport and/or the way the athletes are dressed. For instance, Billings (2008, p. 438) notes that 'all of the sports in which women received the majority of the coverage involved the wearing of swimsuits or leotards'. In their study on coverage of US women's Olympic gold medal winning teams, Jones et al. (1999, p. 184) make a distinction between 'male appropriate sports' that emphasize physical contact through active, aggressive and autonomous behaviour and 'female appropriate sports' that emphasize aesthetics and beauty while discouraging physicality. Similarly Jones (2013, p. 249) explains how sports can be classified into 'feminine sports' and 'masculine sports'. Feminine sports include those that depict females in aesthetically pleasing motions and poses, often emphasizing the erotic physicality of the female body. They also give the appearance of posing little physical risk and being unlikely to cause bodily injury to the athlete. Feminine sports tend to be individual-oriented, where an athlete competes against herself/himself or towards a pre-set standard of excellence, such as a personal best, world record or an opponent's score. Masculine sports require bodily contact, conflict or face-to-face opposition, or heavy equipment, padded uniforms or protective armour. Masculine sports tend to be team-oriented, with athletes competing directly against others in a challenge for power and control.

How do the choices of the Dutch TV broadcaster and the Dutch TV audiences fit into this picture? In contrast to what was observed by Billings (2008), for the sports in which women wear swimsuits or leotards (that is, gymnastics, beach volleyball and swimming, labelled as 'pretty sports' below) in the Netherlands women's events did not receive the majority of coverage. In fact, women's broadcasts received 42.7 per cent of all TV time for these sports, which is 3 percentage points more than the overall women's share of 39.6 per cent for all other sports. So although relative to other sports Dutch television did broadcast a slightly higher share of women's events for these 'pretty sports', it is far from being a majority share. Dutch TV viewers do show a clear preference for 'pretty sports' though. The overall average rating for swimming, gymnastics and beach volleyball equals 9.0, which is significantly higher than the 7.4 average rating for all other sports. But this preference is not related to the gender of the athletes, because for both men's competitions (8.8 versus 7.1) and women's competitions (9.4 versus 7.9) a similar difference exists.

Next we turn our attention to the so-called 'aggressive and powerful' sports. Judo and rowing, the only sports in this category in our dataset of Olympic broadcasts, received an almost equal amount of broadcast time on Dutch television for men's and women's competitions resulting in a 47 per cent share for women's events. With a TV rating of 5.7 only, Dutch audiences for these broadcasts were relatively small. The remarkable thing, though, is that an identical TV rating for men's and women's competitions was found. With respect to 'powerful sports', Dutch TV audiences thus show no gender preference, in contrast to what is the case for all other sports.

From these observations we learn that while for 'pretty sports' there is a significant difference between the choices made by the Dutch broadcaster and the preferences of Dutch TV audiences, this difference is almost non-existent with the 'powerful sports'. Therefore, we can conclude there exists a kind of disequilibrium on the 'pretty sports' programmes market (with a shortage in supply of women's competitions) while the 'powerful sports' programmes market appears to be much more in equilibrium.

CONCLUSION

While total broadcast time for women's competitions equalled only two-thirds of total broadcast time for men's competitions (40 per cent versus 60 per cent), overall audience ratings for women's competitions were considerably higher (8.27 versus 7.43). And although of the ten most important Olympic sports on Dutch television five showed higher overall TV ratings for women's events (that is, track & field, swimming, cycling, field hockey and judo), only for swimming did women's competitions actually receive more TV time relative to men's competitions. We can therefore safely conclude that at the London 2012 Olympic Games the popularity of women's events was not adequately reflected in the share of broadcast time on Dutch television. Since the supply of TV broadcasts did not match very well the desires and the demand of the Dutch TV viewers a disequilibrium situation emerged. There are differences across sports though. While for cycling, track & field, field hockey and 'pretty sports' such as swimming and beach volley the supply of broadcasts of women's events did not match the preferences of Dutch TV viewers for these competitions, for rowing and judo a much better balance was found. For these 'powerful sports' we measured a close to equal broadcast time as well as almost identical TV ratings for men's and women's events.

One should still be careful, though, when jumping to conclusions. Other elements not yet fully explored in this text may play a role too. For instance, a higher number of broadcasts of men's competitions is likely to imply that for men's events more qualifying rounds or group stage games were shown. Such competitions will usually have lower TV ratings than Olympic finals, and thus reduce the average TV ratings for men's broadcasts relative to TV ratings for women's broadcasts with a smaller amount of qualifying competitions. A more refined analysis could therefore consist of excluding these competitions and comparing TV ratings for Olympic finals only. Average TV ratings might also be lower for some sports because of the timing of the competition. For instance, rowing competitions take place during the day with smaller TV audiences than prime time competitions. Similarly, events that take place at the weekend will also record higher TV ratings.

Two more remarks are necessary. First, in the analysis only information on TV broadcasts on the free-to-watch television channel NPO 1 was used. In reality, Dutch people also had the opportunity to watch Olympic events via a number of live streams provided by the broadcaster on its website. A more complete picture of preferences for male or female sports broadcasts could be created if information on the viewing of these live streams were also used. TV broadcasters could in fact monitor the interest in the live streams to better adjust their regular Olympic broadcasts on television to the preferences and needs of the public. Second, since we have no information on the gender of the TV viewers, we cannot check whether male and female viewers have similar preferences on broadcasts for men's and women's competitions. We can only talk about Dutch TV viewers as a group.

Nevertheless, even bearing all these considerations in mind we think that based on the results presented here, at least for the Netherlands we can safely reject the often heard market-driven argument of TV channels that 'since women sport is less interesting to TV viewers we favour male sports broadcasts'. In fact, Dutch Olympic broadcaster NPO could have increased its TV ratings significantly by thoughtfully substituting a number of lesser-watched men's competitions for better-watched women's competitions. There thus no longer appears to be any excuse for Dutch media to prefer male competitions over female competitions.

REFERENCES

Billings, A.C. (2008), 'Clocking gender differences: televised Olympic clock time in the 1996–2006 Summer and Winter Olympics', *Television & New Media*, **9**(5), 429–41.

Billings, A.C., J.R. Angelini and A. Holt Duke (2010), 'Gendered profiles of Olympic history: sportscaster dialogue in the 2008 Beijing Olympics', *Journal of Broadcasting & Electronic Media*, **54**(1), 9–23.

Bolotny, F. and J.-F. Bourg (2006), 'The demand for media coverage', in W. Andreff and S. Szymanski (eds), *Handbook on the Economics of Sport*, Cheltenham, UK and Northampton, MA, USA: Edgar Elgar, pp. 112–33.

Capranica, L. and F. Aversa (2002), 'Italian television sport coverage during the 2000 Sydney Olympic Games', *International Review for the Sociology of Sport*, **37**(3), 337–49.

Eastman, S.T. and A.C. Billings (1999), 'Gender parity in the Olympics', *Journal of Sport & Social Issues*, **23**(2), 140–70.

Greer, J.D., M. Hardin and C. Homan (2009), '"Naturally" less exciting? Visual production of men's and women's track and field coverage during the 2004 Olympics', *Journal of Broadcasting & Electronic Media*, **53**(2), 173–89.

Hardin, M., J. Chance, J.E. Dodd and B. Hardin (2002), 'Olympic photo coverage fair to female athletes', *Newspaper Research Journal*, **23**(2), 64–78.

Higgs, C.T. and K.H. Weiller (1994), 'Gender bias and the 1992 Summer Olympic Games: an analysis of television coverage', *Journal of Sport & Social Issues*, **18**, 234–46.

Higgs, C.T., K.H. Weiller and S.C. Martin (2003), 'Gender bias in the 1996 Olympic Games: a comparative analysis', *Journal of Sport & Social Issues*, **27**(1), 52–64.

Independent (2012), *London 2012 Olympics: The Women's Games*, available at http://www.independent.co.uk/sport/olympics/news/london-2012-olympics-the-womens-games-7976835.html (accessed 4 June 2012).

IOC (2013), 'Factsheet women in Olympic movement', International Olympic Committee.

IOC (2014), *Olympic Marketing Fact File*, International Olympic Committee, available at http://www.olympic.org/ IOC_MARKETING/OLYMPIC-MARKETING-FACT-FILE-2012.pdf (accessed 4 June 2015).

IP & RTL Group (2011), *Television 2011, International Key Facts*, Luxembourg.

Jones, D. (2013), 'Online coverage of the 2008 Olympic Games on the ABC, BBC, CBC and TVNZ', *Pacific Journalism Review*, **19**(1), 244–63.

Jones, R., A.J. Murrell and J. Jackson (1999), 'Pretty versus powerful in the sports pages: print media coverage of U.S. women's Olympic gold medal winning teams', *Journal of Sport & Social Issues*, **23**(2), 183–92.

L'Équipe (2014), *TF1 aurait essuyé 50 millions de pertes avec le Mondial*, available at http://www.lequipe.fr/Medias/Actualites/Tf1-bon-mondial-mauvais-comptes/485288 (accessed 4 June 2015).

Licen, S. and A.C. Billings (2012), 'Two perspectives on one competition: Slovenian coverage of artistic gymnastics at the 2008 Summer Olympics', *Science of Gymnastics Journal*, **4**(3), 49–59.

Toohey, K. (1997), 'Australian television, gender and the Olympic Games', *International Review for the Sociology of Sport*, **32**(1), 19–29.

Toutelatélé (2014), *Tour de France 2014: le coût réel pour France Télévisions*, available at http://www.toutelatele.com/tour-de-france-2014-le-cout-reel-pour-France-televisions-62193 (accessed 4 June 2015).

Tuggle, C.A. and A. Owen (1999), 'A descriptive analysis of NBC's coverage of the centennial Olympics: the "Games of the woman"?', *Journal of Sport & Social Issues*, **23**(2), 171–82.

Van Reeth, D. (2014), 'Female gymnasts or male basketball players: gender preferences in TV viewing of the London 2012 Olympic Games', Presentation at DESport seminar, Paris, 16 May.

PART II

Teams and leagues with soft budget constraints

6. Soft budget constraints in European and US leagues: similarities and differences

Rasmus K. Storm and Klaus Nielsen

INTRODUCTION

In contemporary economic literature on professional team sports the European and the North American[1] contexts are commonly contrasted. A typical textbook comparison argues that open European professional team sport leagues (pro leagues) consist of win (or utility) maximizing teams (Késenne, 1996, 2006; Sandy et al., 2004), while closed American 'major' leagues involve franchises that are essentially profit maximizers (Noll, 1974; Cairns et al., 1986; Fort, 2000; Szymanski and Hall, 2003; Késenne, 2006; Szymanski and Zimbalist, 2006).

However, others stress the similarities between the two models in relation to sports organizations and team objectives (Fort, 2000). The adaption of new strategies and aims on both sides of the Atlantic has led scholars to question the archetypical categorizations. On the one hand, it appears that European football has been 'Americanized' (Hoehn and Szymanski, 1999; Nauright and Ramfjord, 2010) with an increasing focus on revenue streams and profit. On the other hand, an increasing awareness of the existence of 'glory seeking' (that is, 'win maximizing') 'sportsmen' owners in American leagues has evolved as well (Vrooman, 2000). Summing up these new observations in the ongoing debate of win versus profit maximization, Késenne argues that:

> it cannot be denied that the gap between the US and Europe is narrowing. Some US economists like Quirk and El-Hodiri and Noll admit that besides making profits winning the championship is also important, even if it reduces profits. In the world of European soccer being the most professional and commercial sport, not only winning but also making profits is becoming part of the game. (Késenne, 2002, p. 96)

This chapter aims to advance a new perspective in the comparison of European and American sport leagues by deploying Kornaï's soft budget constraint (SBC) approach (Kornaï, 1986, 2001, 2014; Kornaï et al., 2003) in a comparison of the closed American and open European pro leagues. Whereas European sport leagues are characterized by the SBC syndrome in exactly the way Kornaï has conceptualized it (Andreff, 2007a, 2007b, 2011; Storm and Nielsen, 2012; Franck, 2013; Storm, 2013), this is not the case with American sport leagues. Expectations of rescue in case of financial trouble and the associated effects on firm level efficiency do not prevail in the USA. However, American major leagues experience softness of budgets in ways that are remarkably similar to the European experience and with similar distortion of resource allocation.

The chapter is structured as follows. First, we present a brief theoretical overview of the SBC theory. Second, we illustrate how win maximization and softness seem to persist in European pro leagues. Third, we enhance our analysis by examining the American context within the same framework showing that in the USA profit seeking takes place in an environment that softens budget constraints in many ways as in Europe. Fourth, we expand the typical binary categorizations of professional team sports clubs (PTSCs) into a multiple set of ideal type categories, that is, a new matrix of various combinations of team objectives and socio-economic environments. Further, we flesh out some directions for further research of the similarities and differences between professional team sports in Europe and the USA on the basis of this new perspective. In a concluding section we discuss the origin of the differences between European and US pro leagues and the future prospects are briefly touched upon.

SOFT AND HARD BUDGET CONSTRAINTS

The SBC idea was introduced by Kornaï at the late 1970s in order to describe a situation where public enterprises were rescued financially by public authorities (Maskin, 1999, p. 421). Kornaï borrowed the budget constraint expression from microeconomic theory of the household that holds limited resources for spending. The nominal limit of expenditure to be covered by household earnings and/or earlier savings, and which the household in principle cannot exceed, is termed its 'budget constraint'.

Projecting this perspective onto the context of state-owned firms in socialist systems in Eastern European countries, Kornaï argues that if an enterprise faces a deficit, two possible situations can occur: 'One is that the firm is left to its own resources. Then the budget constraint is hard . . .' (Kornaï, 2006, p. 257), and persistent losses will mean that it goes bankrupt after a while. On the other hand, should a superior organization, creditor or authority rush to help the enterprise by providing financial aid or assisting the firm in other ways (see below), the enterprise faces a SBC because – in the likelihood of the rescue being repeated in future parallel situations – there is no real curb on the firm's spending. Thus, 'It will survive even if spending exceeds income plus initial capital over a long period' (Kornaï, 2006, p. 257).

Budget constraints were obviously soft in the classical communist 'command economy' (Kornaï, 2014, p. 42). According to Kornaï, this phenomenon also prevailed in the post-Stalinist reform socialism and was especially present in his native Hungary, which took tentative steps towards a more market-driven approach from 1968 onward. Even though profit motives among public firms' managers were lauded by the state, and reforms were implemented, incentives for profit were seriously distorted due to repeated rescues when they failed.

Kornaï distinguishes five conditions for assessing whether firms face hardness or softness (Kornaï, 1980a; Kornaï et al., 2003, pp. 1097–8). Firms face hard budget constraints when the following circumstances are met. (H1): The firm is a price-taker for both inputs and outputs. (H2): The firm cannot influence the tax rules and no individual exemption can be given concerning the volume of tax or dates of collection. (H3): The firm cannot receive any free state or other grants to cover current expenses or as contributions to finance investment. (H4): No credit from other firms or banks can be obtained (all transactions are made in cash). (H5): No external financial investment is possible, that is, investments are dependent on retained profits.

In primitive economies without banking and for households in the classical command economy all five conditions are met, but with these exceptions such ideal type hardness are not found in reality (Kornaï, 1980b, pp. 311–12). Credits and external finance are constituent characteristics of monetary economies, and the economic power to influence prices exists everywhere. Instead, the 'Almost Hard Budget Constraint' (AHBC) resembles a situation closer to what one might find in practice. Cases of AHBCs materialize when one or several of the 'H conditions' of hardness are relaxed while H2 and H3 remain hard. SBCs exist in many forms. Using the framework of Kornaï we may distinguish soft administrative pricing (S1), soft taxation (S2), soft subsidies (S3), soft credit (S4), soft investment finance (S5), and we may add another category, soft accounting (S6), which is of particular relevance in the soft budget context of contemporary pro leagues.[2]

The SBC phenomenon constitutes a syndrome because of its effects on expectations and behaviour. A soft budget is no problem in itself. Specific bailouts may well have economically favourable effects. However, it becomes a problem if expectations of future rescue influence behaviour with wider implications for the economy as such. In socialist economies the implication was widespread shortage. In capitalist economies the consequences are loss of societal wealth and firm/organizational inefficiency as market demand gets out of control, decision makers make irresponsible investments, price- and cost-sensitivity is reduced, the attention of managers changes from productive to rent seeking activities and damage to the morals of society (Kornaï, 2014, p. 38).

Certain environmental conditions have to be in place for SBC to materialize (Kornaï et al., 2003, p. 1107). If the organization in question holds a key (socio-economic) position in the broader society providing important goods and/or services, the likelihood of softness is potentially high. In this sense, the SBC syndrome is not solely an economic phenomenon; it holds significant cultural, political and social characteristics as well (Kornaï, 1986, p. 8). The socialist system and its political and cultural surroundings formed the ideal environment for the SBC syndrome to appear. However, capitalist societies are facing SBCs as well. Typical examples are found in the military, in national healthcare systems and even in the financial sector (Andreff, 2014). Kornaï outlines nine territories susceptible to the SBC syndrome (Kornaï, 2014, pp. 45–51) indicating a wide field of relevance.

The likelihood of softness is potentially high for major professional team sport leagues because of their key (socio-economic) position in the broader society. In the European context it is obvious that this has led to financially unfair play, a growing sporting arms race and various inefficiencies, such as insensitivity to signals from prices and costs (Storm and Nielsen, 2012; Franck, 2013; Andreff, 2014).

SOFT BUDGET CONSTRAINTS IN EUROPEAN PROFESSIONAL FOOTBALL (SOCCER)

Soft budgets prevail in European professional football.[3] Even though some European clubs behave as win maximizers subject to a break-even constraint,[4] many are facing soft environmental conditions that effectively result in a high survival rate despite continuous financial problems (Storm and Nielsen, 2012).

Revenues are growing rapidly mostly because of highly advantageous television deals. However, costs rise even more as a result of the intense competition for player talent and poor management. The result is persistent deficits and growing debts. Paradoxically, survival rates are very high. Bankruptcies are seldom and only seem to occur for clubs in the second tier. State bailouts and sugar daddies come to the rescue and creditors accept non-payment or lasting debt.[5]

A recent report showed operating losses in more than 50 per cent of all top division clubs in Europe with salaries at more than 120 per cent of revenues in more than a quarter of all clubs (UEFA, 2010). The situation in the major leagues and the top clubs seems even worse. SBCs are a significant part of the overall picture even in the 'Big Five' leagues, the Premier League (England), the *Bundesliga* (Germany), *Serie A* (Italy), *Primera Liga* (Spain) and *Ligue* 1 (France), which are the leagues with the biggest turnover in Europe.

As far the English Premier League is concerned, Grant points out that: 'Every so often a club is reported to be on the brink of closure, . . . usually someone is found to stage a rescue package' (Grant, 2007, p. 77). Buraimo et al. (2006) add that the cultural significance of football has made even hard creditors guilty of what could be interpreted as a relaxing of the H4 and H5 conditions of hardness. The English clubs can sustain persistent losses that other firms cannot 'due to a reluctance to call in overdrafts and unpaid bills in recognition of community disapproval that would follow' (Buraimo et al., 2006, p. 41). In its first 15 years of existence the English Premier League experienced an incredible 900 per cent increase in revenue. Even so, every single year, aggregate pre-tax profit was negative. However, only three cases of tier 1–4 insolvency have occurred since 1985 (Beech et al., 2010).

In Italy, where football is indeed a part of the national heritage, several examples of club rescues indicate the existence of softness. The cultural significance of Italian football has resulted in various rescue operations of financially distressed clubs (Foot, 2006). Furthermore, public negligence regarding widespread illegal accounting practices among football clubs – that is, only applying rules when they serve the clubs' interests – has helped prevent clubs from falling into administration (Foot, 2006, p. 491). This can be interpreted as an indirect way of softening environmental conditions, helping the clubs continue to operate despite insolvency. When the famous Bosman ruling in 1996 resulted in great losses in Italian football, the Italian Prime Minister, Romano Prodi, introduced a specific law 'to make up the losses' (Foot, 2006, p. 536). Another example of soft budgets in Italian football is the rescue of Lazio, which in 2005 – facing the threat of immediate financial collapse – came to an agreement with the Italian authorities to pay off its tax debt over 23 years (Morrow, 2006).

In Spain, grand scale rescues of clubs by the government were made in 1985, when subsidies were poured in from public football pools, and again in 1992 when 192 million euros of public debt was cancelled (Barajas and Rodríguez, 2010, p. 53). In addition, it is far from an unknown phenomenon to see local Spanish authorities aiding financially troubled clubs by buying or renting out stadia at subsidized prices. Big clubs like Barcelona and Real Madrid often enjoy soft forms of credit (Ascari and Gagnepain, 2006;

Lago et al., 2006, p. 8; Barajas and Rodríguez, 2010, p. 64; Andreff, 2014). The European Commission has opened three distinct in-depth investigations to verify whether various public support measures in favour of seven Spanish clubs, including Real Madrid and Barcelona, are in line with European Union state aid rules (European Commission, 2013).

Germany is one of the most financially sound leagues in Europe (Kearney, 2010), but softness is also evident here. Dietl and Franck (2007) show that German clubs typically follow the pattern of over-investment characteristic of firms facing SBCs. In another study, Frick and Prinz (2006) conclude that:

> Irrespective of their financial difficulties, it is unrealistic that either Dortmund or Schalke will become insolvent. In this unlikely event, local and regional politicians striving for re-election will outbid one another with suggestions on how to rescue either of the two with taxpayers' money. (Frick and Prinz, 2006, p. 74)

With regard to French football, Andreff (2007a, 2007b) argues that softness appears to dominate the clubs due to fans', patrons', tycoons' or other shareholders' willingness 'to pour money for nothing into clubs that spend more than they earn . . .' (Andreff, 2007b, p. 76) instead of enforcing hard environmental conditions that could ensure better club management. It is an obvious conclusion that expectations and behaviour of European football clubs and the overall effects correspond with the SBC syndrome. There is ample evidence of all six types of softness in European football.

Soft administrative pricing (S1) takes place when a municipal stadium and/or training facilities are made available to clubs at below market fees and when the government buys naming rights to stadia at above market prices. Soft taxing (S2) takes the form of tax exemptions and non-payment of taxes, non-enforcement or amnesty of tax debt. Soft subsidies (S3) are provided by the government in open and hidden forms. Direct and visible subsidies are granted by the government or 'patrons' or 'tycoons' to cancel deficits and debt in order to keep clubs afloat in situations of acute financial problems. Other subsidies take the form of access to guaranteed income generating schemes such as football pools, and also inflated sponsorship deals and other indirect subsidies prevail.

The softness of credit conditions (S4) is reflected in acceptance of overdrafts, unpaid bills and non-enforcement of repayment arrangements with routine postponement and rescheduling of debt. Investments are soft (S5) when the government or other sponsors pay part of the cost or perhaps all of it when clubs build new stadia or other revenue boosting infrastructure. Soft accounting (S6) takes the form of discretionary and even illegal praxis with the purpose of bypassing rules and creative fulfillment of legal conditions and credit criteria with the effect of fooling the creditors. Often, this is accepted or, at least in the Italian case, even encouraged by the government who has also in some cases changed legislation to facilitate softer accounting.

A recent study shows that the introduction of the Union of European Football Associations' (UEFA) Financial Fair Play (FFP) rules has been followed by a reduction in the quality of financial statements of European football clubs (Dimitropoulos, 2015; see also a previous study of Greek football clubs in Dimitropoulos, 2013). The employment of earnings management, conditional accounting conservatism and auditor switching are used as indicators for accounting quality. A study of 84 clubs for a four-year period (2009–12) shows a decline in accounting quality in all three dimensions. It is hard to escape the conclusion that massaging of accounting is applied as a means to avoid FFP-induced penalties without changing behaviour and actual financial outcome.

DO SOFT BUDGETS EXIST IN THE AMERICAN CONTEXT?

This section applies the SBC framework to the American professional team sport context. This is not a straightforward exercise and it requires a note of caution or even a stretch of imagination. We do not claim that the SBC syndrome exists in American sport. It would be to stretch Kornaï's approach too far to include this case in a catch-all exercise. Crucial constituent parts of the SBC approach are formation of expectations, behavioural effects and *ex post* rescue that do not exist in the American sport context. The characteristics we outline below can be seen as effects of monopoly power including capture of regulators. Further, the softening of budgets in the American context can be interpreted as alternative income generating activities that merely increase the budget rather than soften budget constraints.

However, we believe that the perceptual filter of hard and soft budgets developed by Kornaï may shine new light on the way American pro leagues function and the differences and similarities of European and American sport. It reveals institutional arrangements privileging team franchises and league organizations. This fundamentally distorts the market mechanism in a situation similar to the one Kornaï formulated with regard to socialist and post-socialist economies. The effects, however, are not shortages and widespread inefficiencies but rather the creation of super profits among franchise owners, high consumer prices, costs for taxpayers, regulated supply and absence of innovation and creative destruction.

Next, we will show how American professional sport is characterized by phenomena that have striking resembles to S1–S6 in the European context although the softness of budgets rather occurs *ex ante* whereas they are an effect of *ex ante* expectations of *ex post* bailouts in Europe. The focus in the following text is on the major American pro leagues. Most of the evidence is from the National Football League (NFL), which is the most successful league as far as revenue is concerned. The other three major leagues (Major League Baseball, National Basketball Association and National Hockey League) are quite similar to the NFL in relation to the issues in focus in this chapter. This does not exhaust professional team sports in the USA however. There are at least two other types worth mentioning.

First, whereas major league franchises are in reality guaranteed survival because of their legally guaranteed monopoly position this is not at all the case with most other American leagues. Whereas there is a precedence of new prospering leagues – as shown by the successes of MLS (Major League Soccer) and the WNBA (Women's National Basketball Association) – the length of the list of defunct professional sport leagues shows that bankruptcy and closure are real prospects in the US context. Financial distress is indeed a serious survival threat for practically all other sport clubs and league organizations apart from the major leagues. Almost hard budget constraints do indeed prevail in this section of American pro sport.

Second, college team sport is in reality a professional, commercial enterprise with a high income generating potential. However, it is not organized as private businesses and a significant share of the income comes from alumni and other sponsors, that is, a source reminiscent of European sugar daddies.

In the sport economics literature major league US franchise owners are most often assumed to be profit maximizers. However, maximizing profits – or realizing (large) profits, as is the case in the USA (Easterbrook, 2013) – does not necessarily imply that the enterprises in question (in this case the PTSCs) face hard environmental conditions. When firms or organizations face environmental conditions that allow them favourable opportunities to generate supplementary income, a parallel situation to that in which SBCs occur can be in place, as we will seek to explain in more depth below.

Theoretically, such a situation can be illustrated as in Figure 6.1, where Kornaï's approach is applied and advanced as a supplement to Késenne's (1996, 2006) economic model of professional team sports.

The X-axis in the figure measures the amount of player talent a given club holds, and the Y-axis measures seasonal revenue and expenditure. Both revenue and expenditure increases with the overall amount of player talent purchased by the club, with the revenue curve flattening as the amount of playing talent rises.[6]

Revenue and cost

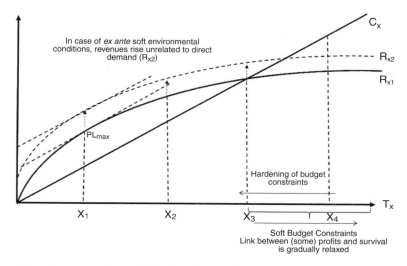

Figure 6.1   An economic model of professional team sports

According to the model, a club will hire talents equal to X_1 on the X-axis, if its objective is to maximize profits, since it is the point where marginal revenue equals marginal costs (illustrated by the punctured line, PL_{max}). If the club is a win maximizer subject to a break-even constraint, the club will recruit talent up until X_3. Should the club instead aim for win maximization subject to a certain level of profit (profit seeking rather than profit maximization), it will hire talent equivalent to maybe X_2. Should the club in question choose to win maximize, and at the same time face a SBC, it will hire more talent than X_3, maybe up until X_4. Depending on the degree of softness, the club is capable of removing the link between profits and survival on a more or less permanent basis with (more or less) persistent deficits as a result.

Yet another situation is possible if the environmental conditions that soften clubs' budget constraints are in place. The club in question could use its privileged position in a given environment to obtain an excess profit instead of striving for a higher winning percentage should the club operate under soft environmental conditions. This is an equivalent – but inverse – situation to the one Kornaï originally dealt with.

As will be argued in the following, the American major league franchises hold positions enabling them to subtract profits that would not be possible to obtain if they were facing hard (or harder) environmental conditions.

Instead, several of the conditions of hardness are relaxed resulting in an inverse situation to that Kornaï argues was institutionalized in the shortage economy. As illustrated by the dotted revenue curve R_{x2}, and the additional arrows, a superficial profit rate is gained should the club have the privilege to raise its revenues[7] without being a direct effect of increased consumer demand,[8] but instead caused by softened environmental conditions.

In reality, the sketched theoretical idea seems, to a large extent, to be an empirical fact. In contrast to the European context, where the clubs' primary objective is to maximize winning percentages subject to a break-even or a SBC, the American professional league system enjoys institutional arrangements that create huge profit potentials due to soft *ex ante* environmental conditions. We now turn to an examination of what can be labelled 'Inverse Softness' following softening of all six conditions of hardness.

Soft Pricing

Traditional economic theory informs us that when an enterprise is a price-maker, competition is distorted and prices are higher and supply lower than the welfare optimum. The closed league model that exists in the American context imposes a cartel-like monopoly power over the sports product lowering competition at the expense of the consumer (Szymanski and Smith, 1997). When franchises are given exclusivity over an urban area (and from other potentially competing leagues) – as is the case in the USA – then restraints are put on supply, thus resulting in consumer prices for the product (the sporting events) above the competitive equilibrium. This is in principle not different from other sectors characterized by economic power including oligopolistic competition. However, the major leagues are unique in the sense that monopoly power is unregulated and fiercely protected and maintained. PTSCs are exempt from anti-trust regulation and the American sport league is effectively an unregulated monopoly and because the sports franchises in the American context are not regulated, 'the monopolists are free to make as much money they can' (Szymanski and Zimbalist, 2006, p. 118).

In other words, the American major league enterprises have unique opportunities to earn super profits because of the environmental conditions. This does not necessarily imply that clubs maximize profits (X_1 in Figure 6.1). The unique monopoly situation means that they can choose to be profit seeking rather than profit maximizing (X_2 in Figure 6.1) and even in this situation be able to earn super profits.

The lucrative and important television rights deals – a massive stream of income in the US major leagues – represent one of the areas where conditions of hardness are relaxed as a result of monopoly power and accommodating institutional conditions. Anti-trust waivers have given the football teams a licence to cooperate in the pricing of television rights. The result is increased consumer prices, restrictions on supply – and super profits. The waivers were granted through the Sports Broadcasting Act from 1961 that obliged the NFL to negotiate television deals as if the NFL were a single entity (Easterbrook, 2013), thereby becoming the only US industry where such cartel behaviour is exempted from anti-trust law (Andreff, 2011, pp. 8–9). In addition, the Act:

> contained a clause authorizing pro football to 'regionalize' coverage. What does that innocuous word mean? It means that the NFL can require that a television station broadcasting within seventy-five miles of an NFL team to show only that team, if it is playing. Normally requiring a publicly regulated local broadcaster to show programming A, while forbidding it to show Programming B, would be restraint of trade. (Easterbrook, 2013, p. 74)

In total, such legislation institutionalizes extremely favourable conditions for PTSCs by means of easing their competitive environment and thus putting them in a position that matches the idea of a price-setter situation in the SBC framework.

Seen from the cost of input side of the franchises, prices on players are restricted by several regulations, which effectively remove the clubs from a price-taker position. First, salary caps and luxury taxes imposed on teams violating salary regulations help to lower the demand for player talent that in turn affects (input) prices for talent. Second, the US league context effectively restricts player mobility and recruitment practices. Roster limits is one particular tool that is used in this way. Rookie drafts – a kind of reverse-order-of-finish draft – put the power in the hands of the clubs regarding input costs in the sense that they hold a restricted right to decide who to employ and how much to spend on their wages.

As the number of jobs is also kept at a fixed rate – for example, in NFL the maximum number of paid positions that can be held by professional players is approximately 1700 – the cost of labour is kept low, because the supply of players aiming for a professional position in the NFL is enormous (Easterbrook, 2013).

Furthermore, player mobility is restricted in the sense that trading for cash is restricted or forbidden (Andreff, 2011, p. 8). Player transfers, being the norm rather than the exception in Europe, are usually barters in the USA (Szymanski, 2004), effectively lowering team competition for players and thus prizes for input costs – in practice, a further softening of the first condition of hardness (H1).

This type of softening budgets can be seen as a typical example of widespread monopoly power. It is an extreme case because of the legal support of behaviour that in other contexts would be considered as violation of anti-trust legislation, but it is not a special case. The following types of softening of budget constraints, on the other hand, represent more extreme instances of softening as a result of the unique societal position of professional team sports.

Soft Taxation

Soft taxation – a relaxation of the second H condition of hardness – is not only prevalent in the European context, it applies to American PTSCs and league organizations such as the NFL as well. For instance, payments of property taxes for privately owned stadia are often based on the principle of 'payments in lieu of taxes' (Easterbrook, 2013). These are negotiated amounts set by the local authorities. Instead of taxes being calculated based on property values, taxes in lieu are typically discounted at a significantly lower level.

Tax favours based on this principle are normally provided to colleges or museums, but sport stadia owners are among those included, leading to a lowering of costs by a H2 relaxation. For example:

> If Forbes is correct, the Jets and Giants combined are worth roughly $3 billion, making $6.3 million annual payment in lieu of taxes the equivalent of two-tenths of 1 percent property tax. Typically businesses pay property taxes that equate to one-half of 1 percent of their value. Individuals pay more . . . that is if an NFL stadium is taxed at all. (Easterbrook, 2013, pp. 59–60)

Dallas Cowboys play in a stadium that is representative of non-taxation cases. To the owner of the Dallas Cowboys, their soft taxation deal is worth around $8 million annually when compared with the normal tax rates in the area (Easterbrook, 2013, p. 60), significantly lowering costs of the franchise.

Not only the private franchises but also the NFL organizations are subject to tax exemptions. Holding status as a non-profit organization, while at the same time being run in a business-like way itself saves the NFL from significant tax obligations (Delaney, 2010). This status seems odd in the sense that the league organization basically helps to secure wealthy owners' profitable businesses. The NFL's non-profit status was secured by legislation that was originally established to ensure chambers of commerce, real estate boards and boards of trade tax exemptions – a perfectly reasonable idea seen from a broader societal point of view. Such organizations are not businesses aiming for profits themselves. Rather, they are aiming to serve objectives relevant to the broader public interest. However, since 1966, the NFL has enjoyed the same privileges:

> While Public Law 89–900 was being negotiated with congressional leaders, NFL lobbyists tossed in the sort of obscure provision that is the essence of the lobbyist's art. The phrase 'professional football leagues' was added to Section 501(c)6 of 26 U.S.C., the international revenue code. (Easterbrook, 2013, p. 66)

The non-profit status that applies to the NFL's headquarters is lucrative, for example, when used to avoid taxation of income by selling NFL logos to lotteries (Easterbrook, 2013, p. 67). Even though the income from logos was meant to fund education, the majority goes to prizes, management companies and payments to local politicians (Easterbrook, 2013, p. 68) to help the professional franchises and the NFL business in general to prosper on a tax-free basis. Such conditions are not what other ordinary kinds of businesses in the US context are facing (Delaney, 2010).[9]

Soft Subsidies and Soft Investment Finances[10]

One of the most significant causes for the profitability of the major leagues in the USA is the fact that league owners receive significant direct or indirect subsidies from public sources that help to finance their ongoing business – activities and investments that they would otherwise have to pay for themselves (Easterbrook, 2013).

Deliberately using their monopoly-like status by holding down the amount of clubs that are allowed to enter the leagues, many large metropolitan cities are still without

> a full complement of teams in the four major leagues. The under-provision of teams, and their ability to relocate almost at will, has forced US cities to pay most (and sometimes all) of the costs of the teams arenas, stadiums and practice facilities. (Sandy et al., 2004, p. 23)

Even though there is overwhelming evidence to conclude that hosting a major sports franchise – or mega events like the Olympics for that matter – does not lead to any significant economic impacts for the host city (Baade, 1987, 1994, 1996; Baade and Dye, 1988; Rosentraub et al., 1994; Tien et al., 2011), the prestige attached to hosting a pro league team has eased the willingness of politicians to subsidize teams. The very real prospect of franchises relocation urges local governments to subsidize existing franchises and to promise subsidies to prospective relocated franchises in a completion with only one winner.

Evidence is plentiful. For instance, in the 1990s, the Governor of Ohio pledged $110 million from the state capital budget for a stadium facility in order to prevent Cincinnati's pro league team from moving (Andranovich et al., 2001, p. 116). In 1985, after taking over the New Orleans Saints, the new owner, Tom Benson, threatened to leave New Orleans. After holding on to his threat for a long period of time, the Louisiana state legislature finally 'voted to give $8.5 million in tax payers money each year to Benson as an "inducement payment" – the actual term used – to keep the Saints . . .' (Easterbrook, 2013, p. 50). In 2009, still under the threat of relocating, the Louisiana Governor leased vacant New Orleans offices from Benson with public money. At that time, the New Orleans office space market was glutted, and the deal effectively granted Benson $5 million in revenue and made the Saints settle for good (Easterbrook, 2013, p. 51). Such initiatives – even though they come in the form of indirect subsidies or 'kickbacks' – must be considered as equivalents to S3 contributing to super profits seen to the franchise owners.

In general, relaxations of H3 and H5 conditions are economically significant. According to Euchner (1999), during a three-year period in the 1990s, $7 billion was either committed or used to build new stadia or refurbish existing ones. Between 1990 and 1998,

> . . . 31 new sports complexes were built for teams in four major league sports, 21 others were under construction, and 30 more were proposed. The extent of this investment is staggering, considering that each facility costs more than $100 million. (Andranovich et al., 2001, p. 117)

Adding to the overall picture, Horne (2007, p. 87) states that by the end of the 1990s 'there were 30 major stadium construction projects in progress – nearly one-third of the total professional sport infrastructure in the USA. The total value was estimated at US$9 billion.' Not all constructions are facilitated by public money alone, but subsidies are high and come with limited demand for public monetary returns.

On average, the public holds a 79 per cent funding share (when upfront and operation costs are taken into account) of facilities used for major league teams (Long, 2005, p. 136). The share is 100 per cent for two-thirds of NFL facilities. This means that the general public basically funds investments on behalf of the football business through subsidies, and that the franchise using the stadia returns a profit on the public subsidies.

The knock-on effects on profitability of such subsidies are huge. When the Pittsburg Steelers sold the naming rights for their stadium – built primarily by public money – to the Heinz Corporation, all $57 million went directly to the Steelers' owner (Easterbrook, 2013). Andranovich et al. (2001) point out that in order to pay for construction costs, special tax zones, travel and leisure taxes and sports lotteries have been introduced:

'These new tools are being used in addition to the traditional mechanisms of issuing bonds and shuffling capital budgets' (Andranovich et al., 2001, p. 117). These are all examples of S5 practices.

According to Long (2005, p. 137) especially newer stadium deals are in the disfavour of the taxpayer. She stresses that it is a myth that operating revenues are able to repay construction costs. 'In reality, operating revenues are almost completely offset by significant ongoing public expenses that are obscured in complex lease agreements' (Long, 2005, p. 137). Horne argues that there is significant scientific evidence to suggest that 'sports mega-events and megaprojects (such as stadium construction) shift public resources to private corporations' (Horne, 2007, p. 88). The lucrative monopoly power of the US pro leagues disproportionally distributes wealth from the consumers to the owners, or 'distorts stadium economy at the expense of tax payers' (Szymanski and Zimbalist, 2006, p. 6).

Generally, the massive subsidies can be interpreted as a specific effect of supply 'shortage' that creates distorted incentives for local governments competing for access to the limited supply.

Soft Credit and Soft Accounting

One of the favourable consequences of NFL's non-profit status is its capability of issuing tax-free bonds to finance stadium facilities. This is equivalent to H4 relaxation – soft credit. It raises the incentive for external investors to pour in capital, thus easing the necessary amount franchise owners have to raise or finance themselves.

From the outset, tax-free bonds were intended to aid local governments or other public organizations, not private profit seeking firms. In Congress proceedings it is explicitly pointed out that they should not be used for business ventures such as pro sports. However, 'Lobbyists for the NFL (and for professional basketball and baseball) have quietly arranged with legislators to alter key words of state and federal law to keep tax-free financing available . . .' (Easterbrook, 2013, p. 67).

In addition, the NFL saves the owners money by lending to them at lower interest rates than the teams could get on their own. In 2008, the NFL programme had $700 million in outstanding loans at 0 per cent interest, that is, soft forms of credit (Delaney, 2010, p. 17).

Long's (2005, 2012) research of public funding for major league sport facilities adds to the overall picture of soft environmental conditions through access to soft credit. This is facilitated through soft accounting. Finding a routine omission procedure regarding the reporting of relevant public costs associated with the construction and operation of major league facilities, Long (2005, p. 140) indicates that various stakeholders have an interest in underreporting public costs because (allegedly inaccurate) low costs serve to justify public spending on facilities. Adjusting for hitherto uncounted construction costs, foregone taxes (due to tax exemptions) and annual operation costs, Long shows how the adjustments reveal the real balance between public and private responsibility for major league stadia. This clearly ends in public 'disfavour', which is softness per se.

There are many other examples of soft accounting, for instance, creative accounting boosting the NFL owner's contribution to the NFL stadium construction programme (Delaney, 2010, p. 17). Such accounting practices among the major league owners are hardly unique in the US business context but add to the overall softening.

TOWARDS AN EXPANSION OF THE THEORETICAL FRAMEWORK

The preceding section adds to the literature on the differences between European and American professional sport leagues by means of applying Kornaï's SBC approach in a novel interpretation of American sport leagues. From this analysis it seems clear that the environment affects budget constraints not only in Europe but also with a kind of inverse result in the US leagues.

The expectations of *ex post* support that characterize the SBC mentality in Europe are turned upside down in the US leagues. Support is institutionalized and provided *ex ante*, but the mechanisms prompting sponsors and creditors to support the PTSCs are similar in the two otherwise contrasting cases. The major league franchises are treated in a similar way to the 'too-big-to-fail' European clubs and similar levels of SBC-induced support is provided. However, the actual forms and delivery of support is *ex ante* rather than *ex post*. In the USA, several institutional arrangements, exemptions and favourable financial conditions are in place in helping the enterprises to realize high levels of profits, which is the core objective of the US PTSCs. The profitability of American major leagues is to a large extent caused by the fact that they face various types of softness that guarantee stability, distort competition and prevent risk-taking in the clubs' decision making and management. Survival is not an issue; it is a question of enhanced super profits. But the mechanisms are largely similar to the ones pointed out by Kornaï. When environmental conditions are soft and the enterprises in question are not faced with the dynamic forces of market competition, wealth is allocated disproportionally – in this case to franchise owners – at the expense of fans, consumers of the sports product and taxpayers.

Other American team sport leagues are in a less fortunate situation. They typically operate with much harder budget constraints and deficits provoke rapid liquidation in the absence of softness. They are profit maximizing or profit seeking but highly vulnerable in the case of downturns. College sport is characterized by a completely different logic that comes closer to the SBC mechanisms. It is not profit maximizing or profit seeking but may generate huge revenue streams and surplus partly because of generous sponsors that provide significant *ex ante* support similar to the support to major league sport clubs.[11]

The specific characteristics of the different types of pro leagues in the USA are distinct from the European league types but there are also similarities that point at the need for a new typology of league types. In the remaining part of this section we will use the insight from the analysis of US professional leagues in an effort to supplement the standard categorization of PTSCs. From this perspective, similarities between Europe and the USA are to be found by pointing to the environmental (soft) conditions that face clubs and franchises,[12] while differences to a large extent are to be identified along the lines of (internal) club objectives. These still seem to be dominated by a win (or utility) maximization approach in Europe compared to a profit maximization or profit seeking approach in the USA. Based on these findings of similarities and differences, a new matrix outlining various ideal types of PTSCs/leagues is shown in Table 6.1.

The matrix is intended to highlight differences and similarities of pro league systems across the Atlantic. It takes internal objectives as well as environmental (external) conditions more thoroughly into account, showing that the distinction between (internal) objectives and (external) environment can serve as a fruitful tool for understanding the US and European contexts specifically and professional team sports in general.

Besides the traditional categorizations, the proposed new category of 'US franchises' is added as a supplement to the overall picture. This is the fifth column (on the far right). Here the PTSCs' primary goal is to aim for the highest possible profit that is also successfully achieved (see row 3: 'Financial result') due to the environmental softness that faces them (see row 2: 'Environmental condition/constraint').

The first and second columns represent the cases described by Kornaï where an enterprise (in this case a PTSC) fails to balance revenues and costs and faces a deficit. If a PTSC faces a hard budget constraint then it will close after a while if it is not able to cover its losses itself (see row 4: 'Survival?') through, for example, earlier savings or initial capital. If the PTSC is rescued from the outside instead, then its budget constraint is soft.

The third column represents the traditional (European) win maximization subject to a break-even constraint case briefly touched upon above

Table 6.1 Ideal type professional team sports clubs

Context	Europe	Europe	Europe	(Mainly) USA	USA
Sporting versus economic club objectives	Win maximization	Win maximization	Win maximization	Profit maximizing	Profit maximizing
Environmental condition/ constraint	HBC	SBC	HBC	HBC	(Inverse) Softness
Financial result	Deficits	Deficits	Break even	Profits/Deficits	Super profits
Survival?	No	Yes	Yes	Yes/No	Yes

(X_3 in Figure 6.1). In such cases, environmental conditions are difficult to determine due to the fact that as long as the enterprise in question breaks even, the question of whether the environmental conditions are hard or soft never really materializes because no deficits are present. Should a deficit occur, then the answer to the question about the character of the budget constraint will surface, which represents a shift to either the first or the second column.

Finally, the fourth column is the ideal type representation of profit maximizing minor leagues in the USA who face hard budget constraints and are forced to fold in case of serious deficits. Profit maximizing clubs under conditions of hard budget constraints exist in Europe as well but they are less prevalent as reflected in few instances of defunct leagues as a result of financial distress.

In practice, other situations may also prevail. The matrix only covers ideal types and, in reality, maximization of profits hardly represents most actual cases. Profitable sport clubs or team franchises are seldom profit maximizers in a literal sense. Rather, they align the profit motive with other goals such as sporting success (win maximization). In the section about US pro leagues we have called this profit seeking. This represents a combination of objectives and is not in this sense an ideal type.[13]

CONCLUSION

This chapter has taken Kornaï's theoretical perspective a step further by applying and advancing it in an analysis of the European versus the American context of professional league sports. Emphasizing differences and similarities in Europe and the USA while simultaneously adding an extra dimension to the SBC approach, we have proposed that profit maximizing subject to a SBC is what characterizes PTSCs in the USA. Differences across the Atlantic mainly concern clubs' primary objectives, and not the environments that face the PTSCs. They are, to a large extent, identical.

However, different institutional (environmental) conditions can make a difference when it comes to the realization of profits across Europe and the USA. A relaxation of (environmental) conditions of hardness eases the possibilities of making a profit, as is the case in the USA, which has institutionalized an inverse kind of softness. This stands in contrast to the European context where conditions *ex ante* seem harder even though expectations of *ex post* support are real and institutionalized.

One may raise the question as to why such similarities – which become differences when it comes to league structures and *ex ante* conditions – of softness have evolved. One simple answer may provide part of the explanation. European PTSCs were not intended as vehicles of profit from the start, as was the case in the USA where the institutional (soft) conditions were put to work more or less from when the pro leagues were established (Szymanski and Zimbalist, 2006, p. 129). In Europe amateurism and non-profit status dominated sport at the beginning. Its leagues became professional only a few decades ago, but they still held onto their original open structure. Supplemented by a very strong foothold in American popular culture, professional sport in the USA has found a permanent way of institutionalizing environmental softness by drawing heavily on political influence and lobbying to secure recurring profits.

The extraordinary exemptions, subsidies and privileges that apply to the pro league teams is due to the fact that sport is such an ingrained part of the American psyche and culture (Nixon II, 1984; Mandelbaum, 2004; Bowers et al., 2011; Silk, 2012). Because of sport's cultural significance the major leagues are able to get away with lobbying and practices that other business sectors are not.

It is likely that the American system will stay on its track of profitability while the European clubs will suffer from a high level of club competition that only allows a very small elite to generate profits (Szymanski and Zimbalist, 2006). The competition structure in the European context – often described as a 'rat race' (Franck, 2013) – makes it very difficult to realize a profit from club activities.[14] If UEFA's Financial Fair Play programme effectively punishes offenders by the letter, and if the European Commission's current investigation into established practices of state aids to sport clubs concludes in real restrictions of the ways in which public authorities can support pro clubs in Europe, the likelihood of future bankruptcies among European PTSCs could potentially grow. On the other hand, a hardening of environmental conditions in Europe may have a positive societal effect if a closer link between break-even or profits and survival is established as anticipated.

NOTES

1. American will be used for North American in the rest of the chapter.
2. How to distinguish empirically between different degrees of hardness and/or softness is an important question but not a theme for discussion in this context.
3. We use football as a prominent case of SBC. The same mechanisms characterize other professional team sports in Europe.
4. A small minority can even be characterized as profit maximizers or profit seekers (Storm, 2013).
5. A unique exception is Glasgow Rangers that was liquidated by the end of the 2011–12 season and relegated to the fourth tier of Scottish league football in spite of its strong cultural role as identity marker for Protestant Scots.

6. This is because the model assumes a diminishing effect on revenue due to declining competitive balance (in turn affecting demand) if the club buys a disproportionate amount of the given talent pool in a league (Késenne, 1996, p. 20).
7. The softness of budget constraints in the American context not only increases revenues but also lowers costs, which can be illustrated by a falling cost curve. This is not included in the figure in order to simplify the illustration.
8. Or a direct effect of hard governing practices or increased productivity inside the organization.
9. According to Delaney (2010): 'The financial results of the NFL's lobbying efforts in the 1960s are probably worth enough to buy several small countries' (p. 6).
10. It is difficult to distinguish between S3 and S5. Public grants or subsidies are often used to finance investments and there is no clear way to distinguish between these two forms of budget constraint relaxation. In this section we will identify relaxations that can be interpreted as equivalents to public grants and subsidies (S3) and (soft) investments (S5).
11. Because of the complexity of this case we shall refrain from an attempt to position college leagues in the following matrix of ideal types.
12. Even though the practical arrangements that make up the specific environments vary across the Atlantic.
13. 'Profit seeking' may be interpreted as utility maximization with profit as one of the variables to maximize. As such, it could perhaps be integrated in the matrix as a sixth ideal type.
14. For a comprehensive discussion of the mechanisms behind the unprofitability of European PTSCs, see Dietl et al. (2008) or Whitney (1993).

REFERENCES

Andranovich, G., M. Burbank and C. Heying (2001), 'Olympic cities: lessons learned from mega-event politics', *Journal of Urban Affairs*, **23**(2), 113–31.

Andreff, W. (2007a), 'French football: a financial crisis rooted in weak governance', *Journal of Sports Economics*, **8**(6), 652–61.

Andreff, W. (2007b), 'Governance issues in French professional football', in P. Rodríguez, S. Kesenne and J. Garcia (eds), *Governance and Competition in Professional Sports Leagues*, Oviedo: Ediciones de la Universidad de Oviedo, pp. 47–78.

Andreff, W. (2011), 'Some comparative economics of the organization of sports: competition and regulation in North American vs. European professional team sports leagues', *European Journal of Comparative Economics*, **8**(1), 3–27.

Andreff, W. (2014), 'Building blocks for a disequilibrium model of a European sports league', *International Journal of Sport Finance*, **9**(1), 20–38.

Ascari, G. and P. Gagnepain (2006), 'Spanish football', *Journal of Sports Economics*, **7**(1), 76–9.

Baade, R.A. (1987), 'Is there an economic rationale for subsidizing sports stadiums?' *Policy Study*, **13**, 1–26.

Baade, R.A. (1994), 'Stadiums, professional sports, and economic development: assessing the reality', Working Paper, Heartland Institute, available at http://news.heartland.org/sites/all/modules/custom/heartland_migration/files/pdfs/8828.pdf (accessed 2 June 2015).

Baade, R.A. (1996), 'Professional sports as catalysts for metropolitan economic development', *Journal of Urban Affairs*, **18**(1), 1–17.

Baade, R.A. and R.F. Dye (1988), 'Sports stadiums and area development: a critical review', *Economic Development Quarterly*, **2**(3), 265–75.

Barajas, A. and P. Rodríguez (2010), 'Spanish football clubs' finances: crisis and player salaries', *International Journal of Sport Finance*, **5**(1), 52–66.

Beech, J., S. Horsman and J. Magraw (2008), 'The circumstances in which English clubs become insolvent', Research Paper, Coventry University.

Beech, J., S. Horsman and J. Magraw (2010), 'Insolvency events among English football clubs', *International Journal of Sports Marketing and Sponsorship*, **11**(3), 236–49.

Bowers, M.T., L. Chalip and B.C. Green (2011), 'Youth sport development in the United States and the illusion of synergy', in B. Houlihan and M. Green (eds), *Routledge Handbook of Sports Development*, Abingdon: Routledge, pp. 173–83.

Buraimo, B., R. Simmons and S. Szymanski (2006), 'English football', *Journal of Sports Economics*, **7**(1), 29–46.

Cairns, J., N. Jennett and P.J. Sloane (1986), 'The economics of professional team sports: a survey of theory and evidence', *Journal of Economic Studies*, **13**(1), 3–80.

Delaney, A.B. (2010), 'Taking a sack: the NFL and its underseved tax-exempt status', Working Paper, available at https://papers.ssrn.com/sol3/papers.cfm?abstract_id=1605281 (accessed 11 December 2014).

Dietl, H.M. and E. Franck (2007), 'Governance failure and financial crisis in German football', *Journal of Sports Economics*, **8**(6), 662–9.

Dietl, H.M., E. Franck and M. Lang (2008), 'Overinvestment in team sports leagues: a contest theory model', *Scottish Journal of Political Economy*, **55**(3), 353–68.

Dimitropoulos, P. (2013), 'The impact of IFRS on accounting quality: evidence from Greece', *Advances in Accounting*, 11/2013, **29**(1), 108–23.

Dimitropoulos, P. (2015), 'The new UEFA Club Licensing Regulations and the quality of financial information: evidence from European football clubs', Research Paper, University of the Peloponese.

Easterbrook, G. (2013), *The King of Sports. Football's Impact on America*, 1st edn, New York: St Martin's Press.

Euchner, C.C. (1999), 'Tourism and sports: the serious competition for play', in D.R. Judd and S.S. Fainstein (eds), *The Tourist City*, New Haven, CT: Yale University Press, pp. 215–32.

European Commission (2013), 'State aid: Commission opens in-depth investigation into public funding of certain Spanish professional football clubs', Press release, 18 December, available at http://europa.eu/rapid/press-release_IP-13-1287_en.htm (accessed 11 December 2014).

Foot, J. (2006), *Calcio: A History of Italian Football*, London: Fourth Estate.

Fort, R.D. (2000), 'European and North American sports differences (?)', *Scottish Journal of Political Economy*, **47**(4), 431–55.

Franck, E. (2013), 'Financial Fair Play in European club football: what is it all about?', *International Journal of Sport Finance*, **9**(3), 193–217.

Frick, B. and J. Prinz (2006), 'Crisis? What crisis? Football in Germany', *Journal of Sports Economics*, **7**(1), 60–75.

Grant, W. (2007), 'An analytical framework for a political economy of football', *British Politics*, **2**(1), 69–90.

Hoehn, T. and S. Szymanski (1999), 'The Americanization of European football', *Economic Policy*, **14**(28), 205–40.

Horne, J. (2007), 'The four "knowns" of sports mega-events', *Leisure Studies*, **26**(1), 81–96.

Kearney, A.T. (2010), *The A.T. Kearny EU Football Sustainability Study: Is European Football Too Popular to Fail?*, Düsseldorf: A.T. Kearney.

Késenne, S. (1996), 'League management in professional team sports with win maximising clubs', *European Journal for Sport Management*, **2**(2), 14–22.

Késenne, S. (2002), 'Improving the competitive balance and the salary distribution in professional team sports', in C. Barros, M. Ibrahímo and S. Szymanski (eds), *Transatlantic Sport: The Comparative Economics of North American and European Sports*, Cheltenham, UK and Northampton, MA, USA: Edward Elgar, pp. 95–124.

Késenne, S. (2006), 'The objective function of a team', in W. Andreff and S. Szymanski (eds), *Handbook on the Economics of Sport*, Cheltenham, UK and Northampton, MA, USA: Edward Elgar, pp. 601–9.

Kornaï, J. (1980a), 'Hard and soft budget constraint', *Acta Oeconomica*, **25**(3–4), 231–45.

Kornaï, J. (1980b), *Economics of Shortage*, Vol. B, Amsterdam: North Holland Publishing.

Kornaï, J. (1986), 'The soft budget constraint', *Kyklos*, **39**(1), 3–30.

Kornaï, J. (2001), 'Hardening the budget constraint: the experience of the post-socialist countries', *European Economic Review*, **45**(9), 1573–99.

Kornai, J. (2006), *By Force of Thought: Irregular Memoirs of an Intellectual Journey*, Cambridge, MA: MIT Press.

Kornaï, J. (2014), 'The soft budget constraint', *Acta Oeconomica*, **64**(Suppl.), 25–79.

Kornaï, J., E. Maskin and G. Roland (2003), 'Understanding the soft budget constraint', *Journal of Economic Literature*, **41**(4), 1095–136.

Lago, U., R. Simmons and S. Szymanski (2006), 'The financial crisis in European football: an introduction', *Journal of Sports Economics*, **7**(1), 3–12.

Long, J.G. (2005), 'Full count: the real cost of public funding for major league sports facilities', *Journal of Sports Economics*, **6**(2), 119–43.

Long, J.G. (2012), *Public-private Partnerships for Major League Sports Facilities*, Oxford: Routledge.

Mandelbaum, M. (2004), *The Meaning of Sports: Why Americans Watch Baseball, Football, and Basketball and What They See When They Do*, New York: Public Affairs.

Maskin, E.S. (1999), 'Recent theoretical work on the soft budget constraint', *American Economic Review*, **89**(2), 421–5.

Morrow, S. (2006), 'Impression management in football club financial reporting', *International Journal of Sport Finance*, **1**(2), 96–108.

Nauright, J. and J. Ramfjord (2010), 'Who owns England's game? American professional sporting influences and foreign ownership in the Premier League', *Soccer & Society*, **11**(4), 428–41.

Nixon II, H.L. (1984), *Sport and the American Dream*, New York: Leisure Press.

Noll, R.G. (1974), 'Attendance and price setting', in R.G. Noll (ed.), *Government and the Sport Business*, Washington, DC: Brookings Institution, pp. 115–58.

Rosentraub, M.S., D. Swindell, M. Przybylski and D.R. Mullins (1994), 'Sport and downtown development strategy. If you build it, will jobs come?', *Journal of Urban Affairs*, **16**(3), 221–39.

Sandy, R., P.J. Sloane and M.S. Rosentraub (2004), *The Economics of Sport: An International Perspective*, Basingstoke: Palgrave Macmillan.

Silk, M. (2012), *The Cultural Politics of Post-9/11 American Sport*, New York: Routledge.

Storm, R.K. (2013), 'Kommercielle sportsklubber: følelser eller forretning?' ('Professional team sports clubs in Europe: emotional attachments or a profitable business?'), PhD Thesis, University of Southern Denmark, Odense.

Storm, R.K. and K. Nielsen (2012), 'Soft budget constraints in professional football', *European Sport Management Quarterly*, **12**(2), 183–201.

Szymanski, S. (2004), 'Is there a European model of sports?', in R. Fort and J. Fizel (eds), *International Sports Economic Comparison*, Westport, CT: Praeger, pp. 19–37.

Szymanski, S. and S. Hall (2003), 'Making money out of football', Unpublished manuscript, The Business School, Imperial College London.

Szymanski, S. and R. Smith (1997), 'The English football industry: profit, performance and industrial structure', *International Review of Applied Economics*, **11**(1), 135–53.

Szymanski, S. and A.S. Zimbalist (2006), *National Pastime: How Americans Play Baseball and the Rest of the World Plays Soccer*, Washington, DC: Brookings Institution Press.

Tien, C., H.C. Lo and H.W. Lin (2011), 'The economic benefits of mega events: a myth or reality? A longitidinal study on the Olympic Games', *Journal of Sport Management*, **25**, 11–23.

UEFA (2010), *The European Footballing Landscape. Licensing Benchmarking Report. Financial Year 2009*, Nyon: UEFA.

Vrooman, J. (2000), 'The economics of American sport leagues', *Scottish Journal of Political Economy*, **47**(4), 364–98.

Whitney, J.D. (1993), 'Bidding till bankrupt: destructive competition in professional team sports', *Economic Inquiry*, **31**(1), 100–115.

7. Governance of professional team sports clubs: agency problem and soft budget constraint

Wladimir Andreff

INTRODUCTION

When studying and assessing corporate governance, mainstream economics refers to the principal-agent model in a context where organizations (firms) operate in a competitive market and whose residual claimants maximize their revenues leading to profit maximization. Transferring such analysis to professional team sports leagues and clubs is not straightforward since a league actually does not operate in a genuine competitive market. A league is a monopoly on the supply side of its product market and a monopsony on the demand side of its major input (talent) market; both markets are not purely or even practically competitive. By the same token, tied by the co-production of their games and league rules, clubs behave as members of a cartel and benefit, through league revenue redistribution, from a windfall rent derived from the league monopoly and monopsony positions. Thus, even if teams are assumed to be profit maximizers, like they are supposed to be in closed North American professional team sports leagues, a team's access to profit is driven by a specific economic environment of monopoly pricing, supply side restriction on quantities and demand side bargaining power that usually guarantee a profit that includes monopoly and monopsony rents, on the one hand. On the other hand, profit maximization is the best hindrance against lasting deficits and debts, and keeps clubs from running under a soft budget constraint.

Now when teams do not actually maximize profit, as assumed to be the case in open European professional team sports leagues, absent profit maximization neither hinders clubs' soft budget constraints from emerging nor the clubs' cumulative financial deficits and debts. Clubs then clearly operate in a universe alien to the principal-agent model and the analysis of clubs' budget constraints must prevail. League downstream monopolistic and upstream monopsonistic strategies, without a profit objective, would be geared towards alleviating budget constraints, and clubs would be able to take it easy and be run under a soft budget constraint. A lax management tolerating recurrent deficits would be the most evident consequence of such a weak governance structure due to market power of the league and clubs. However, lasting club deficits would, at the end of the day, raise the issue of league financial stability without which the continuity of fixtures and the credibility of sporting outcomes might be in jeopardy. If this were the case, the question of hardening clubs' budget constraints would urgently call for appropriate solutions.

This chapter starts with an overview of how the standard principal-agent model specifies the preconditions for good and bad corporate governance when residual claimants aim at maximizing their profit. How well the principal-agent approach can fit with profit-maximizing professional sports teams in North American leagues and with European football clubs whose shares are floated in stock markets is then assessed. When clubs are not-for-profit organizations, if their budget constraints are soft, they are often driven into bad governance practices, mismanagement, recurrent deficits, bad debts, payment arrears and bail-outs; this is exemplified by European and French professional football. The resulting financial instability of a league incurs a risk of distorting the sporting contest, which calls for financial regulation to improve club governance: some recommendations are followed by a brief assessment of the French football league auditing system, and the Union of European Football Associations' (UEFA) Financial Fair Play through the lens of the previous analysis.

CORPORATE GOVERNANCE: PRINCIPAL-AGENT MODEL AND PROFIT MAXIMIZATION

A major difficulty in evaluating the governance structure of an organization is that actual models of corporate governance often represent second-best solutions to the standard principal-agent problem. They basically address the issues of governing large corporations, primarily stockholding companies. North American professional sport teams usually are not stockholding companies even though they are assumed to be profit-maximizing entities. Several European professional sports clubs have adopted the juridical form of a stockholding company in the past two decades; even when their shares are floated in a stock market they do not behave as expected by the principal-agent model.

The Principal-agent Model: A Profit-maximizing Objective

An agency relationship arises whenever one or more individuals, called principals, hire one or more other individuals, called agents, to perform some service and then delegate decision-making authority to the agents. The primary agency relationships in business are those: (a) between the owners and employees; (b) between stockholders (owners) and managers; and (c) between debt-holders, if any, and owners. Since the principal (owner) has less information than the agent (manager, employee) about what the latter is doing within the organization, a moral hazard situation emerges that may drift into adverse selection in decision-making. Thus, in a commercial enterprise, the principal must design a suitable procedure for inciting agents to act according to his or her owner's interest, that is, maximizing profit and the share value of the corporation. Therefore, efficient management requires appropriate incentives sent by the principal to agents (Laffont and Martimort, 2003).

At first glance, agency relationships do exist in professional sports teams: (a) between the owner(s) and recruited players; (b) between owners or stockholders – if the club is a stockholding company – and managers and coaches; and (c) between debt-holders and owners if the club is indebted. If an owner's utility is that its team wins, the service requested from players, coaches and managers is to behave in such a way as to win as many games as possible on the pitch (win-maximizing teams); these employees must be rewarded and incited accordingly in terms of salaries and bonuses. If instead the team owner's objective is to make as much money as possible, a first priority service requested from managers is to raise revenues over costs (profit-maximizing teams), a behaviour quite close to that of other firms – outside the sports industry – in a market economy. If the team holds debts, the owners are committed to repay.

The essence of an agency problem is the separation of finance and management or – in standard terminology – of ownership and control that emerged in big corporations, in particular in the interwar US economy. This separation had been put forward since the 1930s as the major characteristic of managerial capitalism in the making (Berle and Means, 1932) and emphasized by those theoreticians (Galbraith, 1967) who assumed that corporate governance, held up by managers, was becoming independent from ownership in corporations of market economies. With the separation of ownership and control in joint stock companies, important decision-makers (managers) do not bear a substantial share of the wealth effects of their decisions. The principal-agent model is both a reaction against the idea and practices of managerial capitalism and an attempt to go beyond the corporate control theory that prevailed after Berle and Means in which, if no controlling owner or group of owners has a majority or a blocking minority of shares – bigger than that of any other coordinated group of shareholders (Andreff, 1996) –, a corporation will be insider controlled by managers. Coming back to a Coasian contractual view of the firm (Coase, 1937), the latter was henceforth analysed as a nexus of written and unwritten contracts (Jensen and Meckling, 1976), an analysis that resulted in the principal-agent model (Fama and Jensen, 1983).

Agency problems arise because contracts are not written and enforced without cost. Agency costs include the costs of structuring, monitoring, and bonding a set of contracts among agents with conflicting interests, plus the residual loss incurred because the cost of full enforcement of contracts exceeds the benefits (Fama and Jensen, 1983, p. 327). The residual risk is borne by those who contract for the rights to net cash flows: they are the residual claimants; but the decision process is in the hands of professional managers whose interests for increased managerial revenues and in-kind benefits are not identical to those of residual claimants, usually stockholders whose objective is profit maximizing[1] to get dividends or a shareholder value increase. Expanding shareholders' supervision over managers derives from considering the shareholders as the only genuine owners of corporations with the exclusion of any other stakeholders. As residual claimants of the firm's net income, they are assumed to stand last in line for the distribution of gains or losses and, thus, have the appropriate incentives to make accurate discretionary strategic decisions (Easterbrook and Fischel, 1991).

In designing the contract that specifies what the manager does with the funds provided by the financier-shareholder, the manager and the financier have to fix how the returns will be divided among them and since complete contracts (predicting all the future events) are technologically infeasible, they have to allocate residual control rights – that is, the rights to make decisions in circumstances not fully foreseen by the contract (Grossman and Hart, 1986). But the financiers – as outsiders to the firm – are not qualified or informed enough to decide what to do – the very reason they hired managers who are qualified and fully informed insiders. As a consequence, managers end up with substantial residual control rights and therefore discretion to allocate funds as they choose. Managers can expropriate shareholders by entrenching themselves and staying on the job even if they are no longer competent or qualified to run the firm (Shleifer and Vishny, 1989). Poor managers who resist being replaced are a frequent manifestation of the agency problem – an occurrence that is not alien to professional sports clubs.

Owners and Managerial Discipline

The capacity to monitor managers – and through them other employees – is crucial for shareholders. When shareowners are able to monitor and discipline managers, profits are higher than otherwise, profit maximization is effective. Large shareholders address the agency problem in that they both have a general interest in profit maximizing and enough control over the firm's assets to have their interests respected (Shleifer and Vishny, 1997); they are controlling owners and form a 'hard core' of block-holders (Andreff, 1992). Quite logically, the principal-agent model leans towards establishing such hard cores of monitoring shareholders: Shleifer and Vishny (1997) argue in favour of block shareholdings, no matter who the block-holders are since they will be able to fire and replace undisciplined managers (those who do not maximize profit) – a so-called contractual discipline. Corporate governance will be efficient and avoid loss-making under such discipline.

A second solution to the agency problem is a well-functioning capital market, in particular a stock market. Initial public offerings (IPOs) and stock trade are supposed to provide strong corporate governance as well. Discipline over managers is exercised by the capital market through its effects on the firm's stocks and through mechanisms such as takeovers (Hart, 1995). In particular, hostile takeovers play a role in disciplining managers. Once taken over by another firm, some or most incumbent managers will be fired; this permanent challenge to management is coined a takeover discipline. However, with dispersed share ownership this lever for good corporate governance suffers from weaknesses such as a general inability by numerous shareholders to monitor and collectively discipline managers, a system of incentives that orients managers towards short-term goals and an emphasis on financial manoeuvres to boost financial results at the expense of sound business practices and the long-term development of the firm's productive potential.

Finally, if a company is repeatedly in the red and accumulates increasing debts over time, debt-holders rights over owners will be exercised in calling for and obtaining the company's liquidation; this again is likely to threaten incumbent managers and discipline their decisions – a so-called bankruptcy discipline.

Strong and Weak Corporate Governance Structures

Strong corporate governance structures is such that managers, and through them employees, are submitted to the three aforementioned sorts of discipline, namely in stockholding companies; this is a fundamental prerequisite for good governance. When facing managerial entrenchment shareholders may get rid of incumbent managers as soon as there is a competitive market for managerial talents, an efficient capital market with a possible threat for a corporation to be taken over if unsatisfied shareholders sell their stocks and an enforced bankruptcy law.

Therefore, in the perspective of the principal-agent model, all corporate governance structures can be ranked on a scale at the lower end of which are found state-owned enterprises where shareholders are non-existent and all decisions are taken by bureaucrats. Then follow insider-controlled (by managers, employees) organizations. On the top of the hierarchy stand companies outsider controlled by banks, core shareholders or a single powerful owner. Strong corporate governance structures are the ones that operate under:

a. Outsider control by owners whether they are a hard core of monitoring shareholders, a tycoon, family members of a former tycoon, banks or institutional investors (including investment funds) or a coalition of such owners (Andreff, 2000a).
b. Insider control by a big boss, being both the single owner and top manager (that is, the tycoon himself), which often happens before a firm's incorporation and its shares are offered to the public; with an individual owner-manager, ownership and control go together. In tying together residual claims and residual control in a same owner-manager, a firm (a football club) bears the full financial impact of his or her decisions (Franck, 2010). If the roles of owner and manager are combined in the same person, this person will supply the first-best level of effort and the principal-agent problem will not exist. Of course, the owner-manager may choose to take his or her income in the form of perquisites or a high salary, but the cost of these perquisites simply reduces the profits that he or she will receive as the owner of the firm.

For the principal-agent model, weak corporate governance structures are those where insider control is at work; this pertains to situations in which chief officers, senior executives, managers or personnel have the last say on strategic decisions, namely recruitment and finance. Insider control may result from managers being empowered to make the latter decisions and practice self-appointment or remaining uncontrolled by dispersed shareholders; it may also result from management buy-outs where the director and managers immediately use their supervision and cash flow rights in such a way as to take over all the enterprise's residual revenue and strip the most interesting assets (Andreff, 2006a). Even worse from the principal-agent model standpoint, employee buy-outs and ESOP (employee stock ownership programmes) transfer strategic decisions to employees whose objectives are neither profit maximizing nor good jobs and high salaries for managers but to avoid being made redundant and resist downward pressures on wages.

ASSESSING CLUB GOVERNANCE FROM A PRINCIPAL-AGENT PERSPECTIVE

Since they are assumed to be profit maximizing, do professional teams in North American sports leagues have good governance from the viewpoint of the principal-agent model? Moreover, in European football a number of professional clubs were transformed into stockholding companies and some proceeded with IPOs in the past two decades.[2] Did this lead to improved governance?

Ownership and Governance in North American Professional Sports Teams

The principal-agent model usually is not referred to when studying North American professional team sports leagues even less so with the purpose of checking whether teams enjoy good or suffer from bad governance. One of the rare references to this model (Miceli, 2004) argues that the reserve clause provides mutual benefits to players (agents) and owners (principals), beyond the bargaining approach to contracting, or the conflicting views emerging in players' strikes and owners' lock-outs. The concept of residual claimants has been applied to sports league governance (Ross, 2007) but, to the best of our knowledge, not yet to sports team governance. Here, the aforementioned lessons drawn from the principal-agent model are geared towards assessing team profitability and governance.

First, notice that in North American team sports leagues based on a franchise system, teams are not stockholding companies in Major League Baseball (MLB), the National Football League (NFL), the National Basketball Association (NBA) and the National Hockey League (NHL) and are not floated in the stock market; in NFL, IPOs are simply not allowed. Indeed, in 2014, 102 teams (82 per cent of the 122 teams in these four major sports leagues) are both owned and managed by one single rich owner or in some cases two co-owners, many of them listed by Forbes among the richest people in the USA; this is so for 31 teams in NFL, 26 teams in MLB, 24 teams in NBA and 21 teams in NHL (see Table 7A.1 in the appendix). The 20 remaining teams are nearly all owned by a commercial company[3] (outsider control) with the exception of Green Bay Packers. The latter is a publicly traded non-profit company with a strict limitation on how many shares anyone can buy, with the consequence that the company is owned by 364,122 minority shareholders. This is the only North American professional sports team that may be suspected, in a principal-agent perspective, of being held up by insiders since it is extremely complicated coordinating over 360,000 owners in order to supervise team managers. But Green Bay Packers has been profitable every year since 2003 (Table 7.1) and its managers have succeeded in governing this business in such a way as to increase the asset value of the team by 126 per cent over 12 years (Table 7.2). Potential insider control has not drifted into bad governance.

For all other 121 teams either owned by one rich big boss or under a large outsider control, are the expectations of the principal-agent model confirmed? In all these cases, it is assumed that bearing the contractual residual risk on the rights to net cash flows, each single rich owner or outsider-controlling company must behave as the residual claimant. It must discipline managers with a view to maximizing the team's positive residual operating income – profit. Accordingly, contractual discipline is always there, the team is managed by its rich owner or the CEO of an outside commercial company obviously empowered with a contractual discipline capacity since he or she[4] can fire any manager, coach or player in tune with their contract terms; indeed, firing and hiring personnel is a strategic decision and current commitment of team owners in North American leagues. Thus, it remains basically to check profit maximizing, takeover and bankruptcy disciplines in such teams. The principal-agent model would conclude that team governance is good if these three elements complete contractual discipline.

First, it is necessary to observe whether each team actually strives to maximize its profit and most often succeeds in being profitable as assumed in theoretical modelling of North American team sports leagues. Table 7.1 shows many (370) occurrences of operating losses in the four major sports leagues over the past 12 years accounting for 26 per cent out of all the 1434 (122 x 11 + 92 x 1[5]) observed net operating incomes. Thus, it must be concluded that all teams maximize profit but on average more than one-quarter of them fail to be profitable. For the latter, the quality of their governance is called into question. One-quarter of teams/years do not fit with the theoretical model of North American team sports leagues, a point that must be further qualified team by team.

Looking at NFL teams' operating incomes, only 15 operating losses are witnessed over 12 years, 4 per cent of total operating results, with nine teams concerned. NFL fits the best with the profit-maximizing assumption. It shows good governance through its teams' management outcome. Most NFL teams in the red have exhibited a deficit in just one

Table 7.1 Occurrences of operational losses in North American major team sports leagues, 2003–2014, $ million

Major League Baseball	2003	2004	2005	2006	2007	2008	2009	2010	2011	2012	2013	2014
Arizona Diamondbacks	22.2	15.2	18.7									5.8
Atlanta Braves		0.3						0.6				
Boston Red Sox	2.1		11.3	18.5		19.1			1.1			
Chicago White Sox												2.7
Cincinnati Reds												11.6
Cleveland Indians	1.0											1.9
Colorado Rockies		6.3	7.8									
Detroit Tigers	5.3						26.3		29.1		0.4	
Houston Astros	0.8	1.9										
Kansas City Royals	11.2											6.5
Los Angeles Angels of Anaheim	3.7	5.5	30.0	2.6						1.2	12.9	
Los Angeles Dodgers	25.0	19.1	7.4									80.9
Miami (Florida) Marlins	14.0	11.6	11.9	11.9							7.1	8.0
Milwaukee Brewers	6.1											
Minnesota Twins		7.1	0.5									
New York Mets		19.3	11.2	16.1	25.2				6.2	40.8	2.4	
New York Yankees			37.1	50.0		47.3	3.7					9.1
Philadelphia Phillies	11.9	12.5								11.6		20.9
Pittsburgh Pirates	1.6	0.3										
St Louis Cardinals	2.0	11.1	3.9									
Texas Rangers	24.5	28.5									8.7	4.9
Toronto Blue Jays	23.9					1.8					4.8	14.9
Washington Cardinals	9.1	8.3	3.0									

Table 7.1 (continued)

National Football League	2003	2004	2005	2006	2007	2008	2009	2010	2011[a]	2012	2013	2014
Atlanta Falcons					3.4							
Cleveland Browns								2.9	2.9			
Detroit Lions					1.8	3.1			7.7	15.9		15.9
Indianapolis Colts					17.3							
Miami Dolphins					19.1			7.7				
Minnesota Vikings												
New Orleans Saints				4.1			5.7					
Oakland Raiders							2.4					
Seattle Seahawks					2.6							

Nl Basketball Association	2003	2004	2005	2006	2007	2008	2009	2010	2011[a]	2012	2013	2014
Atlanta Hawks		8.4						2.0	7.3	15.0	18.7	3.6
Brooklyn Nets		1.6	7.4	6.1	8.0	1.3	0.9	13.9	10.2	23.6	16.6	19.0
Charlotte Bobcats							4.9	15.1	20.0	25.5	13.3	
Dallas Mavericks		17.7	33.6	17.8	24.4	1.6	13.6	17.4	7.8	3.9		
Denver Nuggets	5.0					4.8	26.3		11.7	1.2		
Detroit Pistons										9.7		
Golden State Warriors	0.6			3.1								
Indiana Pacers		19.7			12.5	1.3	6.5	15.7	16.9	10.5		
Memphis Grizzlies			4.1	15.6	18.5	10.9	3.2	7.1	2.6	24.8	12.5	
Miami Heat							1.1		5.9			
Milwaukee Bucks	8.5	15.1		1.5				7.4	2.0	7.6	0.5	
Minnesota Timberwolves			20.0	5.0		1.9	5.7	6.8	6.7	6.8	4.5	
New Orleans Pelicans	8.3			3.9				0.1	5.9	2.7		2.7
New York Knicks			14.3		39.0	42.2						

	2003	2004	2005[a]	2006	2007	2008	2009	2010	2011	2012	2013[a]	2014
Oklahoma City Thunder				7.8								
Orlando Magic				9.5	20.4	5.7	9.4	2.2	23.1	16.0		
Philadelphia 76ers					6.2	2.8			1.2	10.3	0.8	3.8
Portland Trail Blazers	22.8	85.1	47.0	31.5	15.2	25.1	0.9	20.3		8.1	10.1	
Sacramento Kings		16.8						2.8	9.8			
San Antonio Spurs									4.7			
Seattle Supersonics				7.8		5.7						
Toronto Raptors				1.3								
Utah Jazz									3.9	16.4		
Washington Wizards									5.2	3.4		
National Hockey League	**2003**	**2004**	**2005[a]**	**2006**	**2007**	**2008**	**2009**	**2010**	**2011**	**2012**	**2013[a]**	**2014**
Anaheim Ducks	10.8	22.4		0.2				5.2	8.8	10.8	3.9	3.7
Arizona (Phoenix) Coyotes	21.1	7.8		6.0	11.4	9.7	18.5	20.1	24.0	20.6	8.9	4.6
Atlanta Thrashers	0.9			5.4								
Boston Bruins					0.6	3.0						
Buffalo Sabres	5.3	10.5			4.9	8.9	5.2	7.9	5.9	10.4	1.0	
Calgary Flames	5.8				0.7		0.8					
Carolina Hurricanes	13.0	18.2			7.5	11.5	4.6	7.3	4.8	9.4	3.4	14.0
Chicago Black Hawks					3.6							
Colorado Avalanche	3.9	1.1										
Columbus Blue Jackets				4.0	5.6	7.1	9.9	7.3	13.5	18.7		
Dallas Stars		0.3										
Detroit Red Wings	13.7	16.4							1.4			6.3
Edmonton Oilers	0.1											

Table 7.1 (continued)

National Hockey League	2003	2004	2005a	2006	2007	2008	2009	2010	2011	2012	2013a	2014
Florida Panthers	9.2	3.7		1.9	7.1	9.4	13.6	9.6	7.0	12.0	7.7	15.6
Los Angeles Kings		5.1							1.9			
Minnesota Wild					1.7			2.3	6.0	3.9	13.6	5.4
Montreal Canadiens	5.4											
Nashville Predators	2.8			1.1	9.4	1.3	5.7	5.5	7.8	3.4	0.8	
New Jersey Devils	9.4	13.9		6.7	15.3				5.6		4.2	2.2
New York Islanders	10.9	9.5		9.2	11.6	8.8	5.6	4.5	7.7	16.0	1.2	2.5
New York Rangers	6.9	3.3										
Ottawa Senators	2.0	5.0					3.8	3.8				
Philadelphia Flyers		4.1				1.8						
Pittsburgh Penguins		0.6							1.6			
San Jose Sharks	8.6				5.1		5.0	6.2	8.0	0.9		
St Louis Blues	29.4	28.8			5.5	8.6	2.7	6.2	2.3	10.0	2.5	6.5
Tampa Bay Lightning	0.7						2.2	7.9	8.4	13.1	5.4	11.9
Washington Capitals	21.0	14.7				6.9	4.9	9.1	7.9	1.0		
Winnipeg Jets				5.4	6.5	6.1	1.8	8.0	4.9			

Note: a. lock-outs; no season at all in NHL 2004–2005.

Source: Forbes.

Table 7.2 Team asset valuation in North American major team sports leagues, 2003 and 2014, $ million

Major League Baseball	2003	2014	Growth (%)	National Football League	2003	2014	Growth (%)
Arizona Diamondbacks	269	585	117	Arizona Cardinals	505	1000	98
Atlanta Braves	423	730	73	Atlanta Falcons	534	1125	73
Baltimore Orioles	310	620	100	Baltimore Ravens	649	1500	131
Boston Red Sox	488	1500	207	Buffalo Bills	564	935	66
Chicago Cubs	335	1200	258	Carolina Panthers	642	1250	95
Chicago White Sox	233	695	198	Chicago Bears	621	1700	174
Cincinnati Reds	223	600	169	Cincinnati Bengals	562	990	76
Cleveland Indians	331	570	72	Cleveland Browns	695	1120	61
Colorado Rockies	304	575	89	Dallas Cowboys	851	3200	276
Detroit Tigers	237	680	187	Denver Broncos	683	1450	112
Houston Astros	327	530	62	Detroit Lions	635	960	51
Kansas City Royals	153	490	220	Green Bay Packers	609	1375	126
Los Angeles Angels of Anaheim	225	775	244	Houston Texans	791	1850	134
Los Angeles Dodgers	449	2000	345	Indianapolis Colts	547	1400	156
Miami (Florida) Marlins	136	500	268	Jacksonville Jaguars	569	965	70
Milwaukee Brewers	206	565	174	Kansas City Chiefs	601	1100	83
Minnesota Twins	148	605	308	Miami Dolphins	683	1300	90
New York Mets	498	800	61	Minnesota Vikings	542	1150	112
New York Yankees	849	2500	194	New England Patriots	756	2600	244
Oakland Athletics	172	495	188	New Orleans Saints	585	1110	90
Philadelphia Phillies	239	975	307	New York Giants	573	2100	266
Pittsburgh Pirates	224	572	155	New York Jets	567	1800	217
San Diego Padres	226	615	172	Oakland Raiders	576	970	68
San Francisco Giants	382	1000	161	Philadelphia Eagles	617	1750	184

Table 7.2 (continued)

Major League Baseball	2003	2014	Growth (%)	National Football League	2003	2014	Growth (%)
Seattle Mariners	385	710	84	Pittsburgh Steelers	608	1350	122
St Louis Cardinals	308	820	166	San Diego Chargers	561	995	77
Tampa Bay Rays	145	485	234	San Francisco 49ers	568	1600	182
Texas Rangers	332	825	148	Seattle Seahawks	610	1330	118
Toronto Blue Jays	166	610	267	St Louis Rams	602	930	54
Washington Nls/Montreal Expos	113	700	519	Tampa Bay Buccaneers	671	1225	83
				Tennessee Titans	620	1160	87
				Washington Redskins	952	2400	152

Nl Basketball Association	2003	2014	Growth (%)	National Hockey League	2003	2014	Growth (%)
Atlanta Hawks	206	425	106	Anaheim Ducks	112	365	226
Boston Celtics	274	875	219	Arizona Coyotes	120	225	88
Brooklyn Nets	218	780	258	Boston Bruins	223	750	236
Charlotte Bobcats[a]		410		Buffalo Sabres	95	288	203
Chicago Bulls	323	1000	210	Calgary Flames	97	451	365
Cleveland Cavaliers	222	515	132	Carolina Hurricanes	109	220	102
Dallas Mavericks	304	765	152	Chicago Blackhawks	192	825	330
Denver Nuggets	209	495	137	Colorado Avalanche	229	360	57
Detroit Pistons	258	450	74	Columbus Blue Jackets	144	200	39
Golden State Warriors	176	750	326	Dallas Stars	270	420	56
Houston Rockets	255	775	204	Detroit Red Wings	245	570	133
Indiana Pacers	246	475	93	Edmonton Oilers	91	475	422

Los Angeles Clippers	205	575	180
Los Angeles Lakers	426	1350	217
Memphis Grizzlies	198	453	129
Miami Heat	250	770	208
Milwaukee Bucks	168	405	141
Minnesota Timberwolves	213	430	102
New Orleans Hornets/Pelicans	172	420	144
New York Knicks	398	1400	252
Oklahoma City Thunder	207	590	185
Orlando Magic	197	560	184
Philadelphia 76ers	298	469	57
Phoenix Suns	272	565	108
Portland Trail Blazers	270	587	117
Sacramento Kings	259	550	112
San Antonio Spurs	242	660	173
Toronto Raptors	217	520	140
Utah Jazz	226	525	132
Washington Wizards	278	485	74

Florida Panthers	113	190	68
Los Angeles Kings	183	580	217
Minnesota Wild	170	370	118
Montreal Canadiens	170	1000	488
Nashville Predators	101	250	148
New Jersey Devils	145	330	128
New York Islanders	151	300	99
New York Rangers	272	1100	304
Ottawa Senators	117	400	242
Philadelphia Flyers	252	625	148
Pittsburgh Penguins	114	565	396
San Jose Sharks	137	425	210
St Louis Blues	147	235	73
Tampa Bay Lightning	136	230	69
Toronto Maple Leafs	263	1300	394
Vancouver Canucks	125	800	540
Washington Capitals	130	500	285
Winnipeg Jets	110	358	225

Note: a. New expansion team established in 2004.

Source: Forbes.

year (Table 7.1). Some exogenous or team-specific factors unexpectedly diverted these profit-maximizing organizations from being profitable in one year at random. The only NFL team for which good governance may be questioned is the Detroit Lions since 2007. A part of the response lies in the Lions being one of the three smallest NFL teams, its last championship win dates back to 1957 and it has not yet played in the Super Bowl. It is not easy to govern and manage.

In MLB, 23 teams made at least one operating loss while seven teams were never in the red in 2003–14; 77 losses account for 21 per cent of all operating results. On average, MLB teams have less good governance than NFL ones. If those ten teams having achieved a loss only once or twice over 12 years are put aside, one is left with 13 teams with a questionable quality of governance. In particular, Arizona Diamondbacks, Boston Red Sox, Detroit Tigers, Anaheim Angels, Miami Marlins, New York Mets and New York Yankees were in the red, on average, one year out of two. They do not fit well with either the profit-maximizing or the good governance assumptions although all of them are owned by a rich tycoon.

Another assumption to consider is if either these tycoons behave as sugar daddies, in the same way as some rich owners of European football clubs, or they maximize another financial variable than profit, for instance, the team's asset value. In MLB, average team asset value has increased from $295 million in 2003 to $811 million in 2014 – a 175 per cent increase – whereas asset valuation has grown by 117 per cent for Arizona Diamondbacks, 207 per cent for Boston Red Sox, 187 per cent for Detroit Tigers, 244 per cent for Anaheim Angels, 268 per cent for Miami Marlins, 61 per cent for New York Mets and 194 per cent for New York Yankees, that is, those teams in the red. A growing asset value objective is likely to be relevant for the four teams whose asset value has augmented more than league average, but for the other two it is less likely to be so; bad governance is at the corner. The New York Mets have made only one play-off appearance in 2006, and in 2010 they hired a new general manager and another new manager; probably bad governance to be improved. Arizona Diamondbacks were awarded a franchise in 1998 and had won one World Series championship as early as 2001 but have not reached efficient governance since then. By comparison, average NFL team asset value has increased from $630 million in 2003 to $1428 million in 2014 – a 127 per cent increase – with the Detroit Lions, St Louis Rams, Cincinnati Reds, Baltimore Orioles and San Diego Padres in deficit and quite below this average. However, overall NFL and MLB must be considered as representative of the North American model with profit-maximizing teams and good governance, but with a few exceptions.

The picture is quite different with NBA and NHL. In NBA, 124 operating losses (34 per cent of all results) have surfaced over 12 years affecting 25 teams out of 30. One-third of the league's activity is plagued with team deficit. The Brooklyn Nets have been in the red 11 seasons out of 12, the Memphis Grizzlies and Portland Trail Blazers ten seasons, the Dallas Mavericks and Minnesota Timberwolves nine seasons and the New Jersey Nets eight seasons. For these six teams recurrent annual deficits falsify the profit-maximizing hypothesis though they are all owned by rich tycoons. With a $107 million deficit accumulated by the Memphis Grizzlies over 2004–12, its former owner Michael Hesley (the team was bought by Robert J. Pera in 2012) could hardly avoid being coined a sugar daddy. The Russian oligarch Mikhail Prohorov could also afford a cumulative $83 million deficit since he had acquired the Brooklyn Nets in 2010. As in European football, investment by a sugar daddy must be one major cause of a team's soft budget constraint and subsequent bad governance.

The furthest from the theoretical model of North American leagues is NHL: 29 out of 30 teams have been at least once in deficit between 2003 and 2014 with 154 occurring operating losses over 11 seasons – 47 per cent of all operating results. In NHL 12 (40 per cent of all) teams have been more often in the red than in the black (Table 7.1). This compares with UEFA data about European professional football clubs despite the fact that 11 out of these 12 teams are owned by a rich tycoon, except the Washington Capitals that is controlled by Monumental Sports and Entertainment. On the other hand, those nine teams controlled by a commercial company are not at all (Toronto Maple Leafs) or not often in deficit with the exception of the San Jose Sharks, Washington Capitals and Winnipeg Jets. Bad governance by rich tycoons does not fit with the principal-agent perspective whereas outsider control is not an absolute guarantee for good governance in NHL teams. Overall, NBA and NHL teams do not verify well the profit-maximizing assumption and a number of them are not well governed according to the standard principal-agent view.

It is now considered whether some NBA and NHL teams are asset value maximizing. In NBA, average team value has grown from $240 million in 2003 to $634 million in 2014, a 165 per cent increase, while in NHL it has increased from $159 million to $490 million, a 209 per cent growth. The growth in NBA team value compares with the MLB's. In NHL, average team value paradoxically grows faster whereas many teams are unprofitable, but the fastest growing asset values are those of the Vancouver Canucks, Montreal Canadiens, Edmonton Oilers, Pittsburgh Penguins, Toronto Maple Leafs and Calgary Flames, that is, the most profitable teams. The assumption of bad governance in a great deal of other NHL teams is strengthened by this contrast. So bad that it drove the owners into a one-year long tough lock-out in 2004–05, and a shorter one in 2013, which is not the best way of managing a labour social conflict whose very existence is a sign of bad governance.

When a team is no longer profitable in its urban area in North American leagues, its owner is left with two options: looking to relocate the team or sell it. Relocation is submitted to the agreement of a qualified majority of incumbent team owners in the league and may not play a disciplining role that compares to takeover or bankruptcy discipline on managers; all the more, the same managers can be moved with the team to its new location.[6] While selling the team to a new owner is a threat to entrenched managers since they may be fired sooner or later by the new owner. Asset sale is a proxy for takeover discipline in the context of North American leagues where team shares are not floated on the stock market. If team sales are frequent enough, they fuel potential threat hanging over managers' heads to make their management more effectively profit-oriented.

Sticking to the 2000s, 12 NFL teams have been entirely or partly (majority shares) sold to new owners: the New York Jets to Robert 'Woody' Johnson IV in 2000, the Atlanta Falcons to Arthur Blank and the Houston Texans to Robert C. McNair in 2002, the Baltimore Ravens to Stephen Bisciotti in 2004, the Minnesota Vikings to Zygi Wilf, the Kansas City Chiefs to Clark Hunt in 2006, the Miami Dolphins to Stephen M. Ross and the San Francisco 49ers to Jed York in 2009, the St Louis Rams to Stan Kroenke in 2010, the Oakland Raiders to Mark and Carol Davis in 2011, the Cleveland Browns to Jimmy Haslam and the Jacksonville Jaguars to Shahid Khan in 2012. With a big boss change once a year on average, the takeover threat to managers must be rather effective in NFL. Most of those teams were profitable when on sale except the Cleveland Browns and Oakland Raiders, which have been sold one year after the emergence of a deficit that vanished afterwards (an exemplary effective takeover threat). On the other hand, the Minnesota Vikings and Miami Dolphins have exhibited a just one-year deficit right after their acquisition by a new owner, probably due to a rearrangement in the team's governance and management structure.

In MLB, 15 teams were sold since 2000: the Kansas City Royals to David Glass and the Toronto Blue Jays to Rogers Communications in 2000, the Boston Red Sox to John W. Henry and the New York Mets to Fred Wilpon in 2002, the Los Angeles Angels of Anaheim previously owned by the Walt Disney Company to Arturo Moreno in 2003, the Milwaukee Brewers to Mark Attanasio and the Oakland Athletics to Lewis Wolff and John L. Fisher in 2005, the Cincinnati Reds to Robert Castellini and the Washington Nationals to the Lerner family in 2006, the Atlanta Braves by Time Warner to Liberty Media in 2007, the Chicago Cubs to Thomas S. Ricketts in 2009, the Texas Rangers to Ray Davis in 2010, the Houston Astros to Jim Crane in 2011, the Los Angeles Dodgers to Guggenheim Sport Management and the San Diego Padres to Ron Fowler in 2012. Nevertheless, the takeover discipline has not been impressively strong with five-year deficits after 2002 in the case of the Boston Red Sox, and even less with the Anaheim Angels and New York Mets. Nine teams have been sold when profitable, thus apparently not in view of disciplining managers.

A stronger takeover threat in NBA and NHL teams may have countervailed to some extent the above-observed bad governance indices. In NBA, 16 team asset sales occurred from 2000, the Dallas Mavericks to Mark Cuban and the Denver Nuggets to Stan Kroenke in 2000, the Boston Celtics to Boston Basketball Partners LLC in 2003, the Atlanta Hawks to Michael Gearon Jr and the Phoenix Suns to Robert Sarver in 2004, the Cleveland Cavaliers to Dan Gilbert in 2005, the Oklahoma City Thunder to Professional Basketball Club LLC in 2006, the Brooklyn Nets to Mikhail Prokhorov, the Golden State Warriors to Peter Guber and Joe Lacob, the Charlotte Bobcats to Michael Jordan[7] and the Washington Wizards to Ted Leonsis in 2010, the Detroit Pistons to Tom Gores and the Philadelphia 76ers to Apollo Global Management in 2011, the Memphis Grizzlies to Robert J. Pera and the New Orleans Pelicans to Tom Benson in 2012 and the Sacramento Kings to Vivek Ranavidé in 2013.

Six out of these 16 teams were profitable when on sale; the purpose of selling the assets should not have been to impose discipline on to managers. The Atlanta Hawks, Oklahoma City Thunder, Memphis Grizzlies and New Orleans Pelicans have been sold when in deficit and the year after the deficit vanished or significantly decreased; a significant disciplinary effect seems to have bitten the managers. On the contrary, the sale of the Brooklyn Nets, in slight deficit in 2009, started digging a deeper hole in the team's finance. The Detroit Pistons and the Philadelphia 76ers were sold within a year of lock-out when 17 teams were in the red (though not the Detroit Pistons), a year not characterized by league sensible governance that should have eradicated the roots of the social conflict in advance. However, takeover discipline, like in MLB, must not very often be the target of asset sales in NBA.

NHL has met some turmoil with regards to asset sales since the late 1990s: the Quebec Nordiques were sold to the Comsat Entertainment Group and relocated in Denver to become the Colorado Avalanche in 1995, the Los Angeles Kings to Philip Anschutz and Edward P. Roski in 1995, the Pittsburgh Penguins went bankrupt in 1998 and its owner Mario Lemieux was financially rescued by Ronald Burkle becoming co-owner and the Washington Capitals were sold to Ted Leonsis in 1999. The same trend was seen in the 2000s with the San Jose Sharks sold to a group of local investors in 2002, the Anaheim Ducks to Henry and Susan Samueli in 2005, the St Louis Blues to Sports Capital Partners Worldwide,[8] the Chicago Blackhawks to Rocky Wirtz and the Nashville Predators to the Tennessee-based group Del Baggio in 2007 and, after M. Di Baggio being sentenced to jail and bankrupt for fraud, to Thomas Cigarran. The original Winnipeg Jets renamed the Atlanta Thrashers moved to Atlanta in 1999 and back to Winnipeg when sold to True North Sports & Entertainment in 2011. The Toronto Maple Leafs were sold by Maple Leafs Sports & Entertainment to Bell Canada and Rogers Communications in 2012. The Arizona Coyotes (formerly the Winnipeg Manitoba) were sold to George Gosbee in 2013. Finally, the Tampa Bay Lightning were a NHL financial nightmare with a debt and payment arrears equal to a staggering 236 per cent of its asset value; the team was sold to Art Williams in 1998, sold again to Absolute Hockey Enterprises in 2007, then to OK Hockey LLC in 2008 and eventually to Jeffrey Vinik, a Boston investment banker, in 2010. Thus, NHL exhibits both financial and ownership instability, which would hardly deserve a label of good governance.

Bankruptcy discipline had no opportunity to emerge in NFL with no bankruptcy since 2000. This is quite logical in a league with profitable and well-governed teams. In the past recent years, one MLB team went bankrupt, the Texas Rangers in 2010, with a debt facing 30 unsecured creditors, namely $75 million to the Hicks Sports Group and $25 million to Alex Rodriguez, the highest salary player in the league; the team was sold at a bankruptcy auction to Ray Davis. This is the only case of clear-cut mismanagement and bad governance in MLB where bankruptcy discipline is more the exception than the rule. In NBA, the Denver Nuggets sunk into financial dire straits and ownership instability in 1996 due to cost overruns associated with the construction of Pepsi Center. However, bad governance was not sanctioned by bankruptcy, successive owners throwing the hot potato to each other until Stan Kroenke bought the team in 2000.

Given that it is the least profitable and the least well-governed league, bankruptcy is not that rare as a tool for disciplining management in NHL. The Los Angeles Kings went bankrupt in 1995, the Pittsburgh Penguins in 1998 and the Ottawa Senators in 2003. In 1997, John Spano, the New York Islanders' new owner, was sentenced to 71 months in prison for bank and wire fraud in completing his acquisition deal, but no bankruptcy proceeding was initiated, which means that bankruptcy discipline to improve governance was not as harsh as it should have been. In 2008, the Nashville Predators went bankrupt due to unpaid loans and fraudulent behaviour of its new owner W.B. Del Baggio, who was eventually sentenced to jail; Del Baggio's stake in the Predators was sold to pay off his creditors. The Arizona Coyotes incurred massive financial losses and declared bankrupt by the league in 2009; the city of Glendale had to step in and guarantee the team's losses from 2010 to 2012. The team was operated four seasons by NHL itself while the league failed to find a new owner through several bids until George Gosbee acquired the Coyotes in 2013. The Dallas Stars got into financial troubles in 2011, fired the coach and finally filed for a bankruptcy sale at auction; the team was financially managed by the league itself for over a year until Tom Gaglardi's only submitted bid was approved by the end of the year. The New Jersey Devils were on the brink of bankruptcy, including a $30 million debt to meet their payroll, when they were rescued by a sale to Josh Harris in 2013.

Thus, the NHL story differs a lot from what is observed in the three other leagues: bankruptcy is a frequent occurrence to either change a financially unsuccessful team owner or managers, on the one hand. While, on the other hand, bankruptcy is not actually used as a tool for financial discipline and governance improvement since, after bankruptcy the team does not recover its profitability: New York Islanders were still in the red after 1997, as well as the Arizona Coyotes after 2009, the Nashville Predators after 2008 and the New Jersey Devils after 2013. Bankruptcy did not resolve the governance issues. By the same token, NHL is rather far from the standard North American model of a team sports league and the principal-agent approach of good governance, which calls for another explanatory scheme (see below).

Floating Shares of Win-maximizing Clubs did not Improve their Governance

From the standpoint of the principal-agent model, since they are not profit-maximizing organizations European professional sports clubs cannot have good governance satisfying the residual claimants. Many clubs had been turned into stockholding companies in European football leagues during the past two decades or so, and were commercial companies even earlier in English professional football.[9] Overall, 44 European football clubs have experienced an IPO (see Table 7A.2 in the appendix) and, according to the principal-agent model, must have been submitted to stock market discipline: profitability and good governance should have been within reach. Some consider the discipline imposed by financial markets as a powerful tool for reaching good club governance in European football (Barros, 2006) in order to maximize shareholder value (de Barros et al., 2007). In such a hypothesis the listed clubs should be in the black nearly every year and be able to distribute dividends to shareholders.

The hypothesis basically is not confirmed in Table 7.3: most listed European football clubs were continuously in the red with the exception of Benfica, Fenerbahce, Galatasaray, Lazio, Rangers (though with a

Table 7.3 Pre-tax operating net income of listed and delisted European football clubs, 2003–2012, € million

Listed clubs	2003	2004	2005	2006	2007	2008	2009	2010	2011	2012
AFC Ajax	−7.3	15.2	6.0	−6.7	−13.0	12.8	−0.8	−0.8	−0.8	−0.8
AS Roma	−90.4	−12.1	−27.0	10.4	39.2	22.0	2.7	−26.7	−29.1	−59.1
Besiktas	n.a.	n.a.	n.a.	−3.6	1.5	0.8	−10.4	−20.1	−59.2	−33.9
Borussia Dortmund	6.8	−61.8	−72.7	−13.1	16.7	8.8	−0.9	−0.9	20.9	39.2
Celtic	−6.5	−8.9	−9.5	−3.6	23.3	7.0	3.1	−1.6	1.0	−8.2
Fenerbahce	n.a.	8.8	33.2	27.2	29.7	32.3	30.5	31.0	24.5	15.9
Futebol Club do Porto	−15.9	27.8	0.6	−27.3	24.1	10.8	27.2	−1.0	−5.0	−19.0
Galatasaray	n.a.	28.6	19.2	26.6	40.8	42.5	41.9	13.3	−28.2	2.6
Juventus	−6.3	−6.2	−7.7	−17.3	−7.7	−3.9	17.9	−23.3	−99.8	−25.7
Lazio	−144.8	39.3	−25.5	6.7	15.2	29.7	23.4	11.4	7.2	−9.2
Olympique Lyonnais	n.a.	n.a.	18.6	25.3	29.9	31.9	9.9	−53.0	−35.8	−33.6
Rangers Football Club	n.a.	n.a.	n.a.	2.2	−7.2	10.5	−12.8	6.4	2.5	2.7
Sporting Lisboa e Benfica	n.a.	−5.0	2.4	3.0	21.6	3.3	−33.5	6.8	13.9	15.3
Sporting	−25.0	−8.4	62.8	1.9	17.8	−0.6	−12.1	−9.7	−44.0	−40.5
Trabzonspor	n.a.	n.a.	n.a.	13.1	17.7	13.3	21.1	20.6	29.7	5.5

Delisted clubs	2003	2004	2005	2006	2007	2008	2009	2010	2011	2012
Arsenal	n.a.	n.a.	n.a.	26.6	33.8	73.0	72.2	86.1	34.4	63.9
Aston Villa	−16.4	−15.2	−3.6	−11.4	−11.1	−9.7	−8.5	−8.9	−9.0	−9.6
Birmingham City	4.9	8.5	−3.6	−6.6	−20.9	0	−24.7	1.2	−13.8	−4.9
Charlton Athletic	0.4	17.1	3.0	−2.3	−2.3	−2.0	−1.7	−1.8	−1.8	−2.0
Chelsea FC	−46.3	−47.1	−47.9	−48.1	−46.7	−41.1	−35.7	−37.4	−37.9	−40.7
Leeds United	−59.8	−60.9	−61.9	−62.2	−60.3	−53.1	−46.2	−48.3	−49.0	−52.6
Manchester City	−18.6	−22.1	−16.4	−6.9	−10.9	−34.4	−84.4	−149.4	−223.6	−130.1
Manchester United	56.3	40.5	41.2	41.4	40.1	35.4	30.7	32.2	32.6	35.0
Newcastle United	13.3	12.3	7.6	−9.0	−7.7	−6.7	−7.0	−7.1	−7.6	−7.6
Nottingham Forrest	−20.8	−21.2	−21.6	−21.7	−21.0	−18.5	−16.1	−16.8	−17.1	−18.3
Southampton	2.6	7.6	3.5	−1.4	1.7	−3.4	−2.9	−3.1	−3.1	−3.3
Tottenham Hotspur	−9.0	−2.2	8.6	5.0	42.2	10.9	45.4	−0.2	4.5	4.8
Watford	−9.5	−3.7	−1.5	−5.0	8.3	1.1	−1.4	−3.7	−5.7	−5.7

Source: Datastream and Amadeus Database.

197

£14 million deficit in 2014) and Trabzonspor while AS Roma, FC Porto and Olympique Lyonnais were nearly as often in the red as in the black. All other listed clubs were not profitable at all and have run recurrent deficits.

Publicly trading their shares was mainly undertaken by European football clubs in order to repay their debts in the early 2000s, but IPO is a one-shot, short-term solution if it does not trigger improved club governance. Governance did not change since most IPOs' revenues were invested in recruiting superstar players instead of acquiring stadiums, sporting infrastructures and other tangible assets and, of course, without submitting clubs to financial market discipline. If, for instance, M. Aulas, the majority stockholder in Olympique Lyonnais, had been ready to accept financial market discipline, he would not have kept 50.01 per cent of all the club shares when launching the IPO. Club tycoons and managers remain uncontrolled by stakeholders and shareholders, namely fans having bought shares. Public trade of shares should not be considered as a tool for improving listed clubs' governance and profitability. Fenerbahce, Galatasaray, Benfica and Trabzonspor were profitable before their IPOs, which were absolutely not required for triggering (already existing) good governance. European football clubs, whether in the red or in the black. did not distribute any dividends to shareholders, except for Fenerbahce offering a 4 per cent dividend.

The number of listed European football clubs that was culminating at 33 in 2002 fell to 23 in 2014 despite recent IPOs by Rangers, Ruch Chorzow and Teteks Tetovo. Meanwhile, 21 English clubs have been delisted. Some, though profitable (Arsenal, Tottenham), lost interest in the stock market since it did not appear as promising a source of new finance as expected or because a tycoon, head of an investment fund, did not submit to financial market discipline (Malcolm Glazer with Manchester United). All other 18 delisted clubs left the stock market after a continuous sequence of operating losses. Though still listed, Brondby came close to bankruptcy twice in 1992 and 2013. Clubs taken over by rich sugar daddies (Chelsea by Abramovich, Manchester City by Sheikh Mansur and so on) have been delisted and deficits have been lasting if not increasing. This means that IPOs have not fuelled either the expected disciplining shock to former bad governance or an attractiveness effect on actual investors – except sugar daddies – towards clubs in the red. The recipe derived from the principal-agent model is a wrong one.

Switching from a profit-maximizing to a shareholder value perspective, the Dow Jones (DJ) StoXX Europe Football Index covering all listed football clubs does not compare to the Footsie 100 (English listed companies) and the CAC 40 (French listed companies) in terms of stock returns. The DJ StoXX Football Index had nearly always underperformed and did

Table 7.4   The StoXX Europe Football Index, December 2014

Period	Selected	1 month	6 months	1 year	3 years
High	87.90	80.28	87.90	87.90	101.08
	8.9.2014	28.11.2014	8.9.2014	8.9.2014	23.3.2012
Low	71.34	71.34	71.34	70.66	69.57
	17.12.2014	17.12.2014	17.12.2014	27.12.2013	28.8.2013
Price change (%)	−10.45	−6.43	−10.43	−3.41	−17.67

Source: StoXX.com.

provide a nil return to investors even before the subprime crisis, between 2002 and 2007; a marked downturn in the share prices of most floated clubs began in 1997 (Gannon et al., 2006). This is a major reason why football is not attractive to professional and institutional investors. The DJ StoXX Europe Football Index accumulated a 15 per cent loss from 1992 to 2014, including a 40 per cent loss from 2002 to 2014 after a significant increase between its creation in 1992 and 2001 whereas the Dow Jones Industrial Index shows a 300 per cent and the CAC 40 a 50 per cent increase since 1992. At club level, for instance, since its IPO Juventus share has lost 95 per cent of its value (down from 4€ to 0.19€) and Olympique Lyonnais' 88 per cent (from 24€ to 2.82€) while Turkish clubs' shares were up like Galatasaray (+40 per cent). The decline of the DJ StoXX Football Index continues to the present (Table 7.4); it seems to be a structural trend that calls for a renewed explanatory framework suggested in Aglietta et al. (2008).

First, most event studies[10] have exhibited that the value of a football club's floated stock is extremely sensitive to sporting outcomes; wins imply rises in the club's stock value while draws and losses in decisive matches always trigger a depreciation of the market share value. Other news affecting a club's life, such as signing or missing a sponsorship contract or broadcasting rights, selling or buying a superstar player or fans' mood,[11] also affect the stock value. The stock market valuation of many listed clubs have fallen, for several other reasons (Aglietta et al., 2008). One is the illiquidity of the DJ StoXX Football market, that is, the small number of shares issued in the market and very few share trading; another is share price volatility. Low profitability of such investments is inevitable.

More basically, the uncertainty attached to the fundamental value of football clubs is heavily dependent on intangible assets (the non-amortized value of players' contracts). Most football clubs do not own their stadium or other significantly valuable tangible assets with the consequence that their capital is basically relying on the current value of players' contracts.

Thus, the fundamental value of a club is extremely volatile depending on the team and players' performance on the pitch, the good shape or injury of some players, their good or bad relationships with the coach with subsequent effect on their efforts. Consequently, a French legislation passed in October 2006, allowing sport club shares to be publicly offered, has linked IPOs to the acquisition of tangible assets likely to reinforce the club's financial stability and durability. Olympique Lyonnais backed its IPO in 2007 with a project of OL land – a sporting and commercial centre including a 60,000-seat stadium – while FC Istres (2nd division, relegated in 2013 in the 3rd division) linked its IPO to the construction of a hotel and a re-education centre for high level sportsmen and women – which did not avoid FC Istres' share to lose more than 60 per cent since the IPO. European football experience of raising capital through floatation on the stock market has not been convincing. Moreover, it has not really improved club governance and profitability.

Finally, the fitness of the principal-agent approach is even less suitable for European football win-maximizing clubs, even when floated in the stock market, than North American presumably profit-maximizing teams.[12] This requires switching to another train of analysis.

SOFT BUDGET CONSTRAINTS IN WIN-MAXIMIZING CLUBS: DEFICITS AND BAIL-OUTS

When team sports clubs are not-for-profit organizations, they are often run without sticking to their budget constraint; both their governance and financial performance must be referred to another explanatory framework than the principal-agent problem. Moreover, a soft budget constraint (SBC) approach is the one that fits the best with disequilibrium modelling of a team sports league, presented in Chapter 2 of this volume.

Governance in Not-for-profit Organizations: Hard and Soft Budget Constraints

In the principal-agent model (Fama and Jensen, 1983), the survival of non-profit organizations is explained by private donations. One solution to the agency problem consists in not allowing the donors to have alienable residual claims and rights to net cash flows – they are de facto compelled to be kind of sugar daddies. Such was the situation in European professional football when clubs were not-for-profit organizations (like *associations loi 1901* in France, *eingetragener Vereins* in Germany and so on).[13] If in not-for-profit firms no one can claim the right to appropriate the residual, then managers will use potential profits to obtain more non-pecuniary sources of utility (Alchian and Demsetz, 1972); for instance, more wins to be offered to fans, more free tickets diverted to friends, more perks to coaches and players, possibly 'under-the-table' money transfers. Consequently, insider-controlled organizations are not profitable. One of the most damaging effects of such a strategy adopted by rent-seeking managers consists in payment arrears, tax and wage arrears and inter-enterprise commercial debts (Andreff, 2005). This non-payment or delayed payment bad governance reflects the managerial will to take advantage of a SBC met by the firm – as the one that prevailed in former planned economies. On the contrary, good governance is defined by a hard budget constraint whatever the firm's objective – utility or profit maximizing. Such an analytical framework is likely to fit better with win-maximizing clubs in European professional football.

The alternative approach is focused on any organization's budget constraints. Kornaï (1980) originally formulated the concept of a firm's budget constraint to illuminate economic behaviour of socialist enterprises in a shortage economy marked by a double excess demand (see Chapter 2). In this train of thought, hard budget constraint is a concept akin to the principle of profit maximization, though not exactly identical; profit maximization refers to an objective of a firm's decision-maker while hard (or soft) budget constraint refers to an organization's external conditions that constrain it (or not) to stick to its budget, to spend no more than its revenues (or not). Hard budget constraint is a condition for a firm's survival in a (capitalist) market economic environment while it is not in the context of an administratively regulated or planned (socialist) economy: in the latter, a firm's budget constraint is soft. Therefore, an organization or a sports club i has a hard budget constraint if:

$$E_{it} \leq M_{i0} + R_{it}, \forall\, t \tag{7.1}$$

and its budget constraint is soft if:

$$E_{it} > M_{i0} + R_{it}, \forall t \tag{7.2}$$

without going bankrupt, where E_{it} stands for current operational expenditures, M_{i0} initial money endowment and R_{it} current operational revenues of organization i.

Inequality (7.1) implies that the organization is currently profitable or at least balances its budget while (7.2) shows it is in current deficit at date t. When the budget constraint is hard, its economic environment recognizes that the organization will fail in case of continuing losses and financial debts. A SBC prevails if the economic environment does not accept the organization's failure and in some way bails it out; in this case an organization's survival and expansion do not depend on the market. However, the SBC concept is increasingly acknowledged to be pertinent well beyond the realm of enterprises in socialist and transition economies. It is relevant when chronic loss-makers are not allowed to fail or are not driven into bankruptcy because they are bailed out with financial subsidies or other instruments (Kornaï et al., 2003).

Any organization, even though it is not profit-oriented, has a budget constraint: it must cover its expenditures out of its revenues. If it fails to do so and a deficit arises, it cannot survive without intervention. A constraint on liquidity, solvency or debt sets the upper limit on the sustainability of financial deficit. If the latter is no longer sustainable and the organization does not receive any support from other organizations to cover its deficit, there is no other way than liquidating it, which then means that the organization faces a hard budget constraint.

A firm's budget constraint is soft if it is adjusted to recurrent overspending because the firm receives regular assistance from some organization or administration. The very existence of such organizations – coined supporting organizations (Kornaï et al., 2003) – is a prerequisite for the emergence of SBC.

The SBC phenomenon occurs if some supporting organizations are ready to cover all or part of the deficit and bail the indebted entity out. In European football, supporting organizations that may rescue a professional club are the league itself, a tycoon-owner, a local government authority, a bank or a sugar daddy investor.[14] SBC implies *ex post* bailout of loss-making organizations by supporting organizations even if the latter *ex ante* have promised not to bail out: SBC is about rescuing firms in financial distress. A crucial feature of the SBC syndrome is that rescues are not completely unexpected, nor are they limited to once-off bail-out; they include prolonged support to organizations suffering from persistent financial problems. The SBC syndrome is truly at work if organizations can expect to be rescued from financial trouble, and those expectations in turn affect their behaviour. Bail-outs are common among not-for-profit organizations; it is not surprising that they happen to occur in sports clubs insofar as they are not-for-profit organizations. The bailing out process is often indirect or implicit when the organization regularly survives its failure to:

a. pay its suppliers' bills (overdue trade credit or inter-enterprise arrears). Cross-subsidization is typical of firms' SBC (Kornaï et al., 2003). In some big organizations like conglomerates, trusts and cartels, cross-subsidization serves as insurance against failure of some subsidiary or participating business units – this sounds very much like what is observed in team sports leagues (Fort and Quirk, 1995).

b. pay taxes. The tax authority may deliberately overlook mounting tax arrears. The latter are taxes that have been accrued and have come due but have not been paid. Government toleration of tax arrears means, in effect, that distressed firms are being subsidized or, in other words, they have SBCs (Schaffer, 1998).

c. repay its bank loans. The bank willingly tolerates non-performing debt because it actually wishes to assist the organization, or simply definitely does not want to lose previous investments or loans (Dewatripont and Maskin, 1995).

SBC is at work when the means of rescue are lax taxation and fiscal means: subsidies from the state budget or tax concessions or tolerance of tax arrears; easy credit: loans repayment relaxation to no longer financially eligible debtors; and indirect methods of support: inter-enterprise trade credit, strong expectation of rescue, bail-out by a sugar daddy, absence (or scarcity) of bankruptcies and liquidations in a given business and various possibilities of price bargaining with administrative authorities.[15] If repeatedly occurring, these means of rescue trigger a nearly absolute certainty to be rescued that comes out with SBC mentality, the latter being a basic feature of the SBC syndrome. A key measure of the latter is the degree to which organizations are permitted to fail (bankruptcy, liquidation). If there is no enforcement of bankruptcy laws on sports clubs, no exit from the sports leagues industry follows even if a club is technically bankrupt.

Inside an organization or a sports club, the most important consequence of SBC is the attenuation of managerial effort to maximize profits or, when there is no profit motive, to reduce costs, that is, bad governance, something quite common in sports, namely in European football (Andreff, 2007a, 2007b). This usually boosts the organizations' demand for inputs (see Chapter 2) – driving sports clubs into the arms race for superstars – and fuels the propensity to invest by reducing the risk to the investor. Fueled by the competitive interaction between clubs in the league, such overinvestment in playing talent (Dietl et al., 2008) directly inflates clubs' payrolls, including overinvestment in risky ventures such as recruiting 'lemon' players (Andreff, 2014). Clearly SBC drives football not-for-profit organizations into bad governance and lack of financial discipline.[16]

Soft Budget Constraint and Bad Governance in European Football Clubs

Crucial indicators of SBC and bad governance in European professional football are clubs' lasting deficits and the structure of debts, on the one

Table 7.5   Deficits of European football clubs, top division, 2008–2012

Indicators	2008–09	2009–10	2010–11	2011–12	2012–13
Aggregate net losses (€ million) of all	649	1206	1641	1675	1066
European top division clubs (number)	732	733	734	733	729
Number of reporting clubs	644	664	665	679	696
Percentage of loss-making clubs (%)	54	60	61	63	48
Proportion of clubs that breached at least one of the FFP indicators (%)	n.a.	60	56	63	57
Number of qualified clubs that were not granted UEFA licences	3	6	5	4	6
Number of clubs that were refused licences for financial reasons[a]	75	86	62	85	75
Number of clubs spending above 100% of their revenues on wages	55	73	78	81	94

Note: a. Audited financial statements, overdue employee/tax payables, overdue transfer fees or budgets.

Source: UEFA club licensing benchmarking reports.

hand, and, on the other hand, the frequency of bail-outs that in fact substitute for absent bankruptcies. This mismanagement of clubs currently run in the red over a significant number of years is scrutinized below.

Over 700 European top division football clubs exhibited €649 million of net losses in 2008, a figure that grew to €1675 million in 2011 while the proportion of loss-making clubs climbed from 54 per cent to 63 per cent in the same year (Table 7.5). Recurrent deficits reflecting bad club governance are more the rule than the exception and are much more frequent than in North American team sports leagues. In 2012, the foreseeable perspective of Financial Fair Play (FFP) to be fully enforced in 2013–14 must have started to bite so that net losses were down to €1066 million and the proportion of loss-making clubs to 48 per cent.

A downturn in the percentage of clubs that breached at least one FFP indicators, down from 63 per cent in 2011 to 57 per cent in 2012, confirms the first impression. Over recent years for which data are available, the number of clubs that have been refused a license to participate in either the UEFA Champions League or UEFA Europa League has fluctuated down to three and up to seven (in 2013–14) per year. Bad governance and financial dire straits of these clubs did not inspire enough confidence to let UEFA start up one of its football contests with a sufficient guarantee of financial stability. The number of clubs that were refused licenses due to financial reasons, even if they were not qualified

Table 7.6   Debts of European football clubs, top division, 2008–2012

Indicators	2008–09	2009–10	2010–11	2011–12	2012–13
Number of reporting clubs	644	664	665	654	699
Number of clubs reporting negative net equity (debts > assets)	224	245	237	255	266
as percentage of all reporting clubs (%)	35	37	36	38	39
Bank debt and commercial loans (€ billion)	5.5	5.6	5.5	5.1	6.3
Taxes and social security charges (€ billion)	1.4	1.3	1.2	1.4	1.4
Employee payables (€ billion)	n.a	n.a.	0.6	0.7	1.0
Overdue transfer fees (€ billion)	1.6	2.1	2.3	2.3	2.4
Total debt typical of SCB (€ billion)	8.5	9.0	9.6	9.5	11.1
as percentage of total liabilities (%)	49	48	50	52	57

Source: UEFA club licensing benchmarking reports.

on the pitch for a European tier contest, was fluctuating between 62 and 85 (between 9 per cent and 12 per cent of all clubs) per year; financial reasons are unsatisfactory audited financial statements, overdue tax and social security charges payables, overdue transfer fees payment, overdue employee payables and budget problems, all typical features of SBC, in particular payment arrears. Another reason is overspending on inputs, which is the case of some 55 to 94 clubs per year spending above 100 per cent of their current revenues on wages. Mismanagement is at stake and the issue of clubs' bad governance must be on the agenda of all and any reforms in European professional football. Not surprisingly, about 60 per cent of clubs per year did not stick to at least one of the FFP criteria; there is therefore still a long way to go to reach good governance in the UEFA sense, may be even a longer way with reference to the theoretical SBC approach (see below).

With regards to debts resulting from recurrent deficits, between 35 per cent and 39 per cent of European football clubs report bigger debts than assets that is a negative net equity position each year. This proportion has been slightly increasing over the past five years. A significant share of these debts in total liabilities is directly linked to the above-listed elements of the SBC syndrome, and this share has risen from 49 per cent in 2008 to 57 per cent in 2012. This pertains to bank debt and, even more representative of SBC, commercial loans, tax and social security charges arrears, wage arrears (employee payables) and transfer fees payment arrears.

Finally, it is extremely rare that a European football club goes bankrupt. When a club is close to going bankrupt, usually some supporting organization steps in financially to rescue it. Storm and Nielsen (2012) stress that European professional football clubs continually operate on the brink of insolvency without going out of business. Kuper and Szymanski (2009) have shown a very high club survival rate in English football: when in financial dire straits or nearly bankrupt, an English football club either is put by the league under forced administration[17] to clean deficits and debts or finds some organization to bail it out, primarily sugar daddy investors in the past decade. In Italian *Calcio*, the survival rate is extremely high: of the 60 clubs dating back to the league inception in 1929, only two (Legano and Ancona) are out of business today.[18] The survival rate is slightly lower in the Spanish *Liga* (Storm and Nielsen, 2012); however, clubs' owners know that Catalonian or Castilian banks will always help, respectively FC Barcelona and Real Madrid when they sink into important losses (Ascari and Gagnepain, 2006), and football clubs are heavily backed by their respective regions, that is, governments and financial institutions (Barajas and Rodriguez, 2010).

In French football, all the clubs that were once on the brink of bankruptcy, like Bordeaux, Nantes, Red Star, Reims, Saint-Etienne and others, were all rescued by the league, a municipality (before the European Union rules forbid it), or a benevolent not-for-profit looking investor. In Italian football, the whole league was rescued by the *salva calcio* governmental plan[19] in 2002 (Baroncelli and Lago, 2006). Inter Milan survives only due to a €1 billion money injection year after year by Massimo Morati and AC Milan with about €500 million poured into the club by Silvio Berlusconi. Even one German club, Borussia Dortmund, was rescued by an insurance company, Gerling, buying its new issued shares in 2004. Therefore, many clubs are somehow in a situation of moral hazard due to assurance of continuing to survive anyway in the football business (Drut and Raballand, 2012; Franck, 2014).

In fact, every year those football clubs in the red are bailed out by tax authorities that do not ask for taxes to be paid promptly, social security agencies that do not insist social security payments are on time, banks that do not ask that loans are repaid by their due date, suppliers that tolerate payment delays and other clubs that do not ask for exactly 100 per cent of each transfer fee (thus creating an inter-club overdue payment chain). Sometimes clubs are even bailed out by their unpaid players (employee payables) until they threaten to go on work stoppage. All this is driven by an economic and institutional environment where supporting organizations continuously adapt to European football clubs overspending, as contented in the SBC analysis. One implication is that to improve European football clubs' governance one has not only to upgrade their inner management but also harden their budget constraints, which means reforming their supporting organizations or, at least, creating new incentives that would prevent the latter from continuing or avoiding their bailing out behaviour. In other words, a reform that should go far beyond the boundaries of football leagues as such.

Deficits, Debts and Governance in French Football

Though it is one of the least plagued (along with the German *Bundesligua*) by clubs' deficits and debts among the Big Five European football leagues,[20] French *Ligue 1* also exhibits a SBC syndrome despite its requirement that all the clubs complete current annual financial audits by *Direction Nationale de Contrôle de Gestion* (DNCG), an audit placed under the aegis of the *Ligue du Football Professionnel* (LFP). Since 2000, the league has been in deficit every year except in 2005, 2006 and 2007 (Table 7.7). Clubs in the red had a bigger aggregate deficit than aggregate positive operating income of those clubs in the black in all the years but three. The league's net operating loss peaked up in 2009 and once again in 2011. The deficit significantly reduced in 2012 probably with the perspective of coming FFP enforcement.

The question is whether it was only a short-term outcome, like in 2005–07, that French clubs reacted to the new disclosure obligation compelling them to publicize financial accounts from 2002 (Andreff, 2007b). First, some clubs attempted to circumvent the new rule as they were reluctant to have their accounting data disclosed, in particular those clubs in the red; such undisciplined behaviour is a clear sign of bad governance. Moreover, in the past two decades or so, several clubs' chairmen have been sued and sentenced for fake accounting, suspicious contracts signed, embezzlements, irregular player transfers (with black bags and over-invoicing) and abuses of social benefits. Deficits are only the tip of the iceberg as regards bad governance and mismanagement in football clubs.

At club level, the occurrences of deficits are numerous (Table 7.8): 78 out of 200 possible net operating incomes between 2003 and 2012, that is, 39 per cent of the total, comparable to NBA, and lower than NHL, which is presumably affected by a SBC syndrome as well. Deficits are scattered throughout many clubs, exactly 26 of them, in a 20-team league; this results from the promotion-relegation system. Various newly promoted and nearly demoted clubs accrue a deficit. However, the major part of the league's deficit is due to a few clubs whose governance obviously should have been reformed: Paris Saint-Germain (ten years in deficit out of ten), Nantes (eight years), Lens, Lille, Marseille and Rennes (five years); the first two would probably suffer from FFP enforcement.[21]

The French *Ligue 1* aggregate balance sheet exhibits growing debts from €364 million in 2003 to €702 million in 2012 (Table 7.9). So-called

Table 7.7 Cash balance and transfer fee balance in French professional football

€ million	2003–04	2004–05	2005–06	2006–07	2007–08	2008–09	2009–10	2010–11	2011–12	2012–13
Cash balance										
Ligue 1	−35.9	−32.5	27.7	42.7	25.0	−14.7	−114.1	−46.1	−81.7	−4.3
Ligue 2	−8.0	5.5	5.0	4.1	1.8	−18.9	−15.9	−18.9	−47.4	−21.3
Total	−43.9	−27.0	32.7	46.8	26.8	−33.6	−130.0	−65.0	−129.1	−25.6
Transfer fee balance										
Ligue 1	17.9	3.0	14.7	31.7	58.8	41.9	−91.7	73.4	−38.9	−26.8
Ligue 2	15.5	12.2	11.8	20.1	21.1	37.3	16.5	18.5	35.5	−58.1
Total	33.4	15.2	26.5	51.8	79.9	79.2	−75.2	91.9	−3.4	−84.9

Source: LFP/DNCG.

Table 7.8 Occurrences of operational losses in French Ligue 1, 2003–2012, € million

Clubs	2003–04	2004–05	2005–06	2006–07	2007–08	2008–09	2009–10	2010–11	2011–12	2012–13
AC Ajaccio										1.8
AJ Auxerre						7.7	4.7		16.4	
SC Bastia		1.9								
Bordeaux Gir.		1.3						7.0	14.3	7.7
Stade Brestois										2.2
SM Caen						0.5		1.6		
Grenoble Foot						5.4	3.0			
Havre AC						0.1				
Le Mans FC							2.4			
RC Lens		5.5	7.5				13.6	5.9		
LOSC Lille		2.0			3.2	0.3	1.1	5.9		3.1
FC Lorient						3.8				
Ol. Lyonnais	6.5									
Ol. Marseille		10.6					0.5	14.7	8.2	18.9
FC Metz			1.5							
AS Monaco					0.2			0.3		
AS Nancy	6.5	9.7					13.5		2.5	4.1
FC Nantes				3.9		0.1	35.4	35.1	28.0	27.9
OGC Nice				2.7			6.2	1.2	7.8	
Paris St Germain	31.0	17.8	13.5	19.0	12.3	5.4	21.9			
Stade Rennais		6.1	2.4				2.5	0.2	5.5	
FC Sochaux					5.9		11.0		2.4	3.5
AS St Etienne						4.1	2.6			0.7
RC Strasbourg			2.6							
Toulouse FC				0.3			0.2		0.8	
Valenciennes FC							10.9	2.8	4.3	

Source: LFP/DNCG.

Table 7.9 French Ligue 1 balance sheet, € million

Ligue 1	2003–04	2004–05	2005–06	2006–07	2007–08	2008–09	2009–10	2010–11	2011–12	2012–13
Intangible fixed assets[a]	167.1	194.3	262.9	266.6	346.1	339.2	356.5	273.8	443.9	465.2
Other fixed assets	75.8	90.2	102.4	95.2	116.0	103.7	112.2	114.8	128.9	153.7
Circulating assets	265.6	274.3	266.1	339.1	369.4	355.3	348.2	363.0	321.1	351.1
Liquidities	92.5	108.9	187.9	191.9	168.2	149.5	112.4	173.5	114.3	142.6
Total assets	601.0	668.7	819.3	892.8	999.7	947.7	929.3	925.1	1007.8	1112.6
Own capital	139.4	111.7	159.6	208.6	213.4	265.6	189.0	183.7	143.2	167.5
Stockholders' accounts	60.1	53.1	75.2	51.2	61.8	56.6	104.9	100.9	214.6	83.5
Provisions, risks	37.3	37.5	52.5	54.0	34.6	32.7	25.4	29.0	24.6	32.1
Financial debts	66.1	63.0	70.4	71.3	62.4	60.2	94.2	87.2	105.2	105.0
Other debts[b]	298.1	403.4	461.6	507.7	627.6	532.6	515.7	524.3	392.8	597.6
Total liabilities	601.0	668.7	819.3	892.8	999.7	947.7	929.3	925.1	1007.8	1112.6

Notes:
a. Players' transfer fees not yet amortized.
b. Payment arrears, tax and social security contribution arrears.

Source: LFP/DNCG.

other debts are directly linked to SBC since they consist in payment arrears (including transfer fees), tax arrears and social security charges arrears. All these payment arrears represented 82 per cent of total debt in 2003 and 85 per cent in 2012, financial debts to banks always being below 20 per cent. At club level, for instance, in 2012, Bastia, Bordeaux, Montpellier, Nice, Paris Saint-Germain and Troyes had a debt amounting to 100 per cent of payment arrears, Rennes 98 per cent, Ajaccio 96 per cent and Reims 91 per cent. The best managed teams, in a SBC approach, were Valenciennes, resorting to payment arrears for only 44 per cent of its overall debt, Lille 48 per cent and Nancy 58 per cent. Notice that a club's payment arrears on transfer fees are overdue payables to another club so that most clubs' balance sheets are intertwined through a chain of bad debts. The same situation across banks creates a so-called systemic risk, the risk that the whole banking system would collapse if one significant bank were to fail. In a sense, if overdue transfer fees spread too much across clubs this would generate a sort of systemic risk threatening the whole league's financial sustainability in the long run. This cross-subsidization between clubs makes bankruptcy of any one of them – in particular big clubs – dangerous because it can jeopardize the financial stability of the league as a whole and hinder a continuous and smooth sporting contest by leaving fixtures unfulfilled.

All aforementioned bad debts are kind of club bail-outs by supporting organizations. In recent years, another sort of bailing out has appeared in the French *Ligue 1*, similar to that observed in the English Premier League,[22] with clubs taken over by sugar daddy investors. This was the case for FC Nantes by a Polish oligarch, Waldemar Kita, Paris Saint-Germain, of which 70 per cent of shares was purchased by Qatar Sports Investment, AS Monaco bought by Dmitri Rybolovlev, a Russian oligarch, and RC Lens by Hafiz Mammadov, an oligarch from Azerbaijan. Such takeovers that pour new money for free into a club, without any club commitment to better governance, do not trigger new incentives to phase out the SBC syndrome.

Softening the Budget Constraint

European football clubs, in an environment of benevolent supporting organizations, use the means of softening their budget constraint, as expected in Kornaï et al. (2003) and described above. They also resort to quite specific means that do not only play on the cost side of their accounts like overdue taxes, social security charges, wages and transfer fees but on the revenue side as well. Nowadays, they target the major source of European football finance, which is TV rights' revenues, the negotiation of which each domestic league is in a monopoly situation in the face of competing TV companies. The league usually materializes its monopoly market power through auctioning TV rights. TV rights' revenues are then redistributed across clubs enabling them to cover wage hikes that result from the clubs' arms race for superstar players; without such redistribution of the TV godsend, wage inflation would derail all clubs' budgets into the red – it has been underlined that some clubs nevertheless have a payroll bigger than overall revenues.

In recent years the number of TV channels involved in sports broadcasting has substantially increased, triggering fierce competition between TV companies and dramatically pushed up football broadcasting rights. Each European domestic football league exerts monopoly power over competing TV channels on the demand side of the market in allocating broadcasting rights by staging actual auctions. In such auctions, where the highest bidder acquires the rights, broadcasting rights fees have been extremely inflated, so much so that a TV company obtaining the rights is hit by a winner's curse (Andreff, 2014). The most optimistic and therefore incorrect TV company in its valuation of the rights is the highest bidder; it will win the bid and be cursed. Quite a number of sports rights deals have ended up being unprofitable for the TV network (Solberg and Hammervold, 2008), translating into financial losses for the TV channel that won the bid. Several broadcasters have been cursed because they discovered too late they had overpaid for the rights and were thus unable to make the acquisition economically viable. On the other hand, this has meant that auctioning TV rights accrues large amounts of money to a football league that can be – and are – redistributed across the clubs and eases them in softening their budget constraint, in other words, fueling the SBC syndrome. Thus, the league monopoly rent is used to soften clubs' budget constraints. Finally, once the TV rights' godsend is at hand, the league allocates money to clubs to cover their major expenditure, that is, payroll (over)spending due to overinvestment in players (Dietl et al., 2008); this has the same effect as a bail-out.

Since this league strategy is permanent and translates into pushing up TV rights as much as possible in each auctioning process (every fourth year in *Ligue 1*), clubs can trust that the resulting revenue windfall will happen and spend without counting on players' recruitment and wages. Here lies a factor that facilitates mismanagement and does not provide any incentive for better governance, quite the contrary. A sort of vicious circle, from a governance viewpoint (or 'virtuous' circle from a finance collection standpoint), has been witnessed between inflated TV rights' revenues and payroll inflation in French *Ligue 1*. An optimistic interpretation suggests a virtuous circle: TV revenues enable teams to pay high salaries in order to field highly performing squads, whose frequent wins accrue increased TV revenues (Baroncelli and Lago, 2006). Italian *Calcio*, which is the authors' reference, is in the deepest financial crisis and seems difficult to reconcile with the notion of a virtuous circle.

In many football leagues, like *Ligue 1*, the recruitment strategy financed by TV revenues does not translate into sufficient team improvement to produce success in European competitions (Andreff, 2015), as required to achieve substantial gains in revenue. Clubs are not able to recoup their recruitment expenditures, the league has to revert to the broadcasters in view of negotiating an ever higher price for TV rights and so on. The successfully and repeatedly tested direction of causality in the relationship between TV revenues and payroll in *Ligue 1* is significant and validates a vicious circle in which TV revenues determine salaries (Andreff, 2007a, 2011). At the end of the day, this is its monopoly power and the winner's curse in auctioning TV rights that make the league's strategy successful in sustaining league finance and using it to bail out football clubs that are in the red due to excess payrolls.

Even though UEFA FFP sends a signal in the right direction in hardening clubs' budget constraints, it might not be sufficiently onerous to clubs for breaking up the aforementioned vicious circle. A hard budget constraint would preclude clubs from running deficits, and strict enforcement of a financially balanced management would be required. This calls for a reform of European football clubs and leagues together with a new incentivizing policy towards supporting organizations that surround football such as tax authorities, local governments, banks, tycoons and sugar daddy investors.

IMPROVING EUROPEAN FOOTBALL CLUBS' GOVERNANCE AND MANAGEMENT

A few recommendations about football clubs' governance may be deduced from the above analysis. Two current experiences that attempt to curb clubs' rising debts and deficits are then briefly assessed from the standpoint of these recommendations.

Recommendations for Hardening Clubs' Budget Constraints

The principal-agent model calling for profit maximization considers recurrent operating losses as an index of bad governance while the budget constraints approach interprets repeated football club's deficits as a sign of the SBC syndrome and subsequent mismanagement. Both converge towards the same *R1 recommendation*: a halt must be put on accumulating deficits and debts in a club over years by appropriate incentives and a club governance reform.

With regards to debts, a football club, as any business, may have some debt to facilitate smooth management, but the structure of debt matters a lot. A debt that is not based on borrowing money according to the usual eligibility criteria in force in the financial industry necessarily includes a bailing out dimension; this is obviously the case in payment arrears, tax and social security charges arrears, overdue transfer fees and employee payables. The *R2 recommendation* is: clubs' awareness that these bad management practices must urgently be phased out has to be intensified through sticks that are heavy sanctions, such as fines, wage and recruitment restrictions or relegation, and carrots, such as creating club financial ranking achieved by an external auditing body, published alongside the sporting standing. These measures must be completed by governmental policy providing proper incentives to dissuade supporting organizations from continuously accepting to bail out football clubs.

Since bail-outs and SBC survival may be fueled by sugar daddy investors who are, from the very beginning, alien to football business, *R2* is not enough to cut the roots of bail-outs that sustain bad governance. The *R3 recommendation* must be added: investment by sugar daddies in football clubs must be tightly regulated, both limiting investment amount and strictly supervising it, in particular when investment is made at a loss on purpose – the objective of sugar daddies often being to 'buy' prestige, reputation, image or whatever else in buying a football club.

Football clubs' financial accounts must be audited by an independent auditing body whose members must not derive incomes, even a penny, from the football industry (*R4 recommendation*) in order to avoid conflicts of interest and crony relationships between club decision-makers and supervising auditors. These auditors, at least a majority of them, should be appointed from institutions external to football such as non-football-related professional audits, outsider financial experts and sports economists not involved in the football business. Even if some football clubs are reluctant, the *R5 recommendation* is to impose on to clubs, in all UEFA countries, total accounting transparency with regards to financial deals, revenues, transfer fees, individual player wages, paid and unpaid taxes and social security charges; business secret is not a prerequisite in not-for-profit social activities such as organizing football events. Exhaustive data must be collected, registered and publicized, for instance, by the above-mentioned external auditing body, and then open to anyone, first of all to fans. Since any regulation does not make sense if it has not the strength of a rule of law, the *R6 recommendation* obviously is a very stringent enforcement of those measures derived from the five aforementioned recommendations.

Though an overall salary cap over the whole payroll is a question open to debate in European football, capping the highest individual superstar players' salaries and transfer fees is more than advisable since this is the major root of clubs overspending and thus of lasting SBC. This *R7 recommendation* is only complementary to the previous ones, and possibly transitory, because once a club had adopted good governance practice, sharply sticking to its budget constraint it would immediately put a halt on overspending, stopping those wages and transfer fees it could not afford within its budget. Given the negative experience of most football clubs floated on the stock market, the *R8 recommendation* is: since IPOs do not either increase the stock value of a club or improve its governance, it is not really worth attempting them.

Brief Assessment of French DNCG and UEFA Financial Fair Play

The supervision of French professional football clubs' management is entrusted to an auditing body, the above-mentioned DNCG (Gouguet and Primault, 2006). In a nutshell, every season DNCG inspects the financial accounts of all professional football clubs, supervises their bookkeeping, detects instances of misreporting and assesses the clubs' financial situation. Since 2002 it has started publicizing each club's accounts. When a club is in the red, DNCG can use carrot-and-stick tactics to encourage changes of management practice, so that the club's accounts return to the black. The process begins with warnings, advice and recommendations with regards to urgent policy measures to be taken by the clubs' management. If the financial deficit does not disappear, sanctions can be applied: DNCG is allowed to audit the payroll in detail, to prohibit the recruitment of new players for a certain period, to impose fines and, as a last resort, to relegate the club to a lower division. Several clubs have been relegated since 1990 under this provision.

DNCG guarantees that each club will have sufficient financial resources throughout the season to complete its fixture list. The auditing body has prevented French clubs from sinking as deeply into indebtedness as some big Italian, Spanish and English clubs. However, DNCG has not entirely cleaned clubs' accounts from recurrent deficits and debts (Tables 7.7 and 7.9). Questions have been raised as to whether DNCG is an absolutely independent auditor (Andreff, 2007b). All its members are appointed from football backgrounds such as the French Football Federation, the LFP itself and players', coaches' and managers' trade unions. A useful reform would be the appointment of at least 50 per cent of the expert auditors who sit on DNCG from outside the football industry.

UEFA Financial Fair Play regulation pursues several objectives: a break-even requirement to take place from 2013–14; enhanced rules about overdue payables; a monitoring period covering two, latter three financial years; however, the rules are temporarily softened by a principle of acceptable deviation over the first three reporting periods during which a break-even deficit of €5 million per year is tolerated while overall club losses are limited to €45 million over three years, with external investment permitted to cover current deficits in 2013–14 and 2014–15, with the allowance reducing to €30 million by 2017–18. It may be assumed that the allowance would go down to zero in the longer run. Additional objectives are to stop excessive salary and transfer payments; promotion of investment in youth development and infrastructure; encouragement of sensible long-term clubs' financial management; ensuring that professional football clubs make more transparent their dealings with UEFA and settling their debts on time; encouraging clubs not to spend more than they make in income (stopping the SBC syndrome in the above wording). These regulations impose restrictions on acceptable deficits and debts and on the extent of possible bail-outs, but still permit a club to be subsidized by a sugar daddy in a limited way. The final aims are to guarantee financial stability of UEFA football contests and shrink financial disparities (increase fair play) between those European clubs qualified to participate. The supervision and enforcement of FFP rules are the mandate of the Club Financial Control Body.

Both DNCG and UEFA FFP rules claim that $R1$ is a crucial objective for different reasons at least in the long run. As regards $R2$, both have implemented and used sticks (fines, restriction on recruitment and payroll), but rewards that would incite clubs to adopt good governance – such as ranking the best managed clubs – are missing. DNCG went further in sanctions with relegating financially unsafe clubs even below the *Ligue 2* tier. It is not in DNCG and UEFA Club Financial Control Body mandates to either support or put a brake on potential clubs IPOs ($R8$).

DNCG has not refrained or sanctioned any direct (by sugar daddies and so on) or indirect (by tax and social security authorities) bail-out so far; $R3$ is not actually enforced. Even though French football clubs are rigorously audited by professional auditors and football experts, $R4$ is not entirely fulfilled since DNCG members have some vested interests in football business. Since 2002 transparency of French clubs' accounts has increased ($R5$), though any club can, on principle, refuse to validate the data published by DNCG. The enforcement of the whole regulation is not as stringent as it could be ($R6$), for instance, Paris Saint-Germain being in deficit every year (Table 7.8) was not sanctioned by DNCG. No individual salary capping is enforced (*R7*), but a DNCG sanction is that a club's payroll is temporarily capped and its recruitment temporarily frozen.

Beyond already published pros and cons,[23] what about UEFA FFP implementing the set of recommendations drawn from the above analysis? FFP explicitly intends to dissuade sugar daddy investors in limiting the annual inflow of money they are permitted to pour into a club (*R3*), for the sake of fair play. The composition of the Club Financial Control Body is much closer to an independent external auditor than that of DNCG (*R4*) whereas its publicizing of detailed individual clubs' financial accounts has not yet gone as far as the DNCG's (*R5*), despite the regular publication of benchmarking reports since 2008 though with aggregated and not detailed individual club data. FFP enforcement is not the most stringent it could be (*R6*) with two examples: for the sanctioned clubs, like the 14 clubs in 2014 including Paris Saint-Germain and Manchester City, only a percentage of the full fine sentenced is to be effectively paid; a second example consists in allowing the English Football League to increase the deficit permitted to Championship (second division) clubs from £6 million in 2014–15 to £13 million in 2015–16. Salary cap is not an explicit FFP objective per se (*R7*) but curbing excessive inflation in salaries and transfer fees is. The reduction of deficits and limitation of bail-outs may have a downward side effect on payrolls.

This brief assessment shows some complementarities between DNCG and FFP rules that may be quite beneficial for French professional football clubs in that, in a sense, they are going to be 'squeezed' between two sets of rules and consequently more swiftly driven to better governance. Data for 2012–13 (Tables 7.7 and 7.9) exhibit a move in the right direction for deficits, but not yet for debts. It is hope this will happen over the next years.

CONCLUSION

Both the standard principal-agent model and the analysis of budget constraints consider recurrent financial deficits and debts as a significant outcome and an index of bad governance. The former fits well with NFL teams and to some extent MLB teams assessed as rather well governed. The latter is much more in tune with European football clubs whereas the reality of NBA and NHL teams stands somewhere in between. In European football, clubs exhibiting financial dire straits usually enjoy a SBC due to direct bail-outs by sugar daddy investors, local authorities, commercial partners and banks or indirect bailing out by taxation authorities and social security agencies. Hardening clubs' budget constraints is a must to improve their governance but it is not enough because the behaviour of supporting organizations that bail out football clubs is also at stake and calls for substantial reform of the environment surrounding the football industry. From this standpoint, the French football auditing system and UEFA Financial Fair Play are likely to bring significant improvement in clubs' management and governance. The above analysis is a plea for a more comprehensive step further if one wants football clubs to actually reach good governance.

NOTES

1. Therefore, the principal-agent model fits well with the standard economic equilibrium approach.
2. In 2008, among the 700+ European football top division clubs or so, 4 per cent were listed in a stock market, 13 per cent were sporting incorporated entities, 38 per cent were company-based entities, 42 per cent were still not-for-profit associations and 3 per cent were state-funded entities; 54 per cent were under majority owner control, 46 per cent were not, according to UEFA (2008).
3. However, the distinction between a large outsider-owner and a tycoon control is not that clear-cut in some North American teams where the company's CEO is also the tycoon who chairs and runs the sports team.
4. Just four owners out of 122 teams in the four North American major leagues currently are women: Virginia Halas McCaskey owns the Chicago Bears and Carol Davis co-owns the Oakland Raiders in NFL, Jeannie Buss Lalong is co-owner of the Los Angeles Lakers in NBA and Susan Samueli is co-owner of the Anaheim Ducks in NHL.
5. In 2004–05 the NHL season was not played at all due to a lock-out.
6. It happens that managers are reluctant to move with the team as, for example, the Atlanta Thrashers' President, Don Waddell, who refused to move when the team was relocated in Winnipeg under the name of the Winnipeg Jets in 2011.
7. No takeover discipline in this case since it is a new expansion franchise.
8. Since then the St Louis Blues are currently the only team in the four major North American team sports leagues to be owned by a private equity firm.
9. English football clubs have been limited-liability companies since the nineteenth century.
10. Among which are Baur and McKeating (2011), Bell et al. (2009), Bernile and Lyandres (2009), Berument et al. (2009), Edmans et al. (2007), Gannon et al. (2006), Palomino et al. (2009), Saraç and Zeren (2013) and Stadtmann (2006).
11. Since most club shareholders are fans.
12. Another 'paradoxical' finding that raises some doubt about the fitness of the principal-agent model with European football clubs is that increased ownership by managers sometimes contributes positively to their financial performance and viability (Dimitropoulos and Tsagkanos, 2012).
13. Even in more commercialized English football clubs the Football Association (FA) Rule 34 specified that no club should have directors on salaries and put a cap on any dividend payment beyond a minimal amount; FA abdicated the Rule in the 1990s after some clubs had been floated on the stock market (Conn, 1999).
14. There may be corrupt influences in supporting organizations as well as in entities to be rescued, from 'crony' relationships to plain bribery (Kornaï et al., 2003). In football, this pertains sometimes to veiled accounting and cooking the books, embezzlements, money

transfers through fictitious player transfers, naked bribery, money laundering, corruption and match fixing (Andreff, 2000b, 2006b; Hindley, 2003).

15. See in Chapter 2 the preconditions for a firm (team) to have a SBC that are related to economic environment circumstances such as a lax taxation system, free fund allocation by the government, a granted credit system, and endogenized price-making in the firm or bargained with administration (Kornaï, 1980). Henceforth, the firm's demand for inputs and investment funds is nearly infinite. See also Chapter 6.

16. Boycko et al. (1996) have associated the SBC syndrome with the interventions of politicians in firms. Though beyond the scope of this chapter, politicians' intervention in European football is not rare and usually is not geared towards saving clubs' costs (expenditures).

17. Forty English clubs have been subject to insolvency proceedings and entered administration from 1992 to 2007. 'All of these clubs owed more than they could pay, yet in every case the football club survived. Indeed, survival was never really in doubt' (Szymanski, 2010, p. 37) as it used to be with SBC. Administration is a process whereby a company is placed under the management of an insolvency practitioner whose job is to reach an agreement with creditors so that the business will survive.

18. Some European football clubs really in financial dire straits eventually went bankrupt but were very few such as Crystal Palace in 1998, Leicester City in 2001 and Fiorentina in 2002, but no club definitely disappeared as a business from the football industry.

19. The *salva calcio* decree permitted clubs to amortize the asset of players' registration rights over an arbitrary period of ten years rather than over the length of players' contracts, thus improving clubs' reported financial position and performance.

20. In 2012–13, overall *Ligue 1* debt was about €700 million compared to the English Premier League's over €2 billion.

21. UEFA's Club Financial Control Body has already sanctioned Paris Saint-Germain for its financial record over the past three seasons (2011–12 to 2013–14), not due to its cumulative deficit over three years but, according to the press, because of a bail-out of about €100 million disguised in a sponsorship contract with the Qatar sovereign fund. The club has been fined (a €60 million fine of which €20 million are actually to be paid), its 2014–15 payroll has been capped and the club has committed to reduce its deficit from €107 million down to €30 million.

22. Like Al-Fayed taking over Fulham, Abramovich at Chelsea, Gaydamak at Portsmouth, Lerner at Aston Villa, Gudmundsson at West Ham, Hicks and Gillett at Liverpool, Sheikh Mansur at Manchester City, Usmanov at Arsenal and Mittal and then Ecclestone at Queens Park Rangers.

23. Namely Budzinski (2014), Drut and Raballand (2012), Franck (2014), Hamil (2014), Madden (2015), Müller et al. (2012), Peeters and Szymanski (2014), Szymanski (2014) and Vöpel (2013).

REFERENCES

Aglietta, M., W. Andreff and B. Drut (2008), 'Bourse et Football', *Revue d'Economie Politique*, **118**(2), 255–96.

Aglietta, M., W. Andreff and B. Drut (2010), 'Floating European football clubs in the stock market', Economix Working Paper, No. 2010–24, Université de Paris Ouest Nanterre La Défense.

Alchian, A. and H. Demsetz (1972), 'Production, information costs, and economic organization', *American Economic Review*, **62**(5), 777–95.

Andreff, W. (1992), 'French privatization techniques and experience: a model for Central-Eastern Europe', in F. Targetti (ed.), *Privatization in Europe: West and East Experiences*, Aldershot: Dartmouth, pp. 135–53.

Andreff, W. (1996), 'Three theoretical analyses of corporate governance in privatized enterprises', *Emergo: Journal of Transforming Economies and Societies*, **3**(1), 61–74.

Andreff, W. (2000a), 'Privatization and corporate governance in transition countries: beyond the principal-agent model', in E.F. Rosenbaum, F. Bönker and H.-J. Wagener (eds), *Privatization, Corporate Governance and the Emergence of Markets*, Basingstoke: Macmillan, pp. 123–38.

Andreff, W. (2000b), 'Financing modern sport in the face of a sporting ethic', *European Journal for Sport Management*, **7**(1), 5–30.

Andreff, W. (2005), 'Post-Soviet privatization in the light of the Coase theorem: transaction costs and governance costs', in A.N. Oleinik (ed.), *The Institutional Economics of Russia's Transformation*, Aldershot: Ashgate, pp. 191–212.

Andreff, W. (2006a), 'Corporate governance structures in postsocialist economies: towards a Central Eastern European model of corporate control?', in T. Mickiewicz (ed.), *Corporate Governance and Finance in Poland and Russia*, Basingstoke: Palgrave Macmillan, pp. 23–48.

Andreff, W. (2006b), 'Dérives financières: une remise en cause de l'organisation du sport', *Finance et Bien Commun*, **26**(Winter 2006–2007), 27–35.

Andreff, W. (2007a), 'Governance issues in French professional football', in J. Garcia, S. Késenne and P. Rodriguez (eds), *Governance and Competition in Professional Sports Leagues*, Oviedo: Ediciones de la Universidad de Oviedo, pp. 55–86.

Andreff, W. (2007b), 'French football: a financial crisis rooted in weak governance', *Journal of Sports Economics*, **8**(6), 652–61.

Andreff, W. (2011), 'Some comparative economics of the organization of sports: competition and regulation in North American vs. European professional team sports leagues', *European Journal of Comparative Economics*, **8**(1), 3–27.

Andreff, W. (2014), 'The winner's curse in sports economics', in O. Budzinski and A. Feddersen (eds), *Contemporary Research in Sports Economics*, Frankfurt a.M.: Peter Lang Academic Research, pp. 177–205.

Andreff, W. (2015), 'French professional football: how much different?', in J. Goddard and P. Sloane (eds), *Handbook on the Economics of Football*, Cheltenham, UK and Northampton, MA, USA: Edward Elgar, pp. 298–311.

Ascari, G. and P. Gagnepain (2006), 'Spanish football', *Journal of Sports Economics*, **7**(1), 76–89.

Barajas, A. and P. Rodriguez (2010), 'Spanish football clubs' finances: crisis and player salaries', *International Journal of Sport Finance*, **5**(1), 52–66.

Baroncelli, A. and U. Lago (2006), 'Italian football', *Journal of Sports Economics*, **7**(1), 13–28.

Barros, C.P. (2006), 'Portuguese football', *Journal of Sports Economics*, **7**(1), 96–104.

Baur, D.G. and C. McKeating (2011), 'Do football clubs benefit from initial public offerings', *International Journal of Sport Finance*, **6**(1), 40–59.

Bell, A., C. Brooks, D. Matthews and C. Sutcliffe (2009), 'Over the moon or sick as a parrot? The effects of football results on a club's share price', *ICMA Centre Discussion Papers in Finance*.

Berle, A. and G. Means (1932), *The Modern Corporation and Private Property*, New York: Macmillan.

Bernile, G. and E. Lyandres (2009), 'Understanding investor sentiment: the case of soccer', Boston University School of Management Research Paper, No. 2009–13.

Berument, H., N. Ceylan and E. Gozpinar (2009), 'Soccer, stock returns and fanatism: evidence from Turkey', *Social Science Journal*, **46**(3), 594–600.

Boycko, M., A. Shleifer and R. Vishny (1996), 'A theory of privatisation', *Economic Journal*, **106**(435), 309–19.

Budzinski, O. (2014), 'The competition economics of Financial Fair Play', in O. Budzinski and A. Feddersen (eds), *Contemporary Research in Sports Economics*, Frankfurt a.M.: Peter Lang Academic Research, pp. 75–96.

Coase, R. (1937), 'The nature of the firm', *Economica*, **2**(1), 386–405.

Conn, D. (1999), 'The new commercialism', in S. Hamil, J. Michie and C. Oughton (eds), *A Game of Two Halves? The Business of Football*, London: Mainstream, pp. 40–55.

De Barros, C., C.P. Barros and A. Correia (2007), 'Governance in sports clubs: evidence for the Island of Madeira', *European Sport Management Quarterly*, **7**(2), 123–39.

Dewatripont, M. and E. Maskin (1995), 'Credit and efficiency in centralized and decentralized economies', *Review of Economic Studies*, **62**(4), 541–55.

Dietl, H., E. Franck and M. Lang (2008), 'Overinvestment in team sports leagues: a contest theory model', *Scottish Journal of Political Economy*, **55**(3), 353–68.

Dimitropoulos, P.E. and A. Tsagkanos (2012), 'Financial performance and corporate governance in the European football industry', *International Journal of Sport Finance*, **7**(4), 280–308.

Drut, B. and G. Raballand (2012), 'Why does financial regulation matter for European professional football clubs?', *International Journal of Sport Management and Marketing*, **11**(1), 73–88.

Easterbrook, F.H. and D.R. Fischel (1991), *The Economic Structure of Corporate Law*, Cambridge, MA: Harvard University Press.

Edmans, A., D. Garcia and O. Norli (2007), 'Sports sentiment and stock returns', *Journal of Finance*, **62**, 1967–98.

Fama, E.F. and M.C. Jensen (1983), 'Agency problems and residual claims', *Journal of Law & Economics*, **23**(3), 327–49.

Fort, R. and J. Quirk (1995), 'Cross-subsidization, incentives, and outcomes in professional team sports leagues', *Journal of Economic Literature*, XXXIII(September), 1265–99.

Franck, E. (2010), 'Private firm, public corporation or member's association governance structures in European football', *International Journal of Sport Finance*, **5**(2), 108–27.

Franck, E. (2014), 'Financial Fair Play in European club football – what is it all about?', *International Journal of Sport Finance*, **9**(3), 193–217.

Galbraith, J.K. (1967), *The New Industrial State*, Boston, MA: Houghton Mifflin.

Gannon, J., K. Evans and J. Goddard (2006), 'The stock market effects of the sale of live broadcasting rights for English Premiership football: an event study', *Journal of Sports Economics*, **7**(2), 168–86.

Gouguet, J.-J. and D. Primault (2006), 'The French exception', *Journal of Sports Economics*, **7**(1), 47–59.

Grossman, S. and O. Hart (1986), 'The costs and benefits of ownership: a theory of vertical and lateral integration', *Journal of Political Economy*, **94**(4), 691–719.

Hamil, S. (2014), 'Financial Fair Play – why loss making is a problem: the example of the English football league', in O. Budzinski and A. Feddersen (eds), *Contemporary Research in Sports Economics*, Frankfurt a.M.: Peter Lang Academic Research, pp. 35–56.

Hart, O. (1995), *Firms, Contracts, and Financial Structure*, London: Oxford University Press.

Hindley, D. (2003), 'Political football', *Corporate Governance International*, **6**(4), 18–33.

Jensen, M. and W. Meckling (1976), 'Theory of the firm: managerial behavior, agency costs, and ownership structure', *Journal of Financial Economics*, **3**(1), 305–60.

Kornaï, J. (1980), *Economics of Shortage*, Amsterdam: North Holland.

Kornaï, J., E. Maskin and G. Roland (2003), 'Understanding the soft budget constraint', *Journal of Economic Literature*, **XLI**(December), 1095–136.

Kuper, S. and S. Szymanski (2009), *Why England Lose & Other Curious Football Phenomena Explained*, London: Harper Collins.

Laffont, J.-J. and D. Martimort (2003), 'The theory of incentives – the principal-agent model', *Journal of Economics*, **80**(3), 284–7.

Madden, P. (2015), 'Welfare economics of "Financial Fair Play" in a sports league with benefactor owners', *Journal of Sports Economics*, **16**(2), 127–58.

Miceli, T.J. (2004), 'A principal-agent model of contracting in Major League Baseball', *Journal of Sports Economics*, **5**(2), 213–20.

Müller, J.C., J. Lammert and G. Hovemann (2012), 'The Financial Fair Play Regulations of UEFA: an adequate concept to ensure the long-term viability and sustainability of European club football?', *International Journal of Sport Finance*, **7**(2), 117–40.

Palomino, F., L. Renneboog and C. Zhang (2009), 'Information salience, investor sentiment, and stock returns: the case of British soccer betting', *Journal of Corporate Finance*, **15**(3), 368–87.

Peeters, T. and S. Szymanski (2014), 'Financial Fair Play: winners and losers on and off the pitch', in O. Budzinski and A. Feddersen (eds), *Contemporary Research in Sports Economics*, Frankfurt a.M.: Peter Lang Academic Research, pp. 17–33.

Ross, S.F. (2007), 'The concept of the residual claimant and sports league governance', in J. Garcia, S. Késenne and P. Rodriguez (eds), *Governance and Competition in Professional Sports Leagues*, Oviedo: Ediciones de la Universidad de Oviedo, pp. 31–53.

Saraç, M. and F. Zeren (2013), 'The effect of soccer performance on stock return: empirical evidence from "the big three clubs" of Turkish soccer league', *Journal of Applied Finance & Banking*, **3**(5), 299–314.

Schaffer, M.E. (1998), 'Do firms in transition have soft budget constraints? – a reconsideration of concepts and evidence', *Journal of Comparative Economics*, **26**(1), 80–103.

Shleifer, A. and R.W. Vishny (1989), 'Management entrenchment: the case of manager-specific investments', *Journal of Financial Economics*, **25**(1), 123–39.

Shleifer, A. and R.W. Vishny (1997), 'A survey of corporate governance', *Journal of Finance*, **52**(2), 737–83.

Solberg, H.A. and R. Hammervold (2008), 'TV sports viewers – who are they? A Norwegian case study', *Nordicom Review*, **29**(1), 95–110.

Stadtmann, G. (2006), 'Frequent news and pure signals: the case of a publicly traded football club', *Scottish Journal of Political Economy*, **53**(4), 485–504.

Storm, R.K. and K. Nielsen (2012), 'Soft budget constraints in professional football', *European Sport Management Quarterly*, **12**(2), 183–201.

Szymanski, S. (2010), 'The financial crisis and English football: the dog that will not bark', *International Journal of Sport Finance*, **5**(1), 28–40.

Szymanski, S. (2014), 'Fair is foul: a critical analysis of UEFA Financial Fair Play', *International Journal of Sport Finance*, **9**(3), 218–29.

UEFA (2008), *The European Club Licensing Benchmarking Report*, Nyon: UEFA (and next issues).

Vöpel, H. (2013), 'Is Financial Fair Play really justified? An economic and legal assessment of UEFA's Financial Fair Play rules', Research Paper No. 2013–79, Hamburgisches Weltwirtschaftsinstitut.

APPENDIX

Table 7A.1   Ownership in the four major North American team sports leagues

Major League Baseball			National Football League		
Team	Owner	Since	Team	Owner	Since
Arizona Diamondbacks	Ken Kendrick	1995	Arizona Cardinals	Bill Bidwill	1972
Atlanta Braves	*Liberty Media*	2007	Atlanta Falcons	Arthur Blank	2002
Baltimore Orioles	Peter Angelos	1993	Baltimore Ravens	Stephen Bisciotti	2004
Boston Red Sox	John W. Henry	2002	Buffalo Bills	Ralph Wilson	1959
Chicago Cubs	Thomas S. Ricketts	2009	Carolina Panthers	Jerry Richardson	1993
Chicago White Sox	Jerry Reinsdorf	1981	Chicago Bears	Viriginia Halas McCaskey[a]	1983
Cincinnati Reds	Robert Castellini	2006	Cincinnati Bengals	Mike Brown	1991
Cleveland Indians	Larry Dolan	1999	Cleveland Browns	Jimmy Haslam	2012
Colorado Rockies	Charles & Richard Monfort	1992	Dallas Cowboys	Jerry Jones	1989
Detroit Tigers	Mike Ilitch	1992	Denver Broncos	Pat Bowlen[a]	1984
Houston Astros	Jim Crane	2011	Detroit Lions	William Clay Ford Jr	1963
Kansas City Royals	David Glass	2000	Green Bay Packers	*Green Bay Packers, Inc.*	1923
Los Angeles Angels of Anaheim	Arturo Moreno	2003	Houston Texans	Robert C. McNair	2002
			Indianapolis Colts	Jim Irsay	1997
Los Angeles Dodgers	*Guggenheim Baseball Management*	2012	Jacksonville Jaguars	Shahid Khan	2012
Miami Marlins	Jeffrey Loria	2002	Kansas City Chiefs	Clark Hunt	2006
Milwaukee Brewers	Mark Attanasio	2005	Miami Dolphins	Stephen M. Ross[a]	2009
Minnesota Twins	Jim Pohlad	1984	Minnesota Vikings	Zygi Wilf	2005
New York Mets	Fred Wilpon[a]	2002	New England Patriots	Robert Kraft	1995
New York Yankees	Hal Steinbrenner	1973	New Orleans Saints	Tom Benson	1985
Oakland Athletics	Lewis Wolff & John L. Fisher	2005	New York Giants	John Mara & Steve Tisch	2005
Philadelphia Phillies	David Montgomery	2000	New York Jets	Robert Wood Johnson IV	2000
Pittsburgh Pirates	Robert Nutting	1996	Oakland Raiders	Mark & Carol Davis	2011

		Since
San Diego Padres	Ron Fowler	2012
San Francisco Giants	Charles Bartlett Johnson[a]	1992
Seattle Mariners	*Nintendo*	1992
St Louis Cardinals	William Dewitt Jr.	1995
Tampa Bay Rays	Stuart Sternberg[a]	1995
Texas Rangers	Ray Davis	2010
Toronto Blue Jays	*Rogers Communications*	2000
Washington Nationals	Ted Lerner	2006

		Since
Philadelphia Eagles	Jeffrey Lurie	1994
Pittsburgh Steelers	Dan Rooney	1988
San Diego Chargers	Alex Spanos	1984
San Francisco 49ers	Jed York	2009
Seattle Seahawks	Paul Allen	1997
St Louis Rams	Stan Kroenke	2010
Tampa Bay Buccaneers	Malcolm Glazer	1995
Tennessee Titans	Bud Adams	1960
Washington Redskins	Dan Snyder	1999

National Basketball Association

Team	Owner	Since
Atlanta Hawks	Bruce Levenson, Michael Gearon Jr.	2004
Boston Celtics	*Boston Basketball Partners*	2003
Brooklyn Nets	Mikhail Prokhorov	2010
Charlotte Bobcats	Michael Jordan	2010
Chicago Bulls	Jerry Reinsdorf	1985
Cleveland Cavaliers	Dan Gilbert	2005
Dallas Mavericks	Mark Cuban	2000
Denver Nuggets	Stan Kroenke	2000
Detroit Pistons	Tom Gores	2011
Golden State Warriors	Peter Guber & Joe Lacob	2010
Houston Rockets	Leslie Alexander	1993
Indiana Pacers	Herbert Simon	1983
Los Angeles Clippers	Donald Sterling	1981
Los Angeles Lakers	Jim & Jeannie Buss Lalong	1979
Memphis Grizzlies	Robert J. Pera	2012
Miami Heat	Micky Arison	1995

National Hockey League

Team	Owner	Since
Anaheim Ducks	Henry & Susan Samueli	2005
Boston Bruins	Jeremy Jacobs	1975
Buffalo Sabres	Terrence Pegula	2011
Calgary Flames	N. Murray Edwards	1980
Carolina Hurricanes	Peter Kamanos Jr.	1994
Chicago Blackhawks	*Wirtz Corporation*	1954
Colorado Avalanche	*Comsat Entertainment Group*	2000
Columbus Blue Jackets	John P. McConnell	2000
Dallas Stars	Tom Gaglardi	2011
Detroit Red Wings	Mike Ilitch	1982
Edmonton Oilers	Daryl Katz	2008
Florida Panthers	Vincent Viola	2013
Los Angeles Kings	Philip Anschutz, Edward P. Roski	1995
Minnesota Wild	Craig Leopold	2008
Montreal Canadiens	*Molson*	2009
Nashville Predators	Thomas Cigarran	2007

Table 7A.1 (continued)

National Basketball Association			National Hockey League		
Team	Owner	Since	Team	Owner	Since
Milwaukee Bucks	Herb Kohl	1985	New Jersey Devils	Joshua Harris	2013
Minnesota Timberwolves	Glen Taylor	1995	New York Islanders	Charles Wang	2000
New Orleans Pelicans	Tom Benson	2012	New York Rangers	Madison Square Garden Co.	1997
New York Knicks	James Dolan	1997	Ottawa Senators	Eugene Melnyk	2003
Oklahoma City Thunder	Professional Basketball Club LLC	2006	Philadelphia Flyers	Comcast Spectator	1967
Orlando Magic	RDV Sports, Inc.	1991	Phoenix Coyotes	George Gosbee	2013
Philadelphia 76ers	Apollo Global Management	2011	Pittsburgh Penguins	Ronald Burkle & Mario Lemieux	
Phoenix Suns	Robert Sarver	2004	San Jose Sharks	San Jose Sports & Entertainment	2002
Portland Trail Blazers	Paul Allen	1988	St Louis Blues	Tom Stillman	2012
Sacramento Kings	Vivek Ranadivé	2013	Tampa Bay Lightning	Jeffrey Vinik	2010
San Antonio Spurs	Peter Holt	1993	Toronto Maple Leafs	Bell Canada, Rogers Communic.	2012
Toronto Raptors	Maple Leaf Sports & Entertainment	1998	Vancouver Canucks	Francesco Aquilini	2004
Utah Jazz	Larry Miller Sports & Entertainment	1985	Washington Capitals	Monumental Sports & Entertainment	1999
Washington Wizards	Ted Leonsis	2010	Winnipeg Jets	True North Sports & Entertainment	2011

Note: a. Majority owner.

Source: MLB team values: *The Business of Baseball*, http://www.forbes.com/mlb-valuations/ 2014; NFL team values: *The Business of Football*, http://www.forbes.com/nfl-valuations/ 2014; NBA team values: *The Business of Basketball*, http://www.forbes.com/nba-valuations/ 2014; NHL team values: *The Business of Hockey*, http://www.forbes.com/nhl-valuations/ 2014.

Table 7A.2 European football clubs listed in the stock market, weight in December 2010

Listed football club	Country	Weight	IPO date	Delisted football club	Country	IPO date	Delisted
Aalborg Boldspilklub	Denmark	0.53	09.1998	Aberdeen	Great Britain	02.2000	08.2003
AFC Ajax	Netherlands	3.49	05.1998	Aston Villa	Great Britain	05.1997	08.2006
AIK Football	Sweden	0.27	07.2006	Birmingham	Great Britain	04.1997	10.2009
Arhus Elite	Denmark	2.00	12.2004	Bolton	Great Britain	04.1997	06.2002
AS Roma	Italy	6.50	05.2000	Charlton	Great Britain	03.1997	09.2006
Besiktas	Turkey	8.40	02.2002	Chelsea	Great Britain	03.1996	08.2003
Borussia Dortmund	Germany	9.24	10.2000	Leeds	Great Britain	08.1996	04.2004
Brondby IF B	Denmark	2.89	01.1987	Leicester	Great Britain	04.1997	11.2002
Celtic	Great Britain	3.58	09.1995	Manchester City	Great Britain	02.2002	07.2007
Fenerbahce Sportif Hizmet	Turkey	9.38	09.2004	Manchester United	Great Britain	06.1991	06.2005
Futebol Clube de Porto	Portugal	0.51	06.1998	Millwall HLDG	Great Britain	10.1998	12.2011
Galatasaray	Turkey	11.55	02.2002	Newcastle	Great Britain	04.1997	07.2007
Juventus	Italy	9.45	12.2001	Nottingham Forrest	Great Britain	10.1997	04.2002
Lazio	Italy	1.13	07.1998	Preston	Great Britain	09.1995	09.2010
Olympique Lyonnais	France	6.88	02.2007	QPR	Great Britain	09.1995	05.2003
Parken Sport & Entertainment	Denmark	8.80	12.1997	Sheffield United	Great Britain	12.1996	07.2001
Rangers Int Football Club	Great Britain		10.2012	Southampton	Great Britain	04.1994	04.2009
Ruch Chorzow	Poland		03.2011	Sunderland	Great Britain	12.1996	08.2004
Silkeborg	Denmark	0.88	06.2005	Tottenham Hotspur	Great Britain	10.1983	01.2012
Sport Lisboa e Benfica	Portugal	2.37	05.2007	Watford	Great Britain	08.2001	06.2011
Sporting	Portugal	0.30	06.1998	West Bromwich	Great Britain	02.1998	01.2005
Teteks Ad Tetovo	Macedonia		03.2012				
Trabzonspor Sportif Yatir	Turkey	6.47	04.2005				
StoXX Index		100.00					

Source: Aglietta et al. (2010) and update.

8. Regulation in leagues with clubs' soft budget constraints: the effect of the new UEFA Club Licensing and Financial Fair Play Regulations on managerial incentives and suspense

Egon Franck

INTRODUCTION

The main pillar of the new Union of European Football Associations' (UEFA) Club Licensing and Financial Fair Play Regulations (FFP), the 'break-even requirement', is defined in Articles 58–63.[1] This new rule requests clubs to live within their own means by and large.[2] More precisely, clubs are in compliance with the break-even requirement if 'relevant expenses'[3] do not exceed 'relevant income'[4] in the reporting periods combined to one so-called 'monitoring period'[5] by more than the 'acceptable deviation'[6] of €5 millon. On top of this 'normal' level of €5 million, the 'acceptable deviation' can currently[7] go up to a level of €45 million, provided that equity participants are willing to inject the respective funds.

A closer look at the notions of relevant income and relevant expenses makes clear that 'football investors' will be confronted with a cap on payroll injections in the future. They can obviously still spend unlimited sums of money by investing in stadia, youth academies or community projects, since such expenditures do not count as relevant expenses and therefore do not enter the break-even calculation. However, 'football investors' are no longer able to rescue a club for licensing purposes if the latter overinvested in salaries and transfers with the result that relevant expenses exceed relevant income by more than the 'total acceptable deviation'.

As I see it, the 'break-even requirement' conveys two messages, one message to club managers and one message to club benefactors.

Hard Budget Constraint for Football Managers

Knowing *ex ante* the size of the maximum external rescue package taken into consideration by UEFA for licensing purposes, football managers will have no more options to soften their clubs' budget *ex post*. There is no longer hope for bailout once payroll expenditures drive relevant expenses to a level that exceeds relevant income by more than the total acceptable deviation. The existence of benefactors willing to donate additional money to cover excessive salary and transfer payments becomes irrelevant for club managers once the maximum external rescue package has been reached.

Cap on Payroll Injections for Football Benefactors

Quite obviously, FFP also sends an entirely new message to actual and potential football club benefactors. In the future even the richest club benefactor of the world will be forced to compete with his team based on payrolls largely financed through income generated in the football market. For the first time in European football, personal wealth and willingness to inject additional money no longer directly translate into higher payrolls, once the total acceptable deviation has been reached.

In this chapter I deal with the following two questions:

- How does the hardening of the budget constraints through FFP affect managerial incentives and decision-making in football clubs?
- How does the cap on payroll injections for benefactors affect suspense in European football competitions?

Since Franck (2014, pp. 195–206) has already devoted much space to the detailed analysis of the fundamental change in managerial incentives and decision-making resulting from the introduction of hard budget constraints, the next section only briefly recapitulates the main arguments and then illustrates the first real-world effects of FFP with some new data that have just become available. With regard to the second question, Franck (2014, pp. 209–10) only provided some basic arguments. Here, the current chapter goes into much more detail in a third section, followed by a short conclusion.

HOW DOES THE HARDENING OF BUDGET CONSTRAINTS THROUGH FFP AFFECT MANAGERIAL INCENTIVES AND DECISION-MAKING IN FOOTBALL CLUBS?

The phenomenon of soft budget constraints has received much attention in the sports economics literature[8] and also in the media.[9] In the following, I rely very closely on Franck (2014, pp. 195–206) to illustrate my own understanding of how soft budget constraints adversely affect managerial incentives and decision-making in football clubs.

The Detrimental Managerial Incentives Resulting from Soft Budget Constraints

Two basic forces shape the investment incentives of clubs in European football. The first force stems from the contest structure of the interlinked national and international competitions. The contest structure produces high-powered incentives to invest in playing strength. Under specific conditions – like, for example, high prize spreads and strong correlations between talent investments and winning probabilities – these incentives lead to a rat race (Akerlof, 1976) with systematic overinvestment, where even profit-maximizing clubs would dissipate resources.[10]

The tendency to overinvest immanent in the contest structure of football competitions encounters a decisive second force, namely a football club environment that is characterized by what Kornaï (1980a, 1980b, 1986) termed 'soft budget constraints'. Very often in European club football some form of supporting organization (Kornaï et al., 2003, p. 1097) – either the state or a private benefactor[11] – steps in with a sufficiently high probability in the case of a deficit and relieves the club from the pressure to 'cover its expenditures out of its initial endowment and revenue' (Kornaï et al., 2003, p. 1097). The perception to run an 'immortal' club shapes the expectations of club managers, adversely affects their expenditure behaviour and increases the overinvestment problem. The rat race turns into a 'zombie race', where an increasing number of clubs operate on the verge of insolvency, chronically expending more than their earnings, but being systematically rescued by external money injections year after year. One could argue that this state of affairs had already been reached in the financial year 2010, when 56 per cent of the 734 European top division clubs were loss-making, total expenditures exceeded total revenues by almost €1.7 billion and 36 per cent of clubs faced a situation with debts larger than reported assets (UEFA, 2012b, pp. 16–18, 54–90).

But what is wrong with the (potential) zombie race situation of

European football? If the football industry is sustainable as a zombie race, where clubs are 'immortal' even if the value of their assets is less than the value of their liabilities, what is the problem? Why should we bother about permanent financial distress if 'the show goes on'?[12]

Unfortunately, the declining price-responsiveness of football clubs operating with soft budget constraint creates some serious problems.

Runaway demand for talent and the emergence of a 'salary bubble'[13]
If a club has a perfectly soft budget constraint,[14] the own price-elasticity of demand becomes zero. As a consequence, the vertical demand curve for player talent – the crucial input into football production – is only determined by other variables and not by the price (Kornaï, 1986, p. 9). It seems reasonable to assume that winning is desirable for club decision-makers and that talent contributes to winning. If the supply of talent is not sufficiently elastic, the direct consequence of the soft budget constraint is the formation of excess demand for player talent. There are good reasons to assume that the supply of talent is inelastic by definition:

> Indeed, the most important input of all – highly talented players – is in extremely limited supply. *This is because the very definition of talented player is inescapably relative – simply put, such a player is one who is better than most others.* (Frank and Bernanke, 2004, p. 113, emphasis in original)

Thus, talent (understood as the capacity of players to be better than most others) becomes extremely scarce and its price gets bid through the roof if enough clubs have soft budget constraints and a very low price-elasticity of demand for talent as a consequence. As soft budget constraints propagate, football becomes a 'talent shortage economy'[15] and a 'salary bubble' emerges, where the wages and transfer fees of the (by definition) limited number of talented players reach levels that are totally unsustainable without systematic new money injections.

Managerial moral hazard: too much risk and too little care[16]
Another consequence of the declining price-responsiveness of football clubs operating with soft budget constraint is risk escalation:

> The firm can start a project even though it may have the subconscious suspicion that the cost will be more than planned and the revenue less. In case of financial failure it will be bailed out. Under such circumstances there is no self-restraint in investment intentions; the demand is not counterbalanced by a 'dead-serious' consideration of revenues and ultimately of supply. (Kornaï, 1986, p. 12)

The emergence of managerial moral hazard behaviour in environments with soft budget constraints is a standard result that has been studied in different contexts. A prominent example is the 'too big to fail' problem in the finance sector,[17] where managers are inclined to take excessive risks because they can expect to be bailed out *ex post*. Franck and Lang (2014) have analyzed money injections in football clubs based on a formal model. As soon as the option to be bailed out with a certain probability is introduced, club decision-makers are induced to take more risk in their investment decisions.

Risk escalation is only one aspect of managerial moral hazard. In the absence of what Kornaï (1986) called 'dead-serious' considerations of revenues and supply, decision-makers do not invest enough of their own time and energy to sort out bad projects and develop good projects. 'Money coming like manna' (Kornaï, 1986, p. 12) triggers waste and profuseness.

Managerial rent-seeking: weak incentives to innovate and develop the business[18]

> Allocative efficiency cannot be achieved when input-output combinations do not adjust to price-signals. Within the firm there is no sufficiently strong stimulus to maximum efforts; weaker performance is tolerated. The attention of the firms' leaders is distracted from the shop floor and from the market to the offices of the bureaucracy where they may apply for help in case of financial trouble. (Kornaï, 1986, p. 10)

Because rent-seeking behaviour is systematically rewarded in organizations with soft budget constraints, their managers invest less effort in developing competitive advantages by 'improving quality, cutting costs, introducing new products or new processes' (Kornaï, 1986, p.10). To the extent that productive efforts can easily be substituted by asking a sugar daddy to compensate for unfavourable developments, organizations with soft budget constraints should be less innovative and their managers less entrepreneurial in a dynamic perspective.

Crowding out incentives for good management[19]

Clubs operating with hard budget constraints find themselves victims of the salary bubble produced by the clubs with soft budget constraints. Maintaining their old level of playing strength by keeping their share of star players would require higher expenditure in the player market. At first sight this could generate an additional incentive to further increase efficiency through better management in order to remain competitive on the pitch. But what if the margin to further increase efficiency through better management becomes too small compared to the magnitude of the money injections of benefactors at their competitors? It seems that these clubs will have no choice but to accept sportive decline or to change sides and start gambling on success and invest more aggressively. If we take into account that sporting decline generates disutility both for decision-makers and club fans, it seems plausible that soft budget constraints of some clubs should intensify the incentives of other clubs to overspend.

Thus, unlimited money injections have a tendency to crowd out business models based on good management. More and more clubs tend to take more risk and chronically expend more than their earnings, hoping to be rescued by external money injections year after year if the gamble on success goes wrong.

The Role of FFP in this Context and Some First Results

The traditional soft budget constraint environment in many European football leagues distorts the price mechanism. It leads to runaway demand for talent, overinvestment in risky ventures and detrimental managerial incentives that encourage moral hazard and rent-seeking and, at the same time, dull the drive to innovate and develop the football business. Moreover, as the soft budget constraint mentality spreads, business models based on good management get crowded out systematically. Against this background FFP can be seen as an instrument to move from a state of affairs with soft budget constraints towards a state of affairs with harder budget constraints.

While it is clear in theory that FFP introduces harder budget constraints, and harder budget constraints should have a positive impact on the incentives for good management, the question remains whether the system will work in practice.

Of course, any evaluation of FFP is bound to be preliminary at the moment. However, first data are available now after the initial two years of break-even assessment through the UEFA Club Financial Control Body (CFCB). The first assessment for the licence season 2013/14 covers the monitoring period consisting of the two reporting periods 2012 and 2013. The second assessment for the licence season 2014/15 covers the monitoring period consisting of the three reporting periods 2012, 2013 and 2014. With the exception of the first licence season 2013/14 all future monitoring periods will always consist of three reporting periods. How does this monitoring regime translate into expected club behaviour?

We should expect to see a clear reaction of the 700+ European top division clubs applying for a licence to enter the UEFA Champions League and Europa League from the reporting period 2012 onwards, since this reporting period is the first one to enter the break-even assessment. And it enters the break-even assessment twice (for the licence seasons 2013/14 and

Table 8.1   Annual growth for the 700+ top division clubs

Year	Wages (%)	Revenues (%)
2008	14.0	7.3
2009	6.0	3.2
2010	9.1	9.0
2011	5.2	3.2
2012	6.9	6.7
2013	4.3	6.7

Source: UEFA.[20]

2014/15). Clubs that do not control their expenditures in 2012 carry over a break-even deficit to 2013, when the total result for 2012 and 2013 is not allowed to exceed the acceptable deviation, and they carry it over to 2014, when the total result for 2012, 2013 and 2014 is not allowed to exceed the acceptable deviation. From the licence season 2015/16 onwards the reporting period 2012 drops out, since a new monitoring period consisting of the reporting periods 2013, 2014 and 2015 becomes relevant. We should therefore expect to see an even clearer club reaction for the reporting period 2013, since this period will be included in three break-even assessments before it drops out.

The question is: Do the data show the expected reaction from 2012 onwards?

Table 8.1 shows the annual growth in wages and revenues for the 700+ top division clubs applying for a licence to participate in European competitions. Wage growth slowed down to 4.3 per cent in 2013, the lowest rate in the last decade. For the first time, revenues increased by a faster rate (6.7 per cent) than wages.

Figure 8.1 shows the aggregate operating results and the aggregate results for the 700+ top division clubs. Operating results refer to losses/profits after wages and all operating costs but before transfer activity, financing and investment/divestment. For the first time since 2008, clubs have reported aggregate operating profits rather than losses. Moreover, since the reporting period 2012, a clear downwards development in the aggregated losses is apparent. These have halved in the first two years of break-even assessment.

These numbers indicate that FFP seems to influence decision-making in football clubs in the intended direction. Of course, it remains to be seen if the data for the financial year 2014 and the following years will confirm this development.

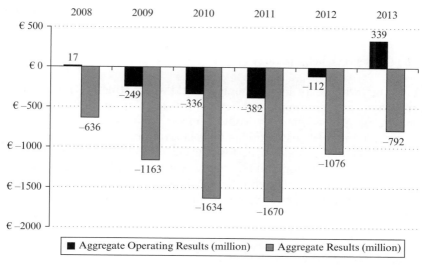

Source: UEFA.²¹

Figure 8.1   Aggregate operating results and aggregate results for the 700+ top division clubs

HOW DOES THE CAP ON PAYROLL INJECTIONS FOR BENEFACTORS AFFECT SUSPENSE IN EUROPEAN FOOTBALL COMPETITIONS?

Does the new cap on payroll injections for benefactors not automatically limit the possibilities of small clubs to challenge big clubs?[22] Since even the richest club benefactor would be forced to compete with a team largely financed through income generated in the football market, he can no longer attack all the bigger clubs in the football hierarchy by spending more money on players, despite having the personal financial means to do so. The idea that FFP might therefore entrench the dominance of already big clubs and destroy suspense in European football competitions has many adherents both in sports economics[23] and the media.[24]

Supporters of this 'ossification of hierarchy' argument must obviously assume that small clubs can only or can better challenge big clubs in a system of unlimited money injections into payrolls. However, are there good reasons for this kind of assumption? Is there a mechanism that systematically allocates unlimited money injections according to a pattern that makes small clubs relatively more competitive? I doubt that such a mechanism exists. It seems more plausible to me that a sort of inverse mechanism is at play, making sure that 'money comes to money'.

The Runners: Doping Analogy

Let's start with an analogy. Assume a world where athletes – for example, marathon runners – would not be able to take any form of performance-enhancing medication. They would compete against each other and sort into a ranking solely based on innate talent, training effort and luck. Now all of a sudden the intake of performance-enhancing medication becomes entirely legal.[25] Every marathon runner would be able to make his own choices about his training efforts and his use of medication. Would this regime of unlimited performance-enhancing medication lead to an equilibrium, where formerly weak runners (underdogs) increase their chances against formerly strong runners (favourites)?

Provided that the incentives to win are strong enough and that the health risks are low (or perceived as low), this will, of course, not be the case. The obvious reason is that favourites will anticipate the danger of losing their rents to 'medicated underdogs' and therefore switch to medication in order to avoid this scenario.

Now assume on top of all this that the providers of medication have special incentives: their medical injection into a runner yields higher utility to them when accompanied by the glamour of victory. To which marathon runners will they offer most/the best of their medication? It seems that the favourites will be even more dominant in the new regime because the enhancement of already high-performing athletes generates a higher winning probability and is more desirable for the medication providers.

In which sense can this analogy be transferred to the competition between football clubs in an environment with potential money injectors? To answer this question, some terminological issues must be clarified first.

The Relationship between the 'Money Injections of the Past' and the 'New' Fair Market Value Transactions with Related Parties

In the past (before FFP) the absorption of club losses through money injected by the owner was a common measure to keep football clubs afloat. It seems to me that much scepticism against FFP is nurtured by the fear that the money that was given to clubs in these 'money injections of the past' will simply disappear and that it will therefore be missing in the football business.[26]

However, the money injections of the past will not simply disappear after FFP as long as they qualify as fair market value transactions with related parties. In the following I will illustrate the relationship by referring to sponsoring as the presumably most important category of transactions, where the fair market value logic of FFP will have to be applied.

Very briefly, the economic logic of football sponsoring can be stated as follows. The media exposure of football clubs is a byproduct of sporting competition. It enables them to sell visibility on the sponsorship market. Sponsors purchase clearly specified rights and services like, for example, the right to name the stadium, the right to place their logos on the player shirts, the right of using players for promotion events and so on.

On the one hand, the sponsor gains direct visibility through media exposure of the football club. For example, as TV, newspapers, magazines and tabloids broadcast the games and other club activities, the logo of the sponsor on player shirts will be exposed to all viewers and readers. If not using football player shirt sponsorship, the sponsor would have to rely on other advertising formats like TV or newspaper ads of a certain duration or location to achieve a comparable 'amount' of exposure.[27]

On the other hand, the association of the sponsor with the club can be a channel to get access to certain desired image attributes associated with the club's brand. A club with an image of playing attractive football, located in a prestigious city, and appealing to a younger international audience delivers more to its shirt sponsor than mere exposure. On top of buying 'units of exposure' the sponsor may augment its own brand by buying 'units of transferred image'.[28]

In essence, the received units of exposure and units of transferred image constitute what the sponsor walks away with when entering into a sponsorship agreement with a club.[29] Provided that the sponsor is knowledgeable and well informed and not under compulsion to buy, there is no reason why the sponsor should pay more for what he walks away with in a particular football sponsorship than in any other deal offering comparable exposure and image transfer elsewhere on the market. Arm's-length sponsorship contracts between unrelated parties will be at fair market value by definition.[30]

Clubs are not dependent on any particular sponsor in such a market, where 'units of exposure and image' are traded. There are many potential buyers of units of exposure and image at any point in time. Indeed, clubs sell certain rights packages to different sponsors in the course of time. For example, shirts sponsors of Bayern Munich have been Adidas, Magirus Deutz, Iveco, Commodore, Opel and Deutsche Telekom (T-Mobile, T-Com, T-Home and Liga total!). The income generated through sponsorship contracts is based on the estimated amount of exposure and image a club can offer in the sponsorship market during the period covered by the contract.

With this economic logic of sponsorship in mind, we can now consider the concept of fair market value transactions with related parties. Quite often owners of football clubs are diversified entities engaged in different businesses. The following two examples illustrate the concept of diversified entity owners. AC Milan is part of the Fininvest Group, which was founded by Silvio Berlusconi. Fininvest S.p.A. is the holding company for one of the world's largest communication groups including Mediaset, currently the biggest private TV company in Italy (Canale 5, Italia 1, Rete 4) and also active in Spain, Mondadori, the leading Italian publisher, Mediolanum, an insurance and banking company, and Medusa Film, a film production company. Bayer AG, the German global conglomerate active in health care, crop science and high-tech materials, is the 100 per cent owner of Bayer 04 Leverkusen Fussball GmbH, which operates the Bayer Leverkusen professional football squad.

The football clubs AC Milan and Bayern Leverkusen apparently can be interpreted as (potential) providers of exposure and image to the various businesses of their owners. The question to be answered is: How much would, for example, Bayer AG have to invest in public relations activities per year in order to achieve a similar level of brand awareness as produced by the Bayer football team? If the corporation Bayer absorbed losses of this level at its subsidiary club, this would be equivalent to the fee paid in a fair market sponsorship deal. Obviously, diversified entity's owners can take the fair market value level of loss absorption incurred for the amount of exposure and image received and write it down as the price of a genuine sponsorship contract with the club in the future.

In the past, diversified entity's owners of football clubs did not feel urged to write down sponsorship contracts clearly specifying transacted rights packages because they could simply inject money and absorb losses in exchange for the publicity received for their other businesses. However, in the future these owners will adapt to FFP and write sponsorship contracts before paying to the club what they owe for the package of exposure and image they receive. Thus, a substantial part of money injections of the past will still flow into football payrolls as regular sponsorship income in the future. The same fair market value logic discussed for the sponsorship example applies to all kinds of transactions with related parties under FFP.

The Nature of the FFP Cap and Why Only Pure Success-seeking Benefactors will be Affected

It cannot be excluded *ex ante* that in some cases owners of football clubs may be willing to pay more than the fair market value for the goods or services transacted with their club. As long as the club does not utilize these generous gifts of its owner to inflate the payroll by covering a break-even deficit above the acceptable deviation, everything is fine. The owner can donate as much money as he pleases for the construction of infrastructure, youth development or community activities.

Clearly, inflated sponsorship contracts are the most likely vehicle to circumvent the cap on benefactor payroll injections introduced through FFP. If, for example, Bayer AG or Fininvest S.p.A. pay more to their subsidiary clubs in a sponsorship agreement than a comparable amount of exposure and image costs in the free market, they would obviously try to inflate relevant income, allowing the clubs to operate at a higher level of relevant expenses before getting into conflict with the break-even rule. *Ceteris paribus*, these clubs would compete with higher playing strength than otherwise identical competitors without benefactors.

It is important to note that only those owner payments (or related party payments) that contribute to club success without creating a fair market reward for the owner (or the related party) – for example, by delivering adequate exposure/image – will be capped (not prohibited!) under FFP.

What types of owners or related parties are affected by such a kind of cap?

The idea that FFP creates an obstacle for true investors looking for a competitive profit from their entrepreneurial activity is quite popular. But how can this be true? Can a true investor transact with his club above fair market value and simply pay more than 'what he walks away with'? How could he survive in the market in such a case? It seems quite obvious that true investors aim to earn and not lose money. Fair market value is the upper bound to their willingness to pay.

Another popular idea is that FFP creates an obstacle for true donators wishing to act as altruistic helpers who do not receive any kind of payback. But why should an altruistic helper insist that his donation must be spent on player salaries and transfers only? Infrastructure, youth development and community activities offer many opportunities to help a club.

Quite obviously, FFP does not handicap true investors and true donators. It only handicaps owners/related parties that attach their help to the pure pursuit of sporting success. The term pure pursuit of sporting success refers to the pursuit of sporting success in excess of the fair market value of sporting success. Let us look at sponsorship contracts again to illustrate the point.

Fair market value sponsorship contracts can, of course, be contingent on the sporting success of a club. For example, as the club advances through the rounds of the Champions League its shirt sponsor receives additional units of exposure and units of transferred image that could be remunerated based on a scheme agreed upon *ex ante* in the contract. But again, the scheme is part of a fair market contract. There is no reason why an unrelated and informed sponsor should not benchmark the price paid for these additional units of exposure and image transfer against alternative offers in the market. *Ceteris paribus*, sponsors will offer higher bids for the same set of specified sponsorship rights at more successful clubs. However, they will pay more money because they receive more units of exposure and image transfer, not because they like success. A fair market value sponsorship remains a 'money against exposure and image' market deal.

In contrast to this, sponsorship agreements considered to be in excess of fair market value under FFP rules single out precisely those owners-related parties that are not or not only dealing 'money against exposure and image'. While there may be something like a true sponsorship component in every agreement between benefactors and their clubs, on top of that the benefactors singled out by FFP rules give additional money because they like success. In contrast to a pure sponsor who pays for the additional exposure and image generated by a more successful team, a benefactor-sponsor is obviously willing to pay for success per se. Put simply: benefactor-sponsors are more than just publicity-seekers, they are genuine success-seekers.

Apparently, it is possible to construct various rational explanations for genuine success-seeking.[31] At a very basic level, it suffices to assume the existence of wealthy individuals with a preference for success in international football. If we imagine a very rich man dreaming about winning the Champions League with his football club more than anything else, his willingness to buy success on the pitch follows by assumption.[32]

Will such success-seeking benefactors inject money into underdog clubs with small market potential? Or will they prefer to spend their money at the clubs already located in the largest markets if they have the choice? This question will be taken up again after considering the incentives of football clubs.

The Incentive of Football Clubs to Maximize Wins

Today, it is widely accepted that European football clubs are best described as win-maximizers subject to some sort of budget constraint. While this view has been developed and elaborated based on theoretical models (for example, Késenne, 1996, 2000) first, Garcia-del-Barro and Szymanski (2009) provided supporting empirical evidence using data on the performance of football clubs in Spain and England.

Put simply, this objective function suggests that European football clubs tend to spend their entire revenues in order to be as successful as possible on the pitch. Quite obviously, an important determinant of club spending power is the market potential of a club.

Clubs are located in cities/regions with a given population, prosperity and national and international prestige. For example, Paris, home of Paris Saint-Germain, clearly outperforms Ajaccio, home of Paris Saint-Germain's competitor AC Ajaccio, on all these dimensions. Moreover, clubs play in leagues that operate in national markets of different size and prosperity. The English Premier League, home of Chelsea, clearly outperforms *Ligue 1*, home of Paris Saint-Germain, in this respect.

It seems reasonable to assume that such local, regional, national and league-specific factors that are out of the clubs' control determine the market potential of the club. Of course, it depends on the quality of the clubs' management and also on factors normally called luck to which extent the market potential can be activated. Well-run clubs will be more successful *ceteris paribus* and attract larger crowds and extract more revenues from their home, national and international audiences. But there is an upper bound to what good club management and good luck can mobilize from a market characterized by a certain combination of local, regional, national and league-specific factors. Market potential describes exactly this upper bound. Thus, market potential sets a limit to the spending power that a club may achieve if properly and luckily run, because certain local, regional, national and league-specific factors remain unalterable. For example, AC Ajaccio has to operate based on certain irrevocable facts, like being located in a town with 65,000 inhabitants and not in a mega-city like Paris or London, playing in *Ligue 1* and not in the English Premier League, that limit its market potential compared to Paris Saint-Germain or Chelsea. Market potential describes an exogenous limit similar to innate talent in the marathon runners' analogy:[33] In the first case, what a club can achieve through management effort is limited by its market potential and in the second case, what an athlete can achieve through training effort is limited by his innate talent.

While the income generated through sponsorship contracts based on the amount of units of exposure and image a club can offer in the sponsorship market is a component of the market potential of a club, payroll injections by a benefactor obviously increase the spending power of the club on top of this market potential. Clearly, the win-maximization objective function suggests that every club will strive to activate its market potential through good management as successfully as possible in order to increase its spending power and become more competitive on the pitch.[34] Moreover, it suggests that the club will welcome and invest in additional wins every other increase in spending power originating from external sources.

Why 'Money Comes to Money' and Primarily Big Market Clubs would Profit from Financial Doping[35]

Which is the likely equilibrium in a market that matches win-maximizing clubs with success-seeking benefactors?

If, for the sake of simplicity, we take quality of management and luck under a *ceteris paribus* clause – for example, by assuming that all clubs are equally well managed and equally lucky in expectation – the longer-term ranking of clubs in a world without benefactors would be a simple reflection of their market potential. Big markets beat smaller markets in expectation.

In this scenario, payroll injections of benefactors work similarly to doping in the marathon runners' analogy. As long as the benefactor subsidizes payrolls, the club is able to perform at a higher level. Once the subsidies fall away, the club falls back to the level dictated by its given market potential. Here too, favourites (clubs with large market potential) will not wish to lose against 'medicated underdogs' (clubs from smaller markets but with payroll injections). Therefore, they will adapt their governance structures and open their doors for benefactors. The consequences of win-maximization seem rather clear: in the end all doors at all clubs will be open for benefactors. Club will welcome and invest in additional wins every increase in spending power originating from external sources. Every club will seek to attract the biggest benefactor possible.

On the other hand, every success-seeking benefactor will prefer to lose his money at the club where the winning probabilities are highest. Obviously, football benefactors will not behave differently from the medication providers in the marathon runners' analogy. As every club is looking for the biggest benefactor possible and every benefactor is looking for the club with the largest market potential available, the result is an equilibrium, where the biggest benefactors support the clubs with the largest market potential (the favourites), making them even more dominant. Unlimited payroll injections contribute to the ossification of the football hierarchy in this scenario. The contrary of what the critics of FFP conjecture will happen.

No wonder that Qatar, presumably the wealthiest potential[36] benefactor active in the world football market at the moment, picked Paris, the biggest free football market in France and one of the biggest, most affluent and prestigious agglomerations of the entire world to pursue its 'Paris Saint-Germain becomes top in Europe' exercise, instead of spending the money in, for example, Ajaccio, Bastia or Reims. Similarly Sheikh Mansour from Abu Dhabi, presumably the second wealthiest potential[37] benefactor in world football, picked a free club in what is considered the capital of football, Manchester, and not a club in Ipswich or Brighton or the Isle of Man. Suffice it to say that the case of Roman Abramovich at Chelsea falls in the same category, as London is not situated in the provinces either.

In sum, the Qatari investment at Paris Saint-Germain has made the club entirely out of reach for its French competitors Lyon, Marseille or Bordeaux for the foreseeable future. Moreover, if the group stage competitors of Chelsea and Manchester City in the Champions League 2013, Olympiacos FC, SL Benfica, RSC Anderlecht, FC Viktoria Plzen, FC Basel, FC Steaua Bucuresti, had the impression that the investments of Roman Abramovich and Sheikh Mansour had flown into already big clubs that are now even more unbeatable for them, not much could be said against it.

Positive, but Presumably Transitory Effects at the Top of the Hierarchy

By definition, success-seeking sugar daddies pick the biggest clubs available for them on the market for corporate control. Paris Saint-Germain, Chelsea and Manchester City that were bought by benefactors are all situated in potentially big markets, without having been at the top of European football hierarchy in the past.[38] Have the new benefactors at these clubs contributed to more suspense in European football?

At first sight, the answer seems to be a matter of perspective. Seen from the perspective of the former competitors of these clubs – for example, from the perspective of Lyon, Marseille or Bordeaux in the case of Paris Saint-Germain – the new owners have destroyed suspense, making their clubs literally unbeatable for the old rivals. However, seen from the top of European football hierarchy, clubs like Chelsea, Manchester City and Paris Saint-Germain, backed by owners with deep pockets, have increased competitive pressures for the incumbents Barcelona, Madrid, Arsenal and Bayern. Thus, it seems that the proponents of the ossification of hierarchy conjecture have a point: increased competition at the top for Madrid, Manchester United, Barcelona, Arsenal and Bayern through benefactors at Chelsea, Manchester City and Paris Saint-Germain has really taken place.

However, European football is not a static industry and the supporters of unrestricted payroll injections should recognize that increased competition at the top is presumably only a transitory phenomenon.

As the competitive pressure for the well-run big market clubs increases, even the biggest market incumbents have stronger incentives to switch to 'medication' in order to stay at the top. Of course, it will take time before some of the biggest clubs, particularly those still operating in association structures like Madrid, Barcelona or Bayern, can change their governance structures and transform their corporate cultures in ways that open the door wider and wider for benefactors.[39] But, given they are win-maximizers, why should they not open the doors for benefactors and instead accept to constantly lose against clubs that from their perspective are 'supported underdogs'? And why should success-seeking benefactors not walk through the doors in Madrid, Barcelona, Munich and so on, once they are open to them? A failure of FFP would presumably accelerate this transition. In the end, 'the deepest pockets' will back the clubs from the biggest markets, entrenching their dominance.

Small market clubs will be further away from the top than ever before, since losing money without the glamour of success is a completely senseless investment plan for success-seeking benefactors. Underdogs will have to compete solely based on their small market potential, while the favourites receive the largest money injections on top of their already huge market potential.

CONCLUSION

First of all, it is worth noting that the main objective of FFP is the preservation of the long-term financial stability of European football. In this respect, the break-even requirement sends an important message to football club managers, a message that will change the way in which clubs are run in the future. After the introduction of FFP, managers will have to field teams based on payrolls that allow them to stay within the hard limit drawn by their football income and the acceptable deviation defined in the FFP regulations. Hard budget constraints terminate the 'too big/ glamorous to fail' problem in the football industry and set an end to the systemic managerial moral hazard and rent-seeking. By introducing hard budget constraints, FFP restores the incentives for good management in an industry that has degenerated to a 'zombie race' with an ever-increasing number of technically bankrupt participants that repeatedly rely on state subventions and/or private money injections.

Second, while it is not a declared objective of FFP to increase competitive balance, it is nevertheless the case that FFP has a positive side-effect on suspense in European football competitions: favourites (clubs with large market potential) will not wish to lose against supported underdogs (clubs from smaller markets but with payroll injections). Therefore, they will increasingly adapt their governance structures and open their doors to benefactors. Since success-seeking benefactors try to spend money where winning probabilities are highest and win-maximizing clubs prefer the largest payroll injection, in the end the benefactors with the deepest pockets get allocated to the clubs with the largest market potential (the favourites), making them even more dominant. In equilibrium, unlimited payroll injections contribute to the ossification of the football hierarchy. Against this background, FFP reduces the gap between favourites and underdogs by forcing favourites to operate within their market potential instead of allowing them to boost salaries with money from benefactors chasing after sporting success.

By bringing the football hierarchy closer together again, the relative importance of good management increases. A well-managed, medium size market club can seriously hope to outperform, at least temporarily, a large market club, if the latter is poorly managed and/or unlucky. There would be no such hope if the large market club had a sugar daddy simply paying for all the mistakes of the clubs' management by pouring in hundreds of millions over the years and hoarding dozens of players. Good management at a club like Lyon is more likely to compensate from time to time the difference in market potential between Lyon and Paris than it is to compensate for the difference in market potential plus the financial resources that could be provided by a benefactor like Qatar. By preventing the deepest pockets from boosting the salaries in the largest markets, FFP revitalizes the importance of management quality in football.

NOTES

1. See UEFA (2012a).
2. The following description of the rule follows closely Franck (2014), pp. 193–4.
3. Article 58(2) clarifies the notion of relevant expenses.
4. Article 58(1) clarifies the notion of relevant income.
5. The 'monitoring period' assessed for the licence season 2013/14 covers the reporting period ending 2013 and the reporting period ending 2012. From then onwards the three previous reporting periods will be assessed for every new licence season. For example, in the 2014/15 licence season the assessment will be performed based on the three reporting periods ending 2014, 2013 and 2012.
6. The notion of 'acceptable deviation' is defined in Article 61.
7. Article 61(2) of the FFP regulations (UEFA, 2012a) explains that the total acceptable deviation will then go down to €30 million for the monitoring period assessed in the licence seasons 2015/16, 2016/17 and 2017/18.
8. See, for example, Andreff (2007, 2011), Storm (2012), Storm and Nielsen (2012) and also Part II of this volume.
9. See Kuper (2009).
10. See Dietl et al. (2008) for an in-depth treatment of this issue.
11. See the detailed discussion of this mechanism in Franck (2014, pp. 197–201).
12. For a range of arguments why football clubs almost always manage to remain viable despite situations of financial distress, see Szymanski (2010).
13. This subsection largely corresponds to Franck (2014, pp. 202–3).
14. Bairner (2012) compared the spending of Chelsea, Manchester City and Paris Saint-Germain on new players in the first 14 months after the respective new owner took control. The numbers (€283.6 million for Roman Abramovich, €234.3 million for

Sheikh Mansour and €212.6 million for the Qatar Investment Authority) are indicative of a perfectly soft budget constraint.

15. The term 'shortage economy' is, of course, borrowed from Kornaï (1980a, 1986).
16. This subsection largely corresponds to Franck (2014, p. 203).
17. See, for example, Stern and Feldman (2004).
18. This subsection largely corresponds to Franck (2014, p. 203).
19. This subsection largely corresponds to Franck (2014, p. 204).
20. The data for this table have been kindly provided by UEFA.
21. The data for this graph have been kindly provided by UEFA.
22. This question has only been treated in a very brief way in Franck (2014, pp. 209–10). Here, I develop my arguments in much more detail.
23. See, for example, Sass (2012) and Vöpel (2011, 2013).
24. See, for example, Thompson (2013) and Daskal (2013).
25. This is, of course, a hypothetical assumption. For a comprehensive analysis of doping at the Tour de France as a dominant strategy in a prisoner's dilemma situation, see Andreff (2015).
26. 'Less money' could translate into lower salaries, less quality on the pitch and unhappier consumers. Madden (2015) has modelled such downward development.
27. The advertising equivalency method, which is often applied to evaluate the alleged value of various public relation activities, seeks to determine the value of a sponsorship by calculating the cost of achieving a comparable amount of exposure by using classical advertising formats; see, for example, Jeffries-Fox (2003).
28. Companies specialized in sponsorship valuation typically capture these more intangible components of value by applying multipliers to the tangible value calculated by using the advertising equivalency method.
29. Of course, direct consumption opportunities for the sponsor, like, for example, access to the games and to hospitality, free merchandise and so on, may also be part of sponsorship agreements. However, these kinds of benefits are an add-on that could also be bought directly without entering into a sponsorship agreement.
30. Fair market value estimates the (highest) price at which a willing seller and a willing buyer who are informed, prudent and knowledgeable and act independently of each other transact a property in an open and unrestricted market. The concept is of utmost importance in tax law and accounting.
31. See Franck (2010) for a detailed discussion.
32. Another rationalization can be constructed, for example, around the phenomenon of positional competition-consumption (see, for example, Frank 2005). In such explanations the central element is that the actual and potential benefactors of football clubs belong to certain comparison groups, for example, sheikhs from the Middle East, Russian oligarchs or political leaders of developing countries. A sheikh supporting a football club can be, of course, interested in the success of the latter because more success generates more exposure and image for his country or enterprises, as has already been described. But, in contrast to a public corporation controlled by the stock market that is equally willing to pay for exposure and image, the sheikhs of the Middle East may derive additional personal utility or disutility from comparisons within their own reference group. Winning the Champions League (or the bid for the World Cup, the bid for the Olympics and so on) may become much more valuable precisely because the members of the respective reference group (the other sheiks, oligarchs or leaders of developing countries) have been outpaced. Again, willingness to pay for sporting success on top of its impact on exposure and image for the country or enterprises is the possible result.
33. It is not important whether market potential is constant over longer periods of time. The crucial point is that the drivers of market potential are not controlled by the club.
34. In the marathon runners' analogy this corresponds to the activation of innate talent through good training in order to maximize performance.

35. To my knowledge, the term 'financial doping' has been coined by Arsène Wenger. See Palmer (2012) for details. For a comprehensive inter-disciplinary reflection of the doping concept, see Schubert and Könecke (2014).
36. The Club Financial Control Body Investigatory Chamber opened an investigation against Paris Saint-Germain for alleged non-compliance with the break-even requirement in 2013. In May 2014, Paris Saint-Germain together with eight other clubs agreed to sign settlement agreements and accept a set of provisions that aim to ensure achievement of break-even compliance with minimal delay. See http://www.uefa.org/disciplinary/news/newsid=2106909.html for details (accessed 2 June 2015). I use the term 'potential' here to make clear that so far it has not been established by any form of legal judgment that the owner of Paris Saint-Germain, Qatar's sovereign wealth fund, injected money into the club in a transaction that was not at fair market value.
37. The content of note 33 also applies – *mutatis mutandis* – to this case.
38. For example, in the season 2007/08 Paris Saint-Germain was close to being relegated to the second division.
39. In the case of Bayern, to open the door completely would even require regulatory adjustments at the level of the league. In the *Bundesliga*, the '50 per cent plus one vote' rule guarantees residual control of the football team to the parent members' association. However, even at Bayern – if the members agree – 49 per cent of the shares could be sold to an investor. Currently, the members' association still owns 82 per cent of the shares of the football team after selling 18 per cent to Adidas and Audi in order to partially finance construction of the Allianz Arena. The members agreed to never sell more than 30 per cent of the shares in the football team, thus taking an even more rigid approach than the league regulation. However, members can always revise decisions if new competitive pressures arise.

REFERENCES

Akerlof, G. (1976), 'The economics of caste and of the rat race and other woeful tales', *Quarterly Journal of Economics*, **90**, 599–617.
Andreff, W. (2007), 'French football: a financial crisis rooted in weak governance', *Journal of Sports Economics*, **8**, 652–61.
Andreff, W. (2011), 'Some comparative economics of the organisation of sports: competition and regulation in North American vs. European professional team sports leagues', *European Journal of Comparative Economics*, **8**, 3–27.
Andreff, W. (2015), 'The Tour de France: a success story in spite of competitive imbalance and doping', in D.J. Larson and D. Van Reeth (eds), *The Handbook of Professional Road Cycling Economics*, Springer (forthcoming).
Bairner, R. (2012), 'PSG turned into a European giant after being taken over by QIA in May 2011, but how has their spending compared to the first 14 month of City and Chelsea's opulent ownerships?', available at http://www.goal.com/en/news/1717/editorial/2012/07/19/3248341/how-psgs-200m-spending-spree-compares-to-abramovichs-chelsea-abu- (accessed 28 December 2012).
Daskal, O. (2013), 'Financial Fair Play – UEFA should seriously consider an alternative to FFP', *Soccerissue*, 29 March, available at http://www.soccerissue.com/2013/03/29/uefa-should-seriously-consider-an-alternative-to-ffp/ (accessed 22 January 2014).
Dietl, H., E. Franck and M. Lang (2008), 'Overinvestment in team sports leagues: a contest theory model', *Scottish Journal of Political Economy*, **55**, 353–68.

Franck, E. (2010), 'Private firm, public corporation or member's association – governance structures in European football', *International Journal of Sport Finance*, **5**, 108–27.

Franck, E. (2014), 'Financial Fair Play in European club football – what is it all about?', *International Journal of Sport Finance*, **9**, 193–217.

Franck, E. and M. Lang (2014), 'Theoretical analysis of the influence of money injections on risk taking in football clubs', *Scottish Journal of Political Economy*, **61**, 430–54.

Frank, R.H. (2005), 'Positional externalities cause large and preventable welfare losses', *American Economic Review*, **95**, 137–41.

Frank, R.H. and B.S. Bernanke (2004), *Principles of Microeconomics*, 2nd edn, New York: McGraw-Hill.

Garcia-del-Barro, P. and S. Szymanski (2009), 'Goal! Profit maximization versus win maximization in soccer', *Review of Industrial Organization*, **34**, 45–68.

Jeffries-Fox, B. (2003), 'A discussion of advertising value equivalency, the Institute of Public Relations Commission on PR Measurement and Evaluation', available at http://www.instituteforpr.org/wp-content/uploads/2003_AVE1.pdf (accessed 6 January 2015).

Késenne, S. (1996), 'League management in professional team sports with win maximizing clubs', *European Journal for Sport Management*, **2**, 14–22.

Késenne, S. (2000), 'Revenue sharing and competitive balance in professional team sports', *Journal of Sports Economics*, **1**, 56–65.

Kornaï, J. (1980a), *Economics of Shortage*, Amsterdam: North Holland.

Kornaï, J. (1980b), 'Hard and soft budget constraint', *Acta Oeconomica*, **25**, 231–45.

Kornaï, J. (1986), 'The soft budget constraint', *Kyklos*, **39**, 3–30.

Kornaï, J., E. Maskin and G. Roland (2003), 'Understanding the soft budget constraint', *Journal of Economic Literature*, **41**, 1095–136.

Kuper, S. (2009), 'Football abandons the fantasy that it is a business', available at http://www.ft.com/intl/cms/s/2/fd77a01c-aa07–11de3ce00144feabdc0.html#axzz2GRMmCmGD (accessed 26 December 2013).

Madden, P. (2015), 'Welfare economics of "financial fair play" in a sports league with benefactor owners', *Journal of Sports Economics*, **16**(2), 127–58.

Palmer, K. (2012), 'Wenger fears "financial doping"', ESPN Global, 21 September, available at http://espnfc.com/feature/_/id/1167069/kevin-pamer:-arsene-wenger-fears--'financial-doping'?cc=5739 (accessed 13 January 2014).

Sass, M. (2012), 'Long-term competitive balance under UEFA Financial Fair Play Regulations', Working Paper No. 5/2012, Otto von Guericke University Magdeburg.

Schubert, M. and T. Könecke (2014), '"Classical" doping, financial doping and beyond: UEFA's Financial Fair Play as a policy of anti-doping', forthcoming in *International Journal of Sport Policy and Politics*, **7**, 63–86.

Stern, G.H. and R.J. Feldman (2004), *Too Big to Fail: The Hazards of Bank Bailouts*, Washington, DC: Brookings Institution Press.

Storm, R.K. (2012), 'The need for regulating professional soccer in Europe: a soft budget constraint argument', *Sport, Business and Management: An International Journal*, **2**, 21–38.

Storm, R.K. and K. Nielsen (2012), 'Soft budget constraints in professional football', *European Sport Management Quarterly*, **12**, 183–201.

Szymanski, S. (2010), 'The financial crisis and English football: the dog that will not bark', *International Journal of Sport Finance*, 5, 28–40.

Thompson, E. (2013), 'Further legal challenge to FFP by Striani and Dupont, Financial Fair Play – latest news', 20 June, available at http://www.financial-fairplay.co.uk/latest-news/further-legal-challenge-to-ffp-by-striani-and-dupont (accessed 26 December 2013).

UEFA (2012a), *UEFA Club Licensing and Financial Fair Play Regulations, Edition 2012*, available at http://www.uefa.com/MultimediaFiles/Download/Tech/uefaorg/General/01/80/54/10/1805410_DOWNLOAD.pdf (accessed 26 December 2013).

UEFA (2012b), *The European Footballing Landscape. Club Licensing Benchmarking Report Financial Year 2010*, available at http://www.uefa.com/MultimediaFiles/Download/Tech/uefaorg/General/01/74/41/25/1744125_DOWNLOAD.pdf (accessed 28 December 2013).

Vöpel, H. (2011), 'Do we really need Financial Fair Play in European club football? An economic analysis', *CESIfo DICE Report*, 3/2011, available at http://hwwi-rohindex.de/fileadmin/hwwi/Publikationen/Externe_PDFs/1210201.pdf (accessed 22 January 2014).

Vöpel, H. (2013), 'Is Financial Fair Play really justified? An economic and legal assessment of UEFA's Financial Fair Play Rules', HWWI Policy Paper 79, available at http://www.hwwi.org/uploads/tx_wilpubdb/HWWI_Policy_Paper_79.pdf (accessed 22 January 2014).

Index